Cana[Mennonite Cookbook

With recipes in Metric and Imperial measures.

OVER 190,000 COPIES SOLD

Stoddart

Published by
Stoddart Publishing Co. Ltd.
34 Lesmill Road
Toronto, Canada
M3B 2T6

Publisher's Note

Our deepest thanks to Rita Kaethler who edited the cookbook,
and arranged and supervised the testing of recipes; and to Pat
Gerber Pauls for continuing and completing the book for
publication.
Color Photos — Courtesy Maple Leaf Mills Ltd.
Food Guide — Courtesy Department of Health & Welfare —
Canada

CANADIAN CATALOGUING IN PUBLICATION DATA

Main entry under title:
Canadian Mennonite cookbook:

Includes index.

ISBN 0-7737-5038-X

I. Cookery, Mennonite. II. Cookery, Canadian.

TX715.C355 1985   641.5   C85-098308

Printed and bound in Canada

CONTENTS

PREFACE

Throughout centuries of recorded history, food has played a leading role as a force behind many great events. This has included conferences, banquets, dinners or other occasions where important decisions have been made.

So, too, food is an important part of every home. Tasty meals, attractively served, can enrich the happiness of a home and its members.

Therefore the recipes selected for this revised edition of the original Altona Women's Cookbook are chosen for their taste, practicality, economy and reliability. It is the sincere hope of the publishers that they will appeal to the average homemaker since they are generally the favorites of many homes.

Twelve editions of the first Altona Women's Institute Cookbook were printed over the years, placing 90,000 copies in the hands of homemakers.

The change in name to the Canadian Mennonite Cookbook was made because the recipes have come from persons across Canada and the distribution of the Cookbooks has been nationwide.

This edition has a new vegetable section and new recipes added to the salad, beverage and other sections. The Mennonite section has been expanded to include recipes from Ontario Mennonite communities. This section has recipes which are the most representative and favorites that Mennonite great-grandmothers have handed down from mother to daughter, many of them by word of mouth, but especially tested for correct measurements and ingredients, to give variety and novelty to your daily menus. We have separated the quick breads from those made with yeast, and reshuffled some of the recipes into different sections.

We were pleased to receive permission to include the new Canada Food Guide for your use in meal planning. The new food guide has four instead of five food groups, and shows the recommended number of servings per day for each age group and indicates serving sizes.

This edition includes conversion of recipes to the metric system of measurement.

We have adopted a new format and attempted to use a uniform style in writing all recipes. The information appears in two columns — Metric and Standard. Where information appears only in the left column, it applies to both metric and standard methods. The mixing procedure appears below and applies to both methods.

Grateful acknowledgement is made not only to the members of the Altona Women's Institute, but to all individuals who have been kind enough to read and make suggestions with regard to recipes or have assisted in testing recipes in their metric form in the preparation of this cookbook.

Pat Gerber Pauls

AN INTRODUCTION TO METRIC COOKING

Canada's conversion to the metric system is well underway, with roadsigns showing distance in kilometres and consumer products displaying centimetre, gram, and kilogram alongside inches, ounces, and pounds. Metric conversion will bring changes in our kitchen measurements also. Metric measures will be phased into our system of measurement over a five year period. You may want to continue using standard measures for your favorite recipes. However, as cookbooks "go metric" and metric measures replace standard ones in the marketplace, persons involved in food preparation may want to be informed of the change in measuring units and how to use them in the kitchen. We have prepared this cookbook to familiarize you with the new system. Recipes appear with both Metric and Standard pan sizes, cooking temperature, yield quantities, and ingredient amounts. Each recipe has been tested in its metric form to assure the same flavor and texture produced by the standard method. Although measures will change methods of measuring and mixing will remain constant.

Following are a few tips on metric cooking which we felt would be of help to you:

Measuring Equipment

Liquid Measures are available in 250 mL volume, graduated in 25 mL divisions, 500 mL and 1000 mL volume, graduated in 50 mL divisions.

Dry Measures — a set of three: a 50 mL, 125 mL and 250 mL measure.

Small Liquid and Dry Measures — a set of five measures: 1 mL, 2 mL, 5 mL, 15 mL and 25 mL.

Ingredients

Volume — Those ingredients which are now measured by volume will continue to be measured by volume, but instead of using cups and tablespoons, mL will be used.

e.g. 200 mL milk

50 mL brown sugar

Mass — Those ingredients which are expressed by weight will continue to be expressed by weight but instead of pounds and ounces, kg and g will be used.

e.g. 1 kg ground beef

170 g canned salmon

Length — The cm is the common unit for expressing length to replace the inch.

e.g. roll out cookie dough to 0.5 cm thick

PAN SIZES

2L CAKE PAN
(20x5 cm)
8x2 in
CAKE PAN

1.5L ROUND CAKE PAN
(23x4 cm)
9x1½ in
CAKE PAN

2.5L CAKE PAN (23x5 cm)
9x2 in CAKE PAN

3.5L CAKE PAN
(33x21x5)
13x9x2 in
CAKE PAN

1L PIE PAN
(23x3 cm)
9x1½ in
PIE PAN

2L JELLY ROLL PAN
(40x25x2 cm)
15x10x¾ in
JELLY ROLL PAN

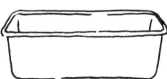

1.5L LOAF PAN
(20x10x7 cm)
8x4x3 in
LOAF PAN

2L LOAF PAN
(23x13x7 cm)
9x5x3 in
LOAF PAN

3L TUBE PAN
(23 x 10 cm)
9x4 in
TUBE PAN

2.5L CASSEROLE
2½ qt.

Oven Temperatures

°C to replace	°F
100	200
120	250
140	275
150	300
160	325
180	350
190	375
200	400
220	425
230	450
240	475
260	500

When baking in ovenproof glassware reduce given temperature 10°C (25°F). For example when using a glass cake pan, bake at 170°C when 180°C is given in recipe.

MENNONITE RECIPES

WHITE BREAD

Metric	Standard
Four 1.5 L loaf pans	Four 8 x 4 x 3 in.
(20 x 10 x 7 cm)	loaf pans
190°C	375°F
45 min.	
Yield: 4 loaves	

Ingredients:

Metric	Standard
5 mL sugar	1 tsp. sugar
125 mL lukewarm water	½ cup lukewarm water
1 pkg. (8 g) active dry yeast	1 pkg. active dry yeast
1.25 L warm water	5 cups warm water
175 mL oil	¾ cup oil
45 mL sugar	3 tbsps. sugar
15 mL salt	1 tbsp. salt
3000 mL flour (approx.)	12 cups flour (approx.)

Grease loaf pans. Dissolve 5 mL (1 tsp.) sugar in lukewarm water. Sprinkle yeast over liquid and let rise in warm place for about 10 minutes. Add remaining ingredients except flour. Gradually add a little flour at a time and beat until smooth. Knead enough flour into mixture to form a stiff smooth elastic dough. Place in greased bowl. Cover and let rise in warm place until double in bulk. Punch down and let rise again till double in bulk. Punch down again and shape into loaves. Place in greased loaf pans. Cover and let rise till double in bulk. Bake till golden brown and sounding hollow when tapped with finger.

Variation:

If you are out of bread and have mixed your white bread, roll out yeast dough after it has risen for about an hour. Cut in rectangles or desired shapes as for rollkuchen. Put a slit in centre of each rectangle. Fry in hot fat until brown on both sides. Drain. Good served warm with soup for lunch.

BROWN BREAD

Metric	Standard
1.5 L loaf pans (20 x 10 x 7 cm)	8 x 4 x 3 in. loaf pans
200°C	400°F
45 minutes	
Yield: 5-6 loaves	

Ingredients:

Metric	Standard
5 mL sugar	1 tsp. sugar
125 mL lukewarm water	½ cup lukewarm water
1 pkg. (8 g) active dry yeast	1 pkg. active dry yeast
1 L warm water	4 cups warm water
125 mL shortening **or** drippings	½ cup shortening **or** drippings
50 mL molasses	¼ cup molasses
5 mL salt	1 tsp. salt
750 mL whole wheat flour	3 cups whole wheat flour
750 mL dark rye flour	3 cups dark rye flour
1000 mL all-purpose flour	4 cups all-purpose flour

Grease five or six loaf pans. Dissolve sugar in lukewarm water. Sprinkle yeast over liquid and let rise in warm place for about 10 minutes. Combine warm water, shortening, molasses and salt in large bowl. Add yeast to molasses mixture. Add part of each flour and beat well till elastic. Knead in remaining flour. Continue kneading till dough is smooth. Grease sides of bowl. Shape dough into ball and place into greased bowl. Cover and let rise in warm place till double in bulk. Shape into five or six loaves and place into greased loaf pans. Pans should be about ½ or ⅔ full. Let rise for ½ hour in warm place. Bake till loaves sound hollow when tapped. Turn out of pans and cool on rack.

Note:

Loaves may be placed on greased cookie sheet when shaped and baked in this traditional way to give the loaf a rounded top.

ZWIEBACK
(Double Buns)

Metric	Standard
190-200°C	375-400°F
15-20 mins.	
Yield: about 6 dz.	

Ingredients:

Metric	Standard
5 mL sugar	1 tsp. sugar
125 mL lukewarm water	½ lukewarm water

Metric	Standard
2 pkg. (g each) active dry yeast	2 pkg. active dry yeast
1.25 L lukewarm water	5 cups lukewarm water
45 mL sugar	3 tbsps. sugar
15 mL salt	1 tbsp. salt
250 mL margarine	1 cup margarine
125 mL shortening	½ cup shortening
3500 mL flour	14 cups flour

Grease several cookie sheets. Dissolve sugar in lukewarm water. Sprinkle yeast over liquid and let rise in warm place for about 10 minutes. Combine yeast mixture with remaining ingredients, except flour. Add a little flour at a time beating well after each addition. Knead in remaining flour to make a smooth soft dough. Place in greased bowl and cover. Set in warm place, to rise till double in bulk. Punch down and let rise again till double in bulk. Punch down and shape dough into buns. Place medium buns on greased cookie sheet about 10 cm (2 in.) apart. Set a little bun (size of a walnut) firmly on top of each medium bun. Let rise till double in bulk. Bake till golden brown.

GLUMS PASKA
(Paska Spread)

Metric	Standard
Yield: about 750 mL	3 cups
1 container (375 g) dry cottage cheese	1 container (16 oz.) dry cottage cheese
3 hard cooked eggs	3 hard cooked eggs
125 mL soft butter	½ cup soft butter
250 mL sugar	1 cup sugar
2 mL vanilla	½ tsp. vanilla

Press first two ingredients through sieve. Mix soft butter and sugar. Combine and mix all ingredients. Mixture should be moist enough to spread. If too dry add a little light cream.

Variation:
Slivered almonds and finely chopped fruit peel may be added for flavor. Refrigerate to store; may also be frozen. A typical well-liked spread for paska.

ZWIEBACK
(Mennonite Double Buns)

Metric	*Standard*
200°C	400°F
15-20 min.	
Yield: 4 doz.	

Ingredients:

Metric	Standard
5 mL sugar	1 tsp. sugar
125 mL lukewarm water	½ cup lukewarm water
1½ pkg. (8 g each) active dry yeast	1½ pkg. active dry yeast
750 mL milk	3 cups milk
2000 mL flour	8 cups flour
10-15 mL salt	2-3 tsps. salt
250 mL shortening	1 cup shortening
50 mL soft butter	3 tbsps. soft butter

Dissolve sugar in lukewarm water. Sprinkle yeast over water and let stand in warm place for 10-15 minutes. Scald milk and cool to lukewarm. Mix ¾ of flour and salt. Rub in shortening to make crumbs of pea size. Make a well, add milk and yeast mixture. Add remaining flour and knead 5-10 minutes. Knead in the butter, 10-15 minutes. Shape dough into a ball and place in slightly greased bowl. Cover and let rise in warm place about one hour. Punch down and let rise again till double in bulk. Pinch off balls of dough, size of small egg. Place on greased cookie sheet 7 cm (1½ in.) apart. Place a smaller ball of dough on top of first ball. Press down firmly. Cover with light tea towel. Let rise in warm place until double in bulk. Bake and serve warm with homemade jam or use cold for vaspa.

PASKA

Metric	*Standard*
Twelve cans (680 mL each)	Twelve 24 oz. cans
120°C	250°F
1 hour	
Yield: 12 medium paska	

Ingredients:

Metric	Standard
15 mL sugar	1 tbsp. sugar
250 mL lukewarm potato water	1 cup lukewarm potato water
2 pkg. (8 g each) active dry yeast	2 pkg. active dry yeast
750 mL light cream	3 cups light cream
750 mL sugar	3 cups sugar

10 eggs separated	10 eggs separated
4000 mL flour	16 cups flour
375 mL butter	1½ cups butter
½ lemon	½ lemon
5 mL vanilla	1 tsp. vanilla

Grease cans lightly. Dissolve 15 mL (1 tbsp.) sugar in lukewarm potato water. Sprinkle yeast over mixture, and let stand for 10-15 minutes. Scald light cream and 125 mL (½ cup) of sugar. Cool, beat egg yolks and add to cream mixture. Beat egg whites and add to cream mixture along with yeast mixture, and about half of flour to make a sponge. Beat together and let rise until light, about 45 minutes. Add remaining sugar, butter grated rind and juice of lemon and vanilla. Knead in remaining flour to make a soft dough. Continue kneading until dough becomes smooth and begins to rise, about 20 minutes. Place dough in lightly greased bowl, cover. Let rise until double in bulk. Shape dough into balls and place into lightly greased tins, about ⅓ full. Let sit in warm place until dough just rises over edge of cans. Place well apart on centre or lower oven rack. Bake until fairly brown and light.

Note:
Cans or loaf pans of any size may be used, but the mushroom shaped paska is the authentic form for this delicious Easter bread.

DUTCH CINNAMON CAKE

Metric	Standard
3 L cake pan (30 x 20 x 5 cm)	12 x 8 x 2 in. cake pan
200° C	400° F
35-40 min.	

Ingredients:

250 mL Sugar	1 cup sugar
250 mL milk	1 cup milk
625 mL flour	2½ cups flour
10 mL baking powder	2 tsps. baking powder
125-175 mL nut meats	½-¾ cup nut meats
50 mL sugar	3 tbsps. sugar
2 mL cinnamon	½ tsp. cinnamon

Grease cake pan. Mix sugar, milk, flour, and baking powder. Place nut meats in bottom of cake pan. Pour dough by spoonfuls into pan. Mix remaining sugar and cinnamon. Sprinkle some over batter. Push bits of butter into batter. Sprinkle remaining sugar/cinnamon mixture over top. Bake until cake springs back when lightly pressed with finger. Serve fresh and warm.

EASTER BREAD

Metric	Standard
Six 1.5 L loaf pans	Six 8 x 4 x 3
(20 x 10 x 7 cm)	in. loaf pans
160-180°C	325-350°F
45 min.	

Ingredients:

Metric	Standard
500 mL raisins	2 cups raisins
5 mL sugar	1 tsp. sugar
125 mL lukewarm water	½ cup lukewarm water
2 pkg. (8 g each) active dry yeast	2 pkg. active dry yeast
250 mL light cream	1 cup light cream
250 mL milk	1 cup milk
300 mL margarine	1¼ cups margarine
6 eggs, separated	6 eggs, separated
5 mL vanilla	1 tsp. vanilla
375 mL sugar	1½ cups sugar
5 mL salt	1 tsp. salt
2500 mL flour	10 cups flour

Lightly grease loaf pans. Wash raisins, dry and roll in flour. Dissolve sugar in lukewarm water and sprinkle yeast over liquid. Let stand 10-15 minutes. Scald light cream and milk, cool slightly. Add margarine. Beat egg yolks and vanilla with sugar and salt. Beat egg whites to soft peaks. Combine all ingredients, mixing in flour to make a soft dough. Knead for a few minutes. Place into lightly greased bowl. Cover and let rise till double in bulk. Punch dough and shape into six loaves. Place in lightly greased loaf pans, about ⅓ full. Let rise in warm place until loaf pans are full or slightly over full. Bake until light and golden brown.

PASKA
(Easter Bread)

Metric	Standard
Six 750 mL cans	Six 24 oz. cans
160°C	325°F
1 hour	

Ingredients:

Metric	Standard
5 mL sugar	1 tsp. sugar
125 mL lukewarm water	½ cup lukewarm water
1 pkg. (8 g) active dry yeast	1 pkg. active dry yeast
375 mL milk	1½ cups milk
125 mL butter	½ cup butter
2 eggs, separated	2 eggs, separated

Metric	Standard
300 mL sugar	1¼ cups sugar
3 whole eggs	3 whole eggs
grated rind of 1 orange	grated rind of 1 orange
5 mL vanilla	1 tsp. vanilla
1750-2000 mL flour	7-8 cups flour

Dissolve sugar in lukewarm water. Sprinkle yeast over liquid and let rise in warm place for about 10 min. Scald milk, remove from heat and add butter. Mix egg yolks with sugar and whip until light. Beat egg whites until foamy. Mix flour, milk mixture, sugar mixture and egg whites to form a soft dough. Knead in last flour and continue kneading dough for about 10-15 mins. Place dough into greased bowl. Cover and let rise in warm place for one hour. Punch down and let rise till double in bulk. Grease cans well and sprinkle with flour or very fine crumbs. Divide dough into six or seven parts. Shape into smooth balls and place into cans. Cans should be only about ⅓ full of dough. Let rise well till dough rises slightly over edge of cans and seems light. Place cans well apart on lower rack in oven. Bake until hollow sounding when tapped and paska is fairly brown. Remove from cans and allow to cool on rack. Frost top part with white icing and sprinkle with fine colourful cake decorations. Place in centre of larger platter, trim with "Easter Grass" coloured eggs and candied eggs. This makes a lovely Easter table centerpiece. Paska should be served with glums paska spread.

SHOO-FLY PIE

Metric	Standard
One 25 cm pie pan	One 10 in. pie pan
190°C	375°F
35 min.	
2 mL baking soda	½ tsp. baking soda
150 mL boiling water	⅔ cup boiling water
150 mL molasses **or** maple syrup	⅔ cup molasses **or** maple syrup
375 mL flour	1½ cups flour
50 mL shortening	¼ cup shortening
125 mL brown sugar	½ cup brown sugar
Pastry for 25 cm (10 in.) pie shell	

Line pie plate with pastry. Dissolve soda in boiling water. Add molasses. Combine sugar, flour, and rub in shortening to make crumbs. Pour ⅓ of the molasses mixture into pie shell. Sprinkle ⅓ of the crumbs over liquid, pour another ⅓ of the liquid over this and repeat adding crumb and liquid until both are used up ending with crumbs on top. Bake. Serve with vanilla ice cream and hot coffee.

FRUIT CRUMB CAKE
(Platz)

Metric	Standard
2 L jelly roll pan (40 x 25 x 2 cm)	15 x 10 x ¾ jelly roll pan
180°C	350°F
30 min.	

Ingredients:

Base:

Metric	Standard
500 mL flour	2 cups flour
30 mL sugar	2 tbsps. sugar
20 mL baking powder	4 tsp. baking powder
1 mL salt	¼ tsp. salt
45 mL shortening	3 tbsp. shortening
1 egg	1 egg
125 mL milk	½ cup milk
2 cans (398 mL each) canned fruit	2 cans (14 oz. each) canned fruit
or 750 mL fresh cut fruit	or 3 cups fresh cut fruit

Topping:

Metric	Standard
125 mL sugar	½ cup sugar
125 mL flour	½ cup flour
30 mL butter	2 tbsps. butter

Grease jelly roll pan. **For base:** sift dry ingredients together. Cut in shortening. Stir egg into milk and add. Mixture will be sticky. Press into greased jelly roll pan. Drain canned fruit (or prepare fresh fruit) and place on dough. **For topping:** mix sugar, flour and butter to form crumbs and sprinkle over fruit. Bake till nicely browned. Cut in squares and serve as tasty snack.

Variation:

Base may be substituted with yeast dough. Roll dough to about 1 cm (½ in.) thickness. Cover with fruit and crumbs as above. Let rise till double in bulk and bake.

APRIKOSEN PLATZ
(Apricot Squares)

Metric	Standard
3 L cake pan (30 x 20 x 5 cm)	12 x 8 x 2 in. cake pan
190°C	375°F
30-35 min.	

Ingredients:

Base:

Metric	Standard
45 mL butter	3 tbsps. butter
45 mL heavy cream	3 tbsps. heavy cream

1 egg	1 egg
50 mL sugar	¼ cup sugar
pinch of salt	pinch of salt
250 mL flour	1 cup flour
10 mL baking powder	2 tsps. baking powder
5 mL vanilla	1 tsp. vanilla

Topping:

1 L fresh apricots	1 qt. fresh apricots
75 mL flour	⅓ cup flour
75 mL sugar	⅓ cup sugar
30 mL butter	2 tbsps. butter

For Base:

Cream butter, cream, egg, sugar and salt. Add and mix remaining ingredients. Press dough into greased pan.

For Topping:

Cover dough with quartered or halved fresh apricots. Combine flour, sugar and butter into crumbs. Sprinkle over apricots. Bake. Broil for a few minutes at the end of baking time to brown crumbs, if desired.

Variation:

Fresh apricots may be substituted by other fruit. Fruit such as plums or rhubarb may need a little extra sugar.

SCHNETKI

Metric	Standard
220°C	425°F
10-12 min.	
Yield: 2½ doz.	

Ingredients:

500 mL flour	2 cups flour
2 mL salt	½ tsp. salt
20 mL baking powder	4 tsps. baking powder
250 mL heavy cream	1 cup heavy cream

Combine dry ingredients. Add cream all at once. Mix just to moisten. Shape dough into ball. Roll out on well floured surface to about 1 cm (½ in.) thickness. Cut in 3 cm (2 in.) squares. Fold to make a roll. Place on lightly greased cookie sheet. Bake till golden. Serve hot with green bean soup or as a snack with homemade jam.

RHUBARB PLATZ

Metric	Standard
2 L jelly roll pan	15 x 10 x ¾ in.
(40 x 25 x 2 cm)	jelly roll pan
180°C	350°F
40 min.	

Ingredients:

Base:

500 mL four	2 cup flour
20 mL baking powder	4 tsps. baking powder
pinch of salt	pinch of salt
250 mL shortening	1 cup shortening
250 mL sour cream	1 cup sour cream
750 mL diced rhubarb	3 cups diced rhubarb
45 mL sugar or less	3 tbsps. sugar or less

Topping:

125 mL sugar	½ cup sugar
125 mL flour	½ cup flour
30-45 mL butter	2-3 tbsps. butter

Sift flour, baking powder and salt. Cut in half of shortening till mixture resembles coarse crumbs, then cut in remaining shortening. Moisten with sour cream. Pat into greased jelly roll pan, fairly thin. Top with diced rhubarb and sprinkle with sugar (amount depending on sweetness of fruit used). Mix topping ingredients into crumbs. Sprinkle over as topping for platz. Bake till golden brown.

Variation: Jam Squares

180°C	350°F
12-15 min.	

Yield: Approx. 4 doz.

Prepare dough as above increasing flour to 750 mL (3 cups). Roll out dough fairly thin on floured surface. Cut in 5-8 cm (2-3 in.) squares. On each, place a dab of jam. Fasten two opposite corners of squares across jam with a toothpick. Bake and cool slightly. Remove toothpicks. Brush on thin icing. Makes a nice, tasty dainty.

PEACH CRUMBLE PIE

Metric	Standard
1 L pie pan (23 x 3 cm)	9 in. pie pan
180°C — 35 min.	350°F
150°C — 10-20 min.	300°F

Ingredients:

Pastry for 1 pie shell	Pastry for 1 pie shell

Filling:

750 mL peeled, sliced peaches	3 cups peeled, sliced peaches
15 mL lemon juice	1 tbsp. lemon juice
5 mL grated lemon rink	1 tsp. grated lemon rind
125 mL sugar	½ cup sugar
15-25 mL cornstarch	1-1½ tbsps. cornstarch

Topping:

125 mL flour	½ cup flour
125 mL sugar	½ cup sugar
2 mL nutmeg **or** cinnamon	½ tsp. nutmeg **or** cinnamon
45-60 mL soft butter	3-4 tbsps. soft butter

Line pie pan with pastry.

For Filling: Place peeled, sliced peaches in bowl. Sprinkle with lemon juice and rind. Combine sugar and cornstarch; add to peaches. Mix well and turn into pie shell. **For Topping:** Combine ingredients in order given. Mix with fork to consistency of crumbs. Sprinkle over peach filling. Bake at high temperature for time given. Reduce heat and bake until filling bubbles. Serve warm with ice cream or plain.

SCHNETKI

Metric	*Standard*
220°C	425°F
12 min.	
Yield: 12-18	

Ingredients:

500 mL flour	2 cups flour
2 mL salt	½ tsp. salt
20 mL baking powder	4 tsps. baking powder
15 mL sugar	1 tbsp. sugar
45 mL shortening	3 tbsps. shortening
125 mL milk	½ cup milk
75 mL heavy cream	⅓ cup heavy cream
1 egg	1 egg

Mix dry ingredients. Cut in shortening. Combine remaining ingredients and add gradually to flour mixture. Knead briefly just till flour disappears. Roll out dough on lightly floured surface, to about 1 cm (¼ in.) thickness. Roll edge up one whole turn. Cut along roll and remove from flat dough. Cut roll across in 7 cm (3 in.) sections. Repeat with remaining dough. Place on ungreased cookie sheet and bake. Schnetki should be golden like tea biscuits. Serve hot with borscht or green bean soup.

ROSINENSTRITZEL
(Raisin Loaf)

Metric	Standard
180°C	350°F
1 hour	
Yield: 10 small loaves	

Ingredients:

5 mL sugar	1 tsp. sugar
125 mL lukewarm water	½ cup lukewarm water
1 pkg (8 g.) active dry yeast	1 pkg active dry yeast
1 L milk	4 cups milk
250 mL shortening	1 cup shortening
1 L raisins	4 cups raisins
50 mL sugar	¼ cup sugar
15 mL salt	1 tbsp. salt
1500 mL flour	6 cups flour
1 egg	1 egg

Grease cookie sheets lightly. Dissolve 5 mL (1 tsp.) sugar in lukewarm water. Sprinkle quick rising yeast over liquid. Let stand 10 minutes. Scald milk, add shortening and cool slightly. Wash raisins, drain and dust with flour. Combine yeast, sugar, salt and part of flour with scalded milk. Beat well, add dusted raisins. Work in remaining flour to make a medium soft dough. Knead for 10-15 minutes. Place in large greased bowl, cover. Let rise one hour in warm place. Punch down and let rise again until double in bulk. Shape in round loaves about the size of a grapefruit. Place on lightly greased cookie sheets about 8-10 cm (3-4 m) apart. Beat egg and brush surface of leaves before baking. Bake until golden brown and light.

ROSINENSTRITZEL
(Raisin Bread)

Metric	Standard
Four 1.5 L loaf pans	Four 8 x 4 x 3 in. loaf pans
(20 x 10 x 7 cm)	
160°C	
1 hour	
Yield: 4 loaves	

Ingredients:

10 mL sugar	2 tsps. sugar
250 mL lukewarm water	1 cup lukewarm water
2 pkg (8 g.) active dry yeast	2 pkg active dry yeast
500 mL raisins	2 cups raisins
500 mL milk	2 cups milk

175 mL shortening	¾ cup shortening
2250 mL flour	9 cups flour
250 mL sugar	1 cup sugar
4 eggs	4 eggs

Grease loaf pans lightly. Dissolve 5 mL (1 tsp.) sugar in lukewarm water. Sprinkle quick rising yeast over liquid. Let stand in warm place for 10-15 minutes. Wash and dry raisins. Scald milk, add shortening and cool to lukewarm. Combine part of flour and remaining sugar in large bowl. Form well in centre and add eggs, milk mixture, yeast mixture and raisins. Beat well adding remaining flour. Knead to a medium soft dough for a few minutes. Place dough in lightly greased bowl. Cover and set in warm place for one hour. Punch down and let rise again until double in bulk. Shape into loaves and place in greased loaf pans. Let rise until double in bulk. Bake for about an hour or until loaves are light and nicely browned. Turn out of pans and let cook on rack.

RAISIN BREAD

Metric	Standard
Two 2 L loaf pans	Two 9 x 5 x 3 in.
(23 x 13 x 7 cm)	loaf pans
160°C	325°F
1 hour	

Ingredients:

125 mL lukewarm water	½ cup lukewarm water
5 mL sugar	1 tsp. sugar
1 pkg (8 g.) active dry yeast	1 pkg active dry yeast
250 mL lukewarm milk	1 cup lukewarm milk
2 eggs, well beaten	2 eggs, well beaten
500 mL raisins	2 cups raisins
125 mL melted shortening	½ cup melted shortening
125 mL sugar	½ cup sugar
1200-1250 mL flour	4½-5 cups flour

Dissolve sugar in lukewarm water. Sprinkle yeast over water, let stand in warm place for about 10 minutes. Add remaining ingredients in order given. Knead thoroughly (about 15 minutes). Shape dough into ball and place in lightly greased bowl. Cover and let rise in warm place till double in bulk. Shape into two loaves and place into greased loaf pans. Cover with tea towel and let rise in warm place till double in bulk. Bake till bread is nicely browned and sounds hollow when lightly tapped. Remove from loaf pans and cool on rack.

KRINGEL

Metric	Standard
200°C	400°F

30 min.
Yield: 3 doz.

Ingredients:

Metric	Standard
125 mL butter	½ cup butter
1250 mL flour	5¼ cups flour
5 eggs	5 eggs
250 mL heavy cream **or** condensed Carnation milk	1 cup heavy cream **or** condensed Carnation milk
125 mL sugar	½ cup sugar
3 L water	3 qts. water
2 mL salt	½ tsp. salt
poppy seed	poppy seed

Grease cookie sheet. Cut butter into 250 mL of flour to make crumbs. Add eggs, cream, sugar and remaining flour to make a fairly hard dough. Knead briefly. Shape dough into rolls 1 cm (½ in.) in diameter and 15 cm (6 in.) in length. Bring ends together to form a circle. Bring water and salt to boil in 5 L (5 qt.) saucepan. Drop kringel into boiling salt water. When kringel rise to top remove carefully with slotted spoon or tongs, and place on greased cookie sheet about 2 cm (1 in.) apart. Sprinkle with poppy seed. Bake until golden brown, shiny and firm.

Note:

Temperature may need to be turned down for the last five minutes of baking.

PEPPERNUTS
(Spice Buns)

Metric	Standard
160°C	325°F

20-25 min.
Yield: About 5 doz.

Ingredients:

Metric	Standard
5 mL sugar	1 tsp. sugar
250 mL lukewarm water	1 cup lukewarm water
2 pkg (8 g. each) active dry yeast	2 pkg active dry yeast
750 mL warm water	3 cups warm water
250 mL melted shortening	1 cup melted shortening
500 mL white **or** yellow sugar	2 cups white **or** yellow sugar
5 mL pepper	1 tsp. pepper

2 mL salt	½ tsp. salt
5 mL cinnamon	1 tsp. cinnamon
2750 mL flour	11 cups flour

Dissolve 5 mL (1 tsp.) sugar in lukewarm water (6 p.m.) Sprinkle yeast over liquid and let stand in warm place for 10 minutes. Combine with remaining ingredients gradually beating in a little flour at a time. Knead in last of flour, dough should be soft. Continue kneading for a few minutes after all of flour has been added. Place dough into lightly greased bowl. Cover and let rise for about four hours. Shape dough into buns and place on greased cookie sheet (11 p.m.). Let rise all night. Bake first thing in the morning (7 a.m.).

HARD PEPPERNUTS

Metric	*Standard*
160°C	325°F
10 min.	
Yield:	

Ingredients:

500 mL water	2 cups water
10 mL aniseed	2 tsps. aniseed
500 mL brown sugar	2 cups brown sugar
5 mL vanilla	1 tsp. vanilla
1500 mL flour	6 cups flour
10 mL baking soda	2 tsps. baking soda
250 mL butter	1 cup butter

Grease cookie sheet. In 1 L. (1 qt.) pot, boil water and aniseed for 15 minutes. Add brown sugar and boil for another 10 minutes. Cool; add vanilla. Mix flour and baking soda. Add along with butter to sugar mixture. Mix to medium soft dough or consistency of bread dough. Chill thoroughly. Shape into long rolls as thick as a finger. Cut into pieces the size of a hazelnut. Place slightly apart on greased cookie sheet. Bake until peppernuts are golden brown. Dust with icing sugar and enjoy this typical Mennonite Christmas cookie.

PEPPERNUTS

Metric	Standard
190°C	375°F
25 mins.	
Yield: 2.5 L	2½ qts.

Ingredients:

375 mL brown sugar	1½ cups brown sugar
125 mL syrup	½ cup syrup
125 mL water	½ cup water
125 mL shortening	½ cup shortening
2 beaten eggs	2 beaten eggs
2 mL cinnamon	½ tsp. cinnamon
2 mL aniseed crushed	½ tsp. aniseed crushed
2 mL cloves	½ tsp. cloves
3 mL soda (dissolved in 15 mL water)	¾ tsp. soda (dissolved in 1 tbsp. water)
1 L flour	4 cups flour

Bring brown sugar, syrup and water to a boil and cool slightly. Add remaining ingredients and mix well. Roll dough into long rolls as thick as your finger. Cut off ¼ inch slices and bake on greased cookie sheet until nicely browned.

AMMONIA KUCHEN

Metric	Standard
180°C	350°F
10-15 min.	
Yield: 4-5 doz.	

Ingredients:

125 mL butter	½ cup butter
375 mL sugar	1½ cups sugar
2 eggs, beaten	2 eggs, beaten
250 mL sour cream	1 cup sour cream
20 mL baking ammonia	4 tsps. baking ammonia
125 mL milk	½ cup milk
1 mL peppermint extract	¼ tsp. peppermint extract
1125-1250 mL flour	4½-5 cups flour

Cream butter, add sugar, beaten eggs, sour cream and mix. Dissolve baking ammonia in part of milk. Add ammonia mixture, remaining milk and peppermint extract. Add flour to make a soft dough. (The softer the dough, the better the cookies). Roll out dough on well floured surface to 1 cm (½ in.) thickness. Cut out with 5 cm (2 in.) cookie cutter. Place on lightly greased cookie sheet and bake. Cookies should be light in colour.

SCHMAUNTCOAKI
(Cream Cookies)

Metric	Standard
190°C	375°F
12-18 min.	
Yield: 5 doz. large	

Ingredients:

2 L flour	8 cups flour
625 mL sugar	2½ cups sugar
20 mL baking powder	4 tsps. baking powder
10 mL baking soda	2 tsps. baking soda
750 mL sour cream	3 cups sour cream
250 mL soft butter	1 cup soft butter
4 eggs	4 eggs
10 mL vanilla	2 tsps. vanilla

Combine dry ingredients. Combine remaining ingredients and add to dry ingredients, mixing well. Roll out on well floured board to 3 cm (½ in.) thickness. Dough will be soft. Cut out with large 5 cm (2 in.) cookie cutter. Place 5 cm (2 in.) apart on greased cookie sheet and bake. Cookies should be white when done and spring back with lightly touched. An old-fashioned, but still well liked cookie.

AMMONIA COOKIES

Metric	Standard
180°C	350°F
12-15 min.	
Yield: 3½ doz. large cookies	

Ingredients:

250 mL shortening	1 cup shortening
375 mL sugar	1½ cups sugar
2 eggs, beaten	2 eggs, beaten
12 mL lemon juice	2½ tsps. lemon juice
250 mL milk	1 cup milk
12 mL baking ammonia	2½ tsps. baking ammonia
8 mL baking powder	1½ tsps. baking powder
1250 mL flour	5 cups flour

Cream shortening. Add sugar, beaten eggs, lemon juice and milk; mix. Sift remaining ingredients. Add to egg mixture and mix well. Dough will be very soft and sticky. Pat out on floured surface to about 1 cm (½ in.) thickness. Cut with 5 cm (2 in.) floured cookie cutter. Place on lightly greased cookie sheet. Bake and cool. Ice with butter icing and sprinkle with coconut.

BLITZ TORTE

Metric	Standard
Two 1.2 L layer cake pans (20 x 4 cm)	Two 8 in. layer cake pans
160°C — 25 min.	325°F
180°C — 30 min.	350°F

Ingredients:

Metric	Standard
75 mL margarine	⅓ cup margarine
125 mL sugar	½ cup sugar
1 mL salt	¼ tsp. salt
2 mL vanilla	½ tsp. vanilla
4 eggs, separated	4 eggs, separated
250 mL sifted cake flour	1 cup sifted cake flour
or	**or**
220 mL all-purpose flour	1 cup minus 2 tbsp. all-purpose flour
5 mL baking powder	1 tsp. baking powder
45 mL milk	3 tbsps. milk
175 mL sugar	¾ cup sugar
125 mL nut meats	½ cup nut meats

Grease layer cake pans. Cream margarine, sugar, and vanilla. Beat egg yolks and add to creamed mixture. Sift cake flour with baking powder. Add dry ingredients alternately with milk to creamed mixture, beginning and ending with flour. Turn batter into greased pans. Beat egg whites to stiff peaks, adding remaining sugar a little at a time. Beat after each addition. Spread with nut meats. Bake at low temperature for 25 minutes. Increase temperature and bake for an additional 30 minutes, as indicated above. Let cool in pans. Remove and put layers together with custard pudding. May be topped with whipped cream.

NAPOLEON'S TORTE

Metric	Standard
190°C	375°F
12-15 min.	
Yield: 12-15 average layers, enough for two cakes	

Ingredients:

Dough:

Metric	Standard
90 mL butter	6 tbsps. butter
125 mL sugar	½ cup sugar
5 mL baking soda	1 tsp. baking soda
250 mL sour cream	1 cup sour cream

2 eggs	2 eggs
750-1000 mL flour	3-4 cups flour

Filling:

1 L milk	1 qt. milk
4 eggs, beaten separately	4 eggs, beaten separately
50 mL cornstarch	¼ cup cornstarch
250 mL sugar	1 cup sugar

Grease cookie sheet lightly.

For Dough:

Cream butter and sugar. Dissolve baking soda in sour cream, mix thoroughly with creamed mixture. Add eggs one at a time, beat well. Add flour to make a soft dough — easy to roll. Roll out thin 0.5 cm (⅛ in.) on well floured surface. Place medium-sized plate on dough and cut out. Transfer each layer to slightly greased cookie sheet. Prick well with fork and bake till light brown. Cool and prepare the followinq:

Filling:

Scald milk in double boiler. Mix egg yolks, cornstach and sugar. Add to milk and boil until thickened, stir occasionally. Remove from heat. Fold in stiffly beaten egg whites. Spoon a little filling onto a large level platter. Place one layer in center of platter. Spoon more filling in center of layer and spread evenly. Continue until layers and filling are used. Do not stack too many layers since they slide off easily and filling may be lost. Chill torte for 2-3 hours before serving with whipped cream, or colourful fruit.

APFELKUCHEN
(Apple Fritters)

Metric	Standard
Yield: 16	

Ingredients:

250 mL flour	1 cup flour
1 mL salt	¼ tsp. salt
3 eggs	3 eggs
125 mL milk	½ cup milk
375-500 mL diced apples	1½-2 cups diced apples
icing sugar	icing sugar

Sift dry ingredients together. Add eggs and milk, beat well. Add pared, diced apples and mix well. Drop batter by spoonfuls into deep hot fat, 190°C (375°F). Fry till golden brown. Serve with sugar.

PIROSHKI
(Minced Meat Tarts)

Metric	Standard
190°C	375°F
15-20 min.	
Yield: Approx. 2½ doz.	

Ingredients:

1 onion, sliced	1 onion, sliced
750 mL meat leftovers	3 cups meat leftovers
2 hard cooked eggs	2 hard cooked eggs
salt and pepper	salt and pepper
to taste	to taste
pastry for	pastry for
double-crust pie	double-crust pie

Saute sliced onion until soft. Do not brown. Put through food chopper along with meat leftovers. (e.g. roast beef or pork) and hard boiled eggs. Mix; add salt and pepper to taste. Roll out pastry on lightly floured surface to about 0.5 cm (⅛ in.) thickness. Cut in 7 cm (3 in.) squares. Place a spoonful of meat mixture on each square. Fold up into triangle or rectangle. Press edges together. Place on ungreased cookie sheet. Bake until nicely browned. Serve with borscht.

Variations:

Sugared, cooked rhubarb or apples may be substituted for meat. Zwieback dough may replace pastry, but let rise on cookie sheet 30-45 minutes before baking.

PIROSHKI (Fruit)

Metric	Standard
200°C	400°F
10-12 min.	
Yield: 4 doz.	

Ingredients:

250 mL lard	1 cup lard
1 L flour	4 cups flour
1 egg	1 egg
5 mL baking powder	1 tsp. baking powder
150 mL milk	⅔ cup milk (Approx.)
1200 mL prepared fruit	4-¾ cups prepared fruit
for filling	for filling

Combine flour and baking powder. Cut in shortening. Make a well in the center; add egg and milk. Mix to form a soft dough.

Roll out to 0.5 cm (¼ in.) and cut into 7.5 cm (3 in.) squares. On each square place 25 mL fruit, and 5 mL (1 tsp.) sugar, gather the flour corners together and seal and sides so that the juice will not run out. Place on an ungreased cookie sheet. Bake until nicely brown.

Note: Fruit for filling may be apples, cherries, gooseberries, apricots, rhubarb or blueberries.

PIROSHKI

Metric	Standard
180°C	350°F
15-20 min.	
Yield: 10-12 doz.	

Ingredients:

Metric	Standard
750 mL sugar	3 cups sugar
375 mL honey	1½ cups honey
500 mL hot water	2 cups hot water
1 pkg. (85 g) lemon **or** orange jello powder	1 pkg. (3 oz.) lemon **or** orange jello powder
2000 mL flour	8 cups flour
10 mL baking soda	2 tsps. baking soda
5 mL cinnamon	1 tsp. cinnamon
2 mL cloves (optional)	½ tsp. cloves
5 mL allspice (optional)	1 tsp. allspice
15 mL baking ammonia	1 tbsp. baking ammonia
5 mL vanilla	1 tsp. vanilla
250 mL cooking oil	1 cup cooking oil
3 eggs plus 2 egg yolks	3 eggs plus 2 egg yolks

Grease cookie sheets. In 2 L (2 qt.) saucepan bring first three ingredients to boil. Add lemon jello powder, cool slightly. Mix dry ingredients together. Add along with remaining ingredients to jello mixture. Dough should be fairly soft. (It is important not to let the dough get cool.) Roll out dough on lightly floured surface to about 1 cm (⅜ in.) thickness. Cut out with round 5 cm (2 in.) cookie cutter. Place a little jam on each cookie. Bring one side over to the other. Press edges together to enclose jam. Put pressed side down on greased cookie sheet. Bake till nicely browned. When cooled frost with "fluffy white icing", using remaining egg whites.

Note: Jam such as apple jam with no added pectin is suggested.

PIROSHKI

Metric	Standard
180°C	350°F
10 min.	
Yield: 18 doz.	

Ingredients:

Metric	Standard
1 L sugar	4 cups sugar
250 mL honey	1 cup honey
500 mL hot water	2 cups hot water
5 mL gelatine, dissolved in 50 mL cold water	1 tsp. gelatine dissolved in ¼ cup cold water
2-2.5 L flour (or enough to make a soft dough)	8-9 cups flour (or enough to make a soft dough)
10 mL soda	2 tsps. soda
15 mL baking ammonia	3 tsps. baking ammonia
5 mL cinnamon	1 tsp. cinnamon
5 mL cloves	1 tsp. cloves
2 mL allspice	½ tsp. allspice
10 mL vanilla	2 tsps. vanilla
250 mL cooking oil	1 cup cooking oil
Jam	Jam

Place sugar, honey, and water in a 2 L (2 qt.) saucepan; bring to a boil, add gelatine and bring to a boil again. Cool slightly. Combine flour, soda, ammonia and spices. Add vanilla and cooking oil. Add flour mixture to heated sugar mixture to form a soft dough. Roll out to 0.5 cm (¼ in.) and cut with a round cookie cutter. Place a little jam on each cookie. Bring one side over to the other and press together. Place pressed side down on greased cookie sheet. Bake until nicely browned. Cool, frost with fluffy white icing. Cover with complete cookie and let icing dry thoroughly before serving.

LEBKUCHEN
(Traditional German Christmas Cookies)

Metric	Standard
180°C	350°F
10-15 min.	
Yield: 5½ doz.	

Ingredients:

Metric	Standard
10 mL potash	2 tsps. potash
75 mL water	⅓ cup water
7 mL baking ammonia	1½ tsps. baking ammonia
300 mL honey	1¼ cups honey
175 mL sugar	¾ cup sugar

Metric	Standard
1050 mL four	4¼ cups flour
2 mL cinnamon	½ tsp. cinnamon
2 mL cloves	½ tsp. cloves
rind of 2 oranges	rind of 2 oranges
1 lemon	1 lemon
2 eggs	2 eggs

Dissolve potash in half of the water. Dissolve baking ammonia in remaining water. Cover both and set aside in warm place for 1 hour. Sift dry ingredients. Put half of dry ingredients, orange and lemon rind in a large bowl. Bring honey and sugar to a boil. Add to dry ingredient mixture; mix well. Add potash and ammonia mixture. Stir until mixture is slightly cool. Add eggs and remaining dry ingredients. Mix; dough will be very sticky. Chill for several hours. Form balls the size of a walnut. Set about 5 cm (2 in.) apart on a lightly greased cookie sheet. Place pan with water on lower rack. Bake until golden brown and cookies are firm when touched with finger. Immerse whole cookies in white icing. A lovely, chewy Christmas cookie.

ROLLKUCHEN
(Crullers)

Metric	Standard
Yield: About 3 doz.	

Ingredients:

Metric	Standard
750 mL flour	3 cups flour
5 mL baking powder	1 tsp. baking powder
2 mL salt	½ tsp. salt
2 eggs	2 eggs
125 mL sour cream	½ cup sour cream
125 mL milk	½ cup milk

Mix dry ingredients together. Add eggs, sour cream and milk; mix well. Roll out dough on floured surface to about 0.5 cm (⅛ in.) thickness. Cut into rectangular pieces. Fry quickly in hot fat, 190°C (375°F), till golden brown, turn once. Drain on paper towel. Serve with borscht on a cold day, with watermelon on a hot summer day.

Variation:

Cut rolled out dough in squares. Place any kind of fruit, such as chokecherries, blueberries, apples, gooseberries, rhubarb or raspberries on each square. Add a little sugar. Fold squares over and pinch edges together securely. Fry quickly in deep fat, turning once. Fry until nicely brown.

ROLLKUCHEN

Metric	Standard
Yield: About 5 doz.	
Ingredients:	
50 mL butter	¼ cup butter
125 mL milk	½ cup milk
750 mL flour	3 cups flour
5 mL salt	1 tsp. salt
3 eggs	3 eggs

Melt butter in small saucepan. Remove from heat and add milk. Combine flour and salt in mixing bowl. Add milk mixture and eggs. Mix well to a smooth, hard dough. Roll out on lightly floured surface as thin as possible; 0.5 cm (⅛ in.). Sprinkle with a little flour to prevent sticking. Cut in rectangles or desired shape. Fry in deep fat 190°C (375°F) till nicely brown, turning once. Drain on paper towel. Serve with Borscht or watermelon on a hot summer day.

PORTZELKY
(New Year's Cookies)

Metric	Standard
Yield: 4-5 doz.	
Ingredients:	
5 mL sugar	1 tsp. sugar
125 mL lukewarm water	½ cup lukewarm water
1 pkg. (8 g) active	1 pkg. active
dry yeast	dry yeast
500 mL raisins	2 cups raisins
250 mL lukewarm milk	1 cup lukewarm milk
2 mL salt	½ tsp. salt
3 eggs	3 eggs
750-800 mL flour	3-3¼ cups flour

Dissolve sugar in lukewarm water. Sprinkle yeast over liquid and let rise for 10 minutes. Wash and dry raisins. Combine yeast mixture, raisins and remaining ingredients. Beat well and cover. Set in warm place to rise till double in bulk. Drop by spoonfuls into deep hot fat, 190°C (375°F). Cook until delicately brown. Sprinkle with icing sugar and serve at New Year's.

Variation:

Leftover portzelky may be placed in slightly greased casserole dish. Pour hot milk over, not quite covering portzelky. Close and bake in 180°C oven for about 45 minutes or until milk is mostly absorbed and portzelky are thoroughly heated. Serve hot.

PORTZELKY
(Yeast Fritters)

Metric	*Standard*
Yield: Approx. 8 doz.	

Ingredients:

Metric	Standard
10 mL sugar	2 tsps. sugar
250 mL lukewarm water	1 cup lukewarm water
2 pkg. (8 g each) active dry yeast	2 pkg. active dry yeast
1 L currants **or** raisins	4 cups currants **or** raisins
500 mL milk	2 cups milk
175 mL sugar	¾ cup sugar
5 mL salt	1 tsp. salt
125 mL melted butter	½ cup melted butter
4 eggs	4 eggs
1500 mL flour	6 cups flour

Dissolve 5 mL (1 tsp.) sugar in lukewarm water. Sprinkle quick rising yeast over liquid, let stand for 10 minutes. Wash currants in warm water, drain well. Heat milk slightly. Add sugar, salt, melted butter eggs and yeast. Add part of flour and beat well by hand. Add raisins, remaining flour and mix thoroughly. Set in warm place to rise till nearly double in bulk. Drop by tablespoonfuls into hot fat, 190°C (375°F). Avoid breaking sponge bubbles. Fry quickly till nicely browned like fritters. Drain on absorbent paper towel and serve.

PFANNKUCHEN
(Pancakes)

Metric	*Standard*
23 cm frying pan	9 in. frying pan
Yield: 1 doz. 23 cm. pancakes	1 doz. 9 in. pancakes

Ingredients:

Metric	Standard
375 mL flour	1½ cups flour
1 mL salt	¼ tsp. salt
5 eggs	5 eggs
550-600 mL milk	2¼-2½ cups milk
melted butter **or** margarine	melted butter **or** margarine

Mix flour and salt. Stir eggs and milk together; pour into flour. Mix well to make a smooth batter. Lightly grease hot frying pan with melted butter. Pour about 75 mL (⅓ cup) batter into pan. Rotate to cover base of frying pan with batter. When bubbles appear on surface, turn pancake. The thinner the pancakes, the better. Serve with syrup, sugar or fruit preserve.

CORN FRITTERS

Metric	Standard
Serves: 4-6	

Ingredients:

6 ears fresh corn	6 ears fresh corn
5 eggs, separated	5 eggs, separated
2 mL salt	½ tsp. salt

Remove milk from corn with corn grater or cut with knife lengthwise through center of kernel raw and scrape with back of knife to remove milk from kernels. Mix corn, milk, egg yolks and salt. Beat egg whites to stiff peaks. Fold into corn mixture. Drop by spoonfuls into hot, well buttered fry pan. Fry on both sides still light brown. Serve immediately with syrup.

PLAIN WAFFLES

Metric	Standard
Serves: 5-6	

Ingredients:

500 mL flour	2 cups flour
10 mL baking powder	2 tsps. baking powder
10 mL sugar	2 tsps. sugar
5 mL salt	1 tsp. salt
500 mL milk	2 cups milk
2 eggs, separated	2 eggs, separated
125 mL melted butter	½ cup melted butter

Combine dry ingredients. Add milk and beat well. Add beaten egg yolks and melted butter. Beat well. Beat egg whites to stiff peaks and fold into mixture. Pour 50-125 mL batter (¼-½ cup) into hot, greased waffle iron, depending on size of iron. Close and bake for about four minutes or until waffle is nicely browned on both sides. Serve hot with waffle or fruit sauce.

KÄSEPFANNKUCHEN
(Cottage Cheese Crêpes)

Metric	Standard
Yield: 20-20 cm pancakes	20 8" pancakes
Serves: 6-8	

Ingredients:

Batter:

750 mL flour	3 cups flour
2 mL salt	½ tsp. salt
3 eggs	3 eggs

15 mL oil	1 tbsp. oil
875 mL-1 L milk	3½-4 cups milk

Cottage Cheese Filling:

500 g dry cottage cheese	1 lb. dry cottage cheese
2 eggs	2 eggs
2 mL salt	½ tsp. salt

For Batter:

Mix ingredients in order given. Beat well to make a fairly thin smooth batter. Lightly grease bottom and sides of hot frying pan. Pour 50-75 mL (¼-⅓ cup) batter into pan. Rotate pan to spread batter evenly around bottom. Remove when both sides are baked and place flat on large plate.

For Cottage Cheese Filling:

Mix ingredients well. Place some filling along one side of crepe. Roll up and place in shallow, lightly greased baking pan. Dot with butter or margarine and bake at 180°C (350°F) for about 30 minutes. Serve with sour cream or cream gravy.

Note: Filled crêpes may also be returned to lightly greased frying pan and baked on low heat for 10-15 minutes.

Variation:

Crêpes may be filled with jam, pie filling, or fruit sauce. These do not need to be baked and make a nice dessert.

BUTTERMILK WAFFLES

Metric	Standard

Serves: 3-4

Ingredients:

500 mL flour	2 cups flour
5 mL salt	1 tsp. salt
3 mL baking soda	½ tsp. baking soda
550 mL buttermilk	2¼ cups buttermilk
125 mL melted butter **or** margarine	½ cup melted butter **or** margarine
2 eggs, separated	2 eggs, separated

Mix dry ingredients and make a well in center of bowl. Add buttermilk, melted butter and egg yolks. Beat egg whites to stiff peaks and fold into above mixture. Pour some batter on a hot, oiled waffle iron and bake briefly until waffles are a golden brown. Serve with syrup, fruit sauce or your favourite topping.

PLUMA MOOS
(Fruit Soup)

Metric	Standard
4 L saucepan	4 qt. saucepan
Serves: 8-10	

Ingredients:

250 mL seedless raisins	1 cup seedless raisins
250 mL dried prunes	1 cup dried prunes
50 mL dried peaches	¼ cup dried peaches
50 mL dried apricots	¼ cup dried apricots
2 L warm water	2 qts. warm water
125 mL cold water	½ cup cold water
125 mL sugar	½ cup sugar
50 mL flour	¼ cup flour
2 mL salt	½ tsp. salt
5 mL cinnamon (optional)	1 tsp. cinnamon (optional)
heavy cream (optional)	heavy cream (optional)

Wash fruit and add warm water. Place over heat and bring to a boil. Simmer until almost tender. Prepare paste with cold water, sugar, flour and salt. Slowly add paste to simmering mixture, stirring constantly. Cook until slightly thickened. Add cinnamon and heavy cream for extra flavour. Serve warm or cold with Mannagrütze if desired.

PLUMA MOOS
(Fruit soup)

Metric	Standard
4 L saucepan	4 qt. saucepan
Serves: About 10	

Ingredients:

1 pkg (340 g) fruit compote	1 pkg (12 oz.) fruit compote
3 cm cinnamon stick	1 in. cinnamon stick
1 star aniseed (optional)	1 star aniseed (optional)
2 L cold water	2 qts. cold water
75-50 mL cornstarch	¼-⅓ cup cornstarch
125 mL sugar	½ cup sugar
1 can (398 mL) bing cherries	1 can (14 oz.) bing cherries

In saucepan, combine fruit compote and spices with cold water. Boil until fruit is tender. Dissolve cornstarch in a little cold water. Add to hot moos; stir. Add sugar and bing cherries with juice. Boil till thickened, stirring occasionally. Serve warm or cold with or with Mannagrütze pudding.

MILK MOOS WITH FRUIT

Metric	Standard
1.5 L double boiler	1½ qts. double boiler

Serves: 6-8

Ingredients:

1 L milk	1 qt. milk
125 mL sugar	½ cup sugar
50 mL flour	3 tbsps. flour
125 mL cold milk	½ cup cold milk
1 can (398 mL)	1 can (14 oz.)
bing cherries	bing cherries

Scald milk in double boiler. Make a thin paste of sugar, flour and cold milk. Add to scalded milk and cook until thickened. Drain bing cherries and add. Simmer just for a few minutes. Serve hot with fried potatoes and ham or sausage. A typical Mennonite meal. Tastes good cold as well.

Variation:

Pears or any other cooked fruit may be used in place of bing cherries.

STACHELBEER MOOS
(Gooseberry Moos)

Metric	Standard
4 L saucepan	4 qt. saucepan

Serves: 6-8

Ingredients:

500 mL gooseberries	2 cups gooseberries
45 mL water	3 tbsps. water
125 mL sugar	½ cup sugar
1.5 L milk	6 cups milk
1 egg	1 egg
30 mL flour	2 tbsps. flour
45 mL milk	3 tbsps. milk
5 mL vanilla (optional)	1 tsp. vanilla (optional)

Simmer gooseberries, water and sugar 6-8 minutes. Add 1.5 L (6 cups) milk, stirring continuously. The more quickly this mixture can be brought to a boil, the more likely curdling can be avoided. Beat egg, flour and 50 mL (3 tbsps.) milk with a beater. When milk and gooseberry mixture is at full boil, add a little of it to egg mixture; stir. Add egg mixture to hot milk; stir continuously. Boil for 2 minutes. Remove from burner, add additional sugar to taste. Flavour with vanilla if desired. May be served hot or cold.

BUTTERMILK SOUP

Metric	Standard
Yield: 3-3.5 L	3-3½ qts.
Serves: 8-10	

Ingredients:

2 L milk	2 qts. milk
1 L buttermilk	1 qt. buttermilk
3 eggs	3 eggs
200-250 mL flour	¾-1 cup flour
pinch of salt	pinch of salt
heavy cream to taste	heavy cream to taste

In heavy 4 L (4 qt.) saucepan heat milk to simmering point. Add buttermilk. Break eggs into bowl, stirring in flour to make a batter of cake sponge consistency. Drop batter by teaspoonfuls into simmering milk mixture. Stir occasionally to keep batter from clinging together. Remove from heat immediately after last batter has been added. Add pinch salt. Serve hot or cold with a little heavy cream. The curdly consistency of this soup is typical, but the taste is nevertheless good.

RINDSUPPE
(Beef Soup)

Metric	Standard
Yield: About 2 L broth	2 qts. broth
Serves: 6	

Ingredients:

1-1.5 kg beef soup bone	2-3 lb. beef soup bone
with meat	with meat
cold water	cold water
1 bay leaf	1 bay leaf
5 whole allspice	5 whole allspice
5 pepper kernels	5 pepper kernels
1 large onion, whole	1 large onion, whole
2-3 carrots, whole	2-3 medium carrots, whole
small bunch parsley	small bunch parsley
10 mL salt	2 tsps. salt
4 large potatoes	4 large potatoes
125 mL rice	½ cup rice

Place soup bone with meat in 4 L (4 qt.) soup pot. Cover with cold water, close. Bring to boil and simmer for one hour, skim occasionally. Add remaining ingredients except potatoes and rice. Bring to boil and simmer for 1½ hours. Strain well and keep broth hot. In a separate pot, boil potatoes, quartered lengthwise, in a little water with salt to taste. In another saucepan, boil rice to fluffy stage with salt to taste. (To serve, scoop broth into bowl). Place rice and potatoes into individual serving bowls. Remove meat from bone and serve on platter with carrots. Choose from ingredients to create a soup of your own liking. An old, traditional way of preparing and serving soup.

GREEN BEAN SOUP

Metric	Standard
4 L soup pot	4 qt. soup pot

Serves: 6-8

Ingredients:

1-1½ kg smoked ham and bone	2-3 lbs. smoked ham and bone
1½ L cold water	1½ qts. cold water
2 whole medium onions	2 whole medium onions
500-750 mL fresh cut green beans	2-3 cups fresh cut green beans
375 mL coarsely grated carrots	1½ cups coarsely graded carrots
bunch fresh parsley	bunch fresh parsley
sprig fresh summer savory	sprig fresh summer savory
50-75 mL sour cream **or** heavy cream	¼-⅓ cup sour cream **or** heavy cream

Combine smoked ham, cold water and whole onions in pot. Boil for 2 hours. Remove ham and onions and strain broth. Add fresh cut green beans, coarsely grated carrots and cubed potatoes to broth. Boil just until tender. Do not overcook. Add parsley and summer savory; boil briefly. Remove herbs from soup. Cut meat from bone and add to soup. Add cream to soup, stir and serve; or, reserve cream to be added to individual soup bowls as served. A refreshing summer soup.

POTATO SOUP

Metric	Standard
4 L soup pot	4 qt. soup pot
Yield: 3 L	3 qts.

Ingredients:

4 medium potatoes, diced	4 medium potatoes, diced
1 medium onion, chopped fine	1 medium onion, chopped fine
2 mL salt	½ tsp. salt
1 L milk	4 cups milk
15 mL butter	1 tbsp. butter

Place potatoes, onion and salt in pot. Cover with cold water, bring to boil and cook until potatoes are tender. Add milk and butter, bring to a boil. Sprinkle with fresh parsley and serve.

Variation:

1 egg	1 egg
0.5 mL salt	⅛ salt
250 mL flour	1 cup flour

Beat egg. Add salt and flour slowly while stirring continuously till dough is in fine crumbs. Sprinkle into soup before adding milk and boil for a few minutes until tender. Then add milk and proceed as above.

SUMMER BORSCHT

Metric	Standard
Yield: About 3 L	3 qts.
Serves: 6-8	

Ingredients:

2 L boiling water	2 qts. boiling water
200-300 g smoked pork **or** sausage, cubed	½ lb. smoked pork **or** sausage, cubed
15 mL salt	1 tbsp. salt
1 L cubed potatoes	1 qt. cubed potatoes
500 mL chopped sorrel	2 cups chopped sorrel
250 mL chopped onion tops	1 cup chopped onion tops
50 mL chopped green dill	¼ cup chopped green dill
15 mL chopped fresh parsley	1 tbsp. chopped fresh parsley
1 bay leaf	1 bay leaf
125 mL heavy cream	½ cup heavy cream

Combine boiling water and cold smoked pork in a 4 L (4 qt.) pot. Cool ½ hour. Add salt and cubed potatoes. Bring to boil and cook for five to ten minutes. Add remaining ingredients, except heavy cream. Bring to boil and cook for 20-30 minutes or until vegetables are done. Remove from heat, add cream and serve. A refreshing, traditional soup.

BORSCHT

Metric	Standard
Yield: 4 L	4 qts.
Serves: 6-8	

Ingredients:

1 kg beef with soup bone	2 lbs. beef with soup bone
3 L cold water	3 qts. cold water
1 L chopped cabbage	1 qt. chopped cabbage
1 carrot sliced	1 carrot sliced
1 large onion chopped	1 large onion chopped
small bunch of parsley	small bunch of parsley
small bunch of dill	small bunch of dill
1 bay leaf	1 bay leaf
salt and pepper to taste	salt and pepper to taste
1 can (540 mL) tomatoes **or**	1 can (19 oz.) tomatoes **or**
1 L fresh tomatoes cut	1 qt. fresh tomatoes cut
500-700 mL cubed potatoes	2-3 cups cubed potatoes
heavy cream **or** sour cream	heavy cream **or** sour cream

Place beef soup bone and water in 6 L (6 qt.) pot. Boil for one hour; skim off foam occasionally. Add chopped cabbage, sliced carrot, chopped onion, herbs and spices. Boil for another hour; adding tomatoes for last half hour. Remove from heat.

Note:

Cubed potatoes may be cooked separately and added to borscht just before serving. Serve with heavy cream to complete borscht and enjoy this typical Mennonite dish.

BORSCHT

Metric	*Standard*
Yield: 4½-5 L	4½-5 qts.
Serves 8-10	

Ingredients:

3 L cold water	3 qts. cold water
200-500 g beef with bone	½-1 lb. beef with bone
15-45 mL pot barley	1-3 tbsps. pot barley
1 small head cabbage	1 small head cabbage
1 medium carrot	1 medium carrot
2 large onions	2 large onions
1 bay leaf	1 bay leaf
8 or more pepper kernels	8 or more pepper kernels
¼ star aniseed	¼ star aniseed
small bunch fresh parsley	small bunch fresh parsley
small bunch fresh dill	small bunch fresh dill
1 can (540 mL) tomatoes	1 can (19 oz.) tomatoes
or tomato juice	**or** tomato juice
heavy cream	heavy cream

In 6 L (6 qt.) pot combine water, beef with bone, and pot barley. Boil about 40 minutes until meat is nearly tender, skim off foam occasionally. Coarsely shred cabbage, slice onions, shred carrot and add to broth. Bring to boil; add spices and herbs. Boil about 30 minutes or until vegetables are tender. Add canned tomatoes, let simmer for 10 minutes. Remove from heat, add salt to taste. Add heavy cream and serve.

SAUERKRAUT BORSCHT

Metric	*Standard*
Yield: about 3 L	3 qts.
Serves: 6-8	

Ingredients:

4 slices side bacon	4 slices side bacon
2 L cold water	2 qts. cold water
4 medium onions	4 medium onions
small piece whole ginger	small piece whole ginger
1 bay leaf	1 bay leaf
1 can (398 mL) sauerkraut	1 can (14 oz.) sauerkraut
small bunch fresh parsley	small bunch fresh parsley
small bunch fresh dill	small bunch fresh dill
3 medium ripe tomatoes cut	3 medium ripe tomatoes cut
or	**or**
1 can (284 mL) tomato juice	1 can (10 oz.) tomato juice
125 mL sugar	½ cup sugar

Chop side bacon and place with cold water in a 5 L (5 qt.) pot. Boil till bacon is almost done. Slice and add onions, whole ginger, bay leaf, and sauerkraut. Boil for a few minutes. Add remaining ingredients and boil briefly. Remove from heat and serve.

DRIED BEAN SOUP

Metric	*Standard*
Yield: About 2.5 L	5 pts.
Serves: 4-6	

Ingredients:

250 mL dried white beans	1 cup dried white beans
1 medium onion, sliced	1 medium onion, sliced
100-200 g ham, salt pork,	¼ lb. ham, salt pork,
or bacon	**or** bacon
2 L cold water	2 qts. cold water
1 bay leaf	1 bay leaf
a few sprigs thyme **or**	a few sprigs thyme **or**
summer savory	summer savory
a few sprigs parsley	a few sprigs parsley
salt and pepper to taste	salt and pepper to taste

Cover dried white beans with water and soak for 6 hrs. or overnight. In 4 L (4 qt.) pot combine all ingredients except herbs and spices. Cover and bring to boil. Simmer until beans are nearly soft, about two hours. Add herbs and spices. Simmer for another half hour, serve.

DRIED BEAN SOUP

Metric	*Standard*
3 hours	2½ qts.
Yield: 2.5 L	
Serves: 6-8	

Ingredients:

500 mL white, dried beans	2 cups white, dried beans
4 medium onions	4 medium onions
200 g salt pork	¼-½ lb. salt pork
4 L cold water	4 qts. cold water
250-500 mL canned tomatoes	1-2 cups canned tomatoes
1 bay leaf	1 bay leaf
pepper and parsley	pepper and parsley
to taste	to taste

Place white dried beans, onions and salt pork and cold water in a 5 L (5 qt.) pot. Bring to boil and simmer until beans are tender. Add remaining ingredients and simmer until beans become very soft and mushy. Add salt to taste and serve.

BUTTERSOUP

Metric	*Standard*
Yield: 2.5 L	2.5 qts.
Serves: 4-6	

Ingredients:

2 L cold water	2 qts. cold water
1 large whole onion	1 large whole onion
1 parsley root **or** small bunch fresh parsley	1 parsley root **or** small bunch of fresh parsley
1 bay leaf	1 bay leaf
5 pepper kernels	5 pepper kernels
5 mL salt	1 tsp. salt
1 small cinnamon stick **or** ¼ star aniseed	1 small cinnamon stick **or** ¼ star aniseed
4 medium potatoes	4 medium potatoes
10 mL butter	2 tsps. butter
15 mL heavy cream	1 tbsp. heavy cream

Combine cold water, onion, spices and herbs in 4 L (4 qt.) pot. Bring to boil and simmer for 30-45 minutes. Peel and cube potatoes, add and boil till tender. Remove onion and herbs. Add butter and cream and serve.

Variation:

Small meatballs and a few noodles may be added to the soup for the last 10-15 minutes of cooking time.

STRING BEAN SOUP

Metric	*Standard*
Yield: 3 L	3 qts.
Serves: 6-8	

Ingredients:

200 g smoked ham	¼-½ lb. smoked ham
3 L cold water	3 qts. cold water
1 L fresh string beans	1 qt. fresh string beans
1-2 medium carrots	1-2 medium carrots
1 medium potato	1 medium potato
250 mL fresh peas	1 cup fresh peas
sprig of parsley	sprig of parsley
sprig of thyme **or** summer savory	sprig of thyme **or** summer savory
light cream	light cream
butter	butter
salt to taste	salt to taste

Place smoked ham in 5 L (5 qt.) pot. Cover with cold water and boil until tender, for about 45 minutes. Cut fresh string beans in 1 cm (½ in.) pieces. Cut carrots into thin slices. Peel and cube potatoes. Add all vegetables to broth. Bring to boil; add parsley and thyme. Boil 20-25 minutes or until vegetables are tender. Add cream, butter and salt to taste. Remove parsley and thyme and serve.

CHICKEN NOODLE SOUP

Metric	Standard
Yield: About 3 L broth	3 qts. broth
Serves: 8-10	

Ingredients:

Metric	Standard
1 1½-2 kg chicken	1 3-4 lb. chicken
4 L water	4 qts. water
10 mL salt	2 tsp. salt
1 medium whole onion	1 medium whole onion
9 parsley stalks **or**	9 parsley stalks **or**
3 parsley roots	3 parsley roots
2 bay leaves	2 bay leaves
pinch of pepper	pinch of pepper
1 cinnamon stick	1 cinnamon stick
(optional)	(optional)
1 star aniseed	1 star aniseed
45 mL butter (optional)	3 tbsps. butter (optional)
fine noodles	fine noodles

Place chicken, water and salt in 8 L (8 qt.) pot. Bring to boil and simmer for one hour. Skim off foam occasionally. Remove practically all fat. Add whole onion, parsley stalks, bay leaves, pinch of pepper and cinnamon stick. Simmer for 1-1½ hours. Add star aniseed, butter and simmer for about half hour. Cook amout of fine noodles desired. Strain and keep hot. Strain soup and add hot noodles; serve. Meat may be removed from bones and added to soup or served whole, separately on platter.

HOME MADE NOODLES

Metric   *Standard*

Serves: 8-10

Ingredients:

750 mL flour	3 cups flour
2 mL salt	½ tsp. salt
3 eggs	3 eggs
75 mL milk	⅓ cup milk

Sift flour and salt into mixing bowl. Break eggs into one side of the flour. Add a little milk and mix with spoon, adding milk until about ⅔ of flour is used up to make a stiff batter. Work in rest of flour until even, firm and hard (harder than bread dough). Cut into five pieces. Roll out very thin 0.2 cm (1/16 in.). Put sheets of dough on clean tea towel or lightly floured table. Let dry somewhat. Then, roll each sheet of dough into a roll and with a sharp knife shred it crosswise into fine noodles, **or** cut dough into strips, about 5 cm (2 in.) wide. Place five or six on top of each other and cut crosswise into fine noodles. The finer, the better. Sift out flour. Cook in slightly salted boiling water for eight minutes. Strain and mix noodles with hot chicken broth just before serving.

Note:

Noodles may be slightly dried after cutting and frozen in plastic bags till ready for use.

HALLAPSE

Metric   *Standard*

Yield: 12-15

Serves: 6

Ingredients:

1 medium cabbage	1 medium cabbage
15-45 mL rice	1½-3 tbsps. rice
500 g ground hamburger	1 lb. ground hamburger
1 egg	1 egg
salt and pepper to taste	salt and pepper to taste
125 mL dairy sour cream	½ cup dairy sour cream
250 mL tomato juice	1 cup tomato juice
15 mL butter	1 tbsp. butter

Bring water to boil in large pot (to fit the size of cabbage). Cut cabbage leaves loose at stem. Steam in boiling water until outer leaves can be easily removed. Remove leaves carefully and return head of cabbage to steam inner leaves as well. Cut away thick end of nib from leaf. Cover rice with water and boil for 10 minutes. Drain and mix with ground hamburger, egg and seasonings. Wrap a heaping tablespoon of this mixture into pliable cabbage leaves. Tuck ends of cabbage leaf in and fasten with toothpick if necessary. Place side by side in large greased skillet. Fry on low temperature until nicely browned. Turn once to brown both sides. Mix dairy sour cream and tomato juice and pour over cabbage rolls. Dot with butter. Bring to boil and simmer for about one hour. Turn cabbage rolls once more. Serve hot.

HALLAPSE

Metric	Standard
4 L casserole dish	4 qt. casserole dish
180°C	350°F
2 hours	
Serves: 6	

Ingredients:

1 small head cabbage	1 small head cabbage
500 g minced beef	1 lb. minced beef
50 mL uncooked rice	¼ cup uncooked rice
1 egg	1 egg
salt and pepper to taste	salt and pepper to taste
125 mL water	½ cup water
30 mL butter	2 tbsps. butter
250 mL tomato juice	1 cup tomato juice

Lightly grease casserole dish. Cut cabbage leaves loose at stem and steam for 10 minutes. Mix minced beef, uncooked rice, egg, salt and pepper. Place heaping tablespoonfuls on each cabbage leaf. Wrap and place with loose side down side in greased casserole dish or roaster. Pour water over and dot with butter. Cook for about 1½ hours. Cover with tomato juice. Continue baking for ½ hour. Serve and enjoy.

RÜHREI
(Scrambled Eggs)

Metric	Standard
Serves: 4	
100 mL flour	6 tbsps. flour
6 eggs	6 eggs
2 mL salt	½ tsp. salt
75 mL milk	⅓ cup milk
25 mL butter **or**	1½ tbsps. butter **or**
margarine	margarine

Mix flour, eggs and salt. Add milk to make a thin batter. Melt butter in frying pan. Pour in egg mixture and fry over medium heat. Cut and turn constantly with spoon till firm and light brown. Serve hot.

WARENIKI
(Cottage Cheese Pockets)

Metric	Standard
Yield: About 24	
Serves: 6-8	

Ingredients:
Dough:

Metric	Standard
50 mL milk	¼ cup milk
50 mL light cream	¼ cup light cream
2 egg whites	2 egg whites
pinch of salt	pinch of salt
375 mL flour	1½ cups flour

Mix milk, light cream and egg whites. Combine flour and salt. Make a well in the center of the dry ingredients. Add milk mixture and stir to form a pliable dough. Shape into smooth ball. Let dough rest for a few minutes to allow better handling.

Filling:

Metric	Standard
1 carton (500 g) dry cottage cheese	1 carton (16 oz.) dry cottage cheese
2 egg yolks	2 egg yolks
salt and pepper to taste	salt and pepper to taste

Combine all ingredients and mix well. Roll out dough on well floured surface to about 0.5 cm (48 in.) thickness and cut in 10-12 cm (2-3 in.) squares. Place a spoonful of filling on each square. Fold one edge over to match the opposite and pinch together, dipping fingers in flour to prevent stickiness. Seal completely. Place pockets on floured surface until ready to boil. Bring to boil 3 L (3 qts.) water with 5 mL (1 tsp.) salt and 15 mL (1 tbsp.) oil. Place pockets one by one into boiling water, about 8-10 at a time. Boil for 5 minutes or until pockets float all on top. Remove with slotted spoon. Drain and dot with butter **or** margarine. Serve with hot cream sauce.

Cream Sauce:

30 mL butter	2 tbsps. butter
125 mL heavy cream	½ cup heavy cream
pinch of salt	pinch of salt

Melt butter, add heavy cream and salt. Bring to a boil, stirring constantly. Serve.

Variation:

Cottage cheese filling may be replaced by fresh fruit such as cherries, plums, blueberries or fruit of your choice. Leftover pockets may be fried in lightly greased pan to a golden crispness and served as part of a delicious supper.

CHICKEN POT PIE

Metric	*Standard*
Yield: About 3.5 L	3-4 qts.
Serves: 6	

Ingredients:

1½-2 kg boiling chicken	3-4 lb. boiling chicken
2.5 L cold water	6 cups cold water
5 mL salt	1 tsp. salt
1 egg	1 egg
50-75 mL milk	¼-⅓ cup milk
pinch of salt	pinch of salt
500 mL flour	2 cups flour
1 large potato	1 large potato
finely chopped parsley	finely chopped parsley
(optional)	(optional)

Place chicken, cold water and salt in 5 L (5 qts.) pot. Bring to boil and simmer until tender. Remove chicken and take meat from bones. Break egg into measuring container, add equal amount of milk. Add pinch of salt and combine with flour to make a stiff dough. Knead in last part of flour. Roll out on floured surface till very thin — 0.5 cm (1/16 in.). Let dry one to two hours. Peel and cut large potato into eight cubes. Cut dough into 4 cm (1½ in.) squares. Drop into boiling broth one at a time. Add finely chopped parsley and cook till potatoes and dough are tender, about 20 minutes. Add chicken meat and bring to a boil. Serve hot.

BUBBAT
(Mennonite Chicken Dressing)

Metric	*Standard*
2 L cake pan (20 cm square)	8 x 8 x 2 in. cake pan
180°C	350°F
20 min.	
Serves: 6	

Ingredients:

250 mL flour	1 cup flour
10 mL baking powder	2 tsps. baking powder
2 mL salt	½ tsp. salt
30 mL sugar (optional)	2 tbsps. sugar (optional)
1 egg, beaten	1 egg, beaten
30 mL shortening, melted	2 tbsps. shortening, melted
75 mL milk	⅓ cup milk
250 mL raisins	1 cup raisins

Mix dry ingredients. Add beaten egg, melted shortening and milk. Mix well and add raisins. Pour into greased cake pan and bake. Serve hot with poultry.

Note:

Mixture may also be used as dressing to stuff chicken.

WURST BUBBAT

Metric	*Standard*
3.5 L cake pan (33 x 21 x 5 cm)	13 x 9 x 2 in. cake pan
180°C	350°F
45 min.	
Serves: 6-8	

Ingredients:

10 mL sugar	2 tsps. sugar
100 mL lukewarm water	½ cup water
1 pkg. active dry yeast	1 pkg. (8 g) active dry yeast
175 mL milk	¾ cup milk
2 eggs, well beaten	2 eggs, well beaten
5 mL salt	1 tsp. salt
15 mL melted margarine	1 tbsp. melted margarine
700-750 mL flour	2¾-3 cups flour
500 g farmer sausage	1 lb. farmer sausage
5 slices side bacon	5 slices side bacon
30 mL Carnation condensed milk	2 tbsps. Carnation condensed milk or light cream

Grease cake pan well. Dissolve sugar in lukewarm water. Sprinkle yeast over water and let stand in warm place for about 10 minutes.

Scald milk and cool to lukewarm. Add yeast mixture, well beaten eggs, melted margarine and flour. Mix well with spoon. Pour into prepared cake pan. Fry side bacon, cool and cut in 2 cm (1 in.) pieces. Peel and slice farmer sausage. Arrange bacon and sausage on dough in a manner that it will be easy to cut later. Let rise for about 45 minutes or until dough almost covers meat. Brush with Carnation condensed milk. Bake on lower rack in oven. Test for doneness with toothpick. Serve hot with soup.

Variation:
Farmer sausage may be replaced by any meat, e.g.: leftover roast, ham or pork or combinations of these.

HOT MUSTARD

Metric	Standard
Yield: 125 mL	½ cup

Ingredients:

50 mL dry mustard	¼ cup dry mustard
50 mL icing sugar	¼ cup icing sugar
50 mL flour	¼ cup flour
15 mL vinegar	1 tbsp. vinegar
2 mL safflo oil	½ tsp. safflo oil
10-15 mL hot water	2-3 tsps. hot water

Combine dry ingredients. Stir in vinegar and safflo oil. Add hot water mixing well. Store in refrigerator.

SCHMORKOHL
(Stewed Cabbage)

Metric	Standard
Serves: 4	

Ingredients:

1.5 L shredded cabbage (white **or** red)	6 cups shredded cabbage (white **or** red)
250 mL dried apples	1 cup dried apples
250 mL prunes	1 cup prunes
150 mL water	⅔ cup water
5 mL salt	1 tsp. salt
45 mL sugar	3 tbsps. sugar
25 mL oil	1½ tbsps. oil

Place all ingredients in 3 L (3 qts.) pot. Cover, bring to boil and simmer 1½-2 hours. Stir occasionally and serve as vegetable.

PICKLED PIGS FEET

Metric	Standard
Yield: 3 jars (455 mL each)	3 pt. jars

Ingredients:

1.5 kg pigs feet	3¼ lbs. pigs feet
cold water	cold water
150 mL white vinegar	⅔ cup white vinegar
90 mL sugar	6 tbsps. sugar
15 mL salt	1 tbsp. salt
5 mL pickling spice	1 tsp. pickling spice
5 pepper kernels	5 pepper kernels

Place clean pigs feet into 4 L (4 qts.) pot. Cover with cold water; bring to boil. Simmer till meat is fairly tender. Skim off foam occasionally. Cool for 8-10 hours. Drain, reserving liquid, and place meat into jars. Combine 325 mL (2⅓ cups) of liquid and remaining ingredients. Bring to boil and simmer for a few minutes. Pour over pigs feet. Cool and refrigerate. Serve cold.

Variation:

Other parts of pig such as ankles, ears, tongue and heart may be substituted for feet.

CUCUMBER SALAD

Metric	Standard
Serves: 4	

Ingredients:

2 large cucumbers	2 large cucumbers
3 mL salt	½ tsp. salt
250 mL buttermilk	1 cup buttermilk
30 mL sour cream	2 tbsps. sour cream
15 mL mayonnaise	1 tbsp. mayonnaise
30 mL milk	2 tbsps. milk
1 mL vinegar	¼ tsp. vinegar
pinch of salt **or**	pinch of salt **or**
celery salt	celery salt
pinch of sugar	pinch of sugar
sprig of fresh dill	sprig of fresh dill
1 hard cooked egg	1 hard cooked egg

Peel and slice cucumbers; sprinkle with salt. Chill for 1-2 hours. Combine remaining ingredients, except dill and egg, and whip until slightly fluffy. Add dill and chopped egg. Chill dressing. Drain cucumbers. Add dressing and serve as a refreshing summer salad.

IKRA

Metric	Standard
Yield: 2 jars (455 ml each)	2 pt. jars

Ingredients:

Metric	Standard
1 medium head cabbage **or**	1 medium head cabbage **or**
1 L cucumbers, peeled and seeded	4 cups cucumbers, peeled seeded
1 medium green pepper	1 medium green pepper
5 large stalks celery	5 large stalks celery
10 large tomatoes	10 large tomatoes
1 medium carrot (optional)	1 medium carrot (optional)
45 mL sugar	3 tbsps. sugar
10 mL salt	2 tsps. salt
5 mL pepper	1 tsp. pepper
125 mL oil	½ cup oil

Chop vegetables (except tomatoes) fine or put through coarse food chopper. Cook tomatoes and strain through medium sieve. Discard solid parts of tomatoes, save juice. Combine all ingredients in 4 L (4 qts.) heavy pot. Bring to boil and simmer for two hours. Stir occasionally, mixture should become fairly thick. Scoop into hot sterilized jars and close immediately to seal. Ikra may also be chilled, then frozen to preserve. Use as pickle or side dish with meat.

IKRA

Metric	Standard
Yield: 1.5 L	3 pts.

Ingredients:

Metric	Standard
1 kg mL shredded carrots	2 lbs. shredded carrots
3 large onions, chopped fine	3 large onions, chopped fine
1 green pepper chopped (optional)	1 green pepper, chopped (optional)
1 small parsley root	1 small parsely root
750 mL tomato juice	3 cups tomato juice
15 mL salt	1 tbsp. salt
50 mL oil	¼ cup oil
125 mL sugar	½ cup sugar

Prepare vegetables. Place in saucepan and add remaining ingredients. Boil until tender, about 1 hour. Pour into clean sterilized jars and close. To seal, place closed jars in canner with warm water. Heat to boiling and boil 5 min. Store in cool dark room.

Notes

BEVERAGES

LEMON SYRUP DRINK

Metric	*Standard*
Yield: 4.5 L	4.5 qts.

Ingredients:

5 lemons	5 lemons
5 oranges	5 oranges
2.5 L boiling water	5 pts. boiling water
3 L sugar	3 qts. sugar
60 mL citric acid	4 tbsps. citric acid
30 mL tartaric acid	2 tbsps. tartaric acid
30 mL epsom salts	2 tbsps. epsom salts

Squeeze juice from fruit. Place fruit peel in boiling water and boil for about 3 minutes. Strain, discard peel. Add sugar and fruit juice to strained liquid. Boil until sugar dissolves. Add acids and salts; stir until all are melted. Remove from heat and pour into sterilized jars to seal. To reconstitute, add 30 mL (2 tbsps.) syrup to each glass of water or to taste. Store in refrigerator.

TEA PUNCH

Metric	*Standard*
Yield: 2½ L	2½ qts.

Ingredients:

2 L cold water	2 qts. cold water
50 mL loose tea leaves **or**	¼ cup loose tea leaves **or**
5 tea bags	5 tea bags
250 mL sugar	1 cup sugar
250 mL cold water	1 cup cold water
Two 5 cm. cinnamon sticks	Two 2 in. cinnamon sticks
15 mL grated lemon rind	1 tbsp. grated lemon rind
10 mL grated orange rind	2 tsps. grated orange rind
125 mL orange juice	½ cup orange juice
50 mL lemon juice	¼ cup lemon juice
125 mL pineapple juice	½ cup pineapple juice

Bring 2 L (2 qts.) cold water to full boil. Pour over tea; let steep 3-5 minutes; strain. Combine sugar, remaining cold water, cinnamon sticks and fruit rinds. Simmer 15 minutes to make syrup. Add syrup and fruit juices to tea. Chill thoroughly. Serve in punch bowl over ice cubes.

VICO

Metric	*Standard*
1 L saucepan	1 qt. saucepan
Yield: approx. 500 mL	2 cups

Ingredients:

125 mL cocoa	½ cup cocoa
375 mL sugar	1½ cups sugar
250 mL water	1 cup water
pinch of salt	pinch of salt
1 mL vanilla	¼ tsp. vanilla

Combine all ingredients and boil for 5 minutes. Cool, bottle and refrigerate. Mix 15-30 mL (1-2 tbsps.) with a cup of milk for a delicious chocolate drink. May also be served undiluted over ice cream as chocolate sauce.

CHOCOLATE DRINK

Metric	*Standard*
Yield: 1½-2 L powder	1½-2 qts. powder

Ingredients:

1 L skim milk powder	4 cups powdered milk
150 mL Coffee Mate	⅔ cup Coffee Mate
250 mL sugar	1 cup sugar
500 mL chocolate drink powder	2 cups chocolate drink powder

Mix all ingredients and store in dry closed jar. Use 75 mL (⅓ cup) chocolate mixture to make 1 cup chocolate drink. Add boiling water, stir and serve.

ORANGE LEMON DRINK

Metric	*Standard*
Yield: about 1.5 L	1.5 qts.

Ingredients:

3 oranges	3 oranges
1 large lemon	1 large lemon
500 mL sugar	2 cups sugar
15 g tartaric acid	½ oz. tartaric acid
1 L boiling water	1 qt. boiling water

Grate rind of oranges and lemon. Mix with sugar and tartaric acid. Pour boiling water over this, cool. Squeeze and add juice from oranges and lemon. Store in refrigerator. Use one part of concentrate to two parts of water or mix to taste. Refreshing summer drink.

ICE TEA

Metric	Standard
Yield: about 4 L	4 qts.

Ingredients:

1.25 L boiling water	5 cups boiling water
8 (2 cups) tea bags	8 (2 cups) tea bags
625 mL orange juice	2½ cups orange juice
150 mL lemon juice	⅔ cup lemon juice
375 mL grapefruit juice	1½ cups grapefruit juice
375 mL fruit sugar **or**	1½ cups fruit sugar **or**
granulated sugar	granulated sugar
1 L ginger ale chilled	35.2 oz. ginger ale chilled

Pour boiling water over tea bags. Let steep for five minutes; remove tea bags. Pour hot tea into large mixing bowl. Add fruit juice and sugar. Stir until sugar is dissolved. Chill until ready to serve. Pour over ice in large punch bowl. Add ginger ale just before serving.

FRUIT PUNCH

Metric	Standard
Yield: Approx. 5-6 L	5-6 qts.

Ingredients:

125 mL sugar	½ cup sugar
1 can (355 mL) frozen lemonade concentrate	1 can (12.5 oz.) frozen lemonade concentrate
1 L water	1 qt. water
2 lemons	2 lemons
2 oranges	2 oranges
2 bananas (optional)	2 bananas (optional)
750 mL frozen strawberries	3 cups frozen strawberries
1 L Ginger ale	1 bottle (35.2 oz.) Ginger ale
1 L 7-up	1 bottle (35.2 oz.) 7-up.

Combine sugar, frozen lemonade and water in large punch bowl. Slice lemons, oranges and bananas and add along with frozen strawberries. Just before serving add Ginger ale and 7-up.

Variation:

Pour part of lemonade and water into jello ring mold. Add strawberries and green maraschino cherries. Freeze. Just before serving, add fruit ring to punch. Pink lemonade may be used for additional colour.

PUNCH

Metric	Standard
Yield: 4.5 L	4½ qts.

Ingredients:

Metric	Standard
1 can (1.36 L) orange juice **or**	1 can (48 oz.) orange juice **or**
1 can (355 mL) frozen orange concentrate	1 can (12 oz.) frozen orange concentrate
1 can (1.36 L) pineapple juice	1 can (48 oz.) pineapple juice
1 can (1.36 L) grapefruit juice	1 can (48 oz.) grapefruit juice
1 can (355 mL) frozen lemonade	1 can (12 oz.) frozen lemonade
1 bottle (796 mL) ginger ale	1 bottle (28 oz.) ginger ale

Combine juices and chill. Just before serving add ginger ale.

Variation:
Use half pink and half yellow lemonade to vary colour and taste. To make an attractive punch bowl, place some thinly sliced lemons, oranges, and whole maraschino cherries into a ring jello mold. Pour water or part of punch (excluding ginger ale) over fruit slices just to cover. Freeze; add more juice to ¾ full. Freeze. At serving time unmold and float in punch.

Metric	Standard
Yield: 1500 mL mix	6 cups mix

Ingredients:

Metric	Standard
500 mL sugar	2 cups sugar
500 mL Tang orange crystals	2 cups Tang orange crystals
250 mL instant tea powder	1 cup instant tea powder
2 (85 g) pkg Tang lemonade	2 (3 oz.) pkg Tang lemonade
5 mL cinnamon	1 tsp. cinnamon
2 mL cloves	½ tsp. cloves.

Mix ingredients together. Store in closed jar. Use 15-30 mL (1-2 tbsps.) of mix per cup of boiling water. A refreshing hot tea for a cold night.

QUICK BREADS

COFFEE CAKE

Metric	Standard
2.5 L cake pan (23 cm square)	9 x 9 x 2 in. cake pan
180°C	350°F
30-35 mins.	

Ingredients:

500 mL sifted flour	2 cups sifted flour
15 mL baking powder	1 tbsp. baking powder
1 mL salt	¼ tsp. salt
50 mL shortening	3 tbsps. shortening
125 mL white sugar	½ cup white sugar
1 egg, well beaten	1 egg, well beaten
175 mL milk	¾ cup milk
125 mL brown sugar	½ cup brown sugar
5 mL cinnamon	1 tsp. cinnamon
125 mL chopped walnuts	½ cup chopped walnuts

Grease cake pan. Sift dry ingredients together. Cream shortening and white sugar. Beat in egg. Add dry ingredients alternately with milk. Turn half the batter into prepared cake pans. Sprinkle half of brown sugar mixture over batter. Add remaining batter and sprinkle rest of brown sugar mixture over top. Bake. Cut in squares and cool before serving.

NUT BREAD

Metric	Standard
3 L loaf pan (25 x 15 x 7 cm)	10 x 6 x 3 in. loaf pan
180°C	350°F
60-70 min.	

Ingredients:

1000 mL flour	4 cups flour
30 mL baking powder	2 tbsps. baking powder
5 mL salt	1 tsp. salt
250 mL brown sugar	1 cup brown sugar
250 mL finely chopped nuts	1 cup finely chopped nuts
1 egg	1 egg
625 mL milk	2½ cups milk

Grease loaf pan well. Sift dry ingredients. Add finely chopped nuts. Beat egg and stir into milk. Add to dry mixture, stir just to mix. Pour into greased loaf pan. Let rise for 45 minutes. Bake till done when tested with toothpick.

BOSTON BROWN BREAD

Metric	Standard
2 L loaf pan (23 x 13 x 7 cm)	9 x 5 x 3 in. loaf pan
190°C	375°F
1 hour	

Ingredients:

Metric	Standard
50 mL butter	¼ cup butter
125 mL brown sugar	½ cup brown sugar
1 egg	1 egg
375 mL flour	1½ cups flour
5 mL baking soda	1 tsp. baking soda
5 mL salt	1 tsp. salt
250 mL all bran	1 cup all bran
250 mL sour milk **or** buttermilk	1 cup sour milk **or** buttermilk
250 mL chopped walnuts	1 cup chopped walnuts
250 mL raisins	1 cup raisins

Grease loaf pan lightly. Cream butter, brown sugar and egg. Sift flour, baking soda and salt. Soak all bran in sour milk. Combine sifted ingredients and bran mixture with the butter mixture. Mix well, adding chopped walnuts and raisins. Pour into prepared loaf pan and bake. Test for doneness with toothpick. Cool partly in pan, then remove and cool on rack.

ORANGE BREAD

Metric	Standard
1.5 L loaf pan (20 x 10 x 7 cm)	8 x 4 x 3 in. loaf pan
180°C	350°F
1 hour	

Ingredients:

Metric	Standard
125 mL raisins	½ cup raisins
10 mL grated orange rind	2 tsps. grated orange rind
375 mL sifted flour	1½ cups sifted flour
150 mL sugar	⅔ cup sugar
10 mL baking powder	2 tsps. baking powder
1 mL salt	¼ tsp. salt
175 mL orange juice	¾ cup orange juice
30 mL butter, melted	2 tbsps. butter, melted
1 egg, beaten	1 egg, beaten

Grease loaf pan. Wash and dry raisins if necessary. Grate orange rind and squeeze juice. Sift dry ingredients together twice. Add raisins. Combine remaining ingredients and add to dry ingredients, STIRRING ONLY UNTIL MOISTENED, like muffins.

Turn into greased loaf pan and bake. Cool; cover well and allow to sit for a day before slicing bread.

BAKING POWDER BISCUITS

Metric	Standard
220-230°C	425-450°F
10-12 min.	
Yield: 2 doz.	

Ingredients:

500 mL flour	2 cups flour
20 mL baking powder	4 tsps. baking powder
2 mL salt	½ tsp. salt
50 mL shortening	¼ cup shortening
150 mL milk **or** light cream	⅔ cup milk **or** light cream

Lightly grease cookie sheet. Mix dry ingredients. Cut in shortening until mixture resembles crumbs. Add milk all at once. Stir until mixture leaves the side of bowl and sticks to spoon. Roll to desired thickness (biscuits double during baking). Cut into squares with knife or round shapes with cookie cutters. Place on greased cookie sheet and bake until golden brown.

Variations:

Cheese biscuits: To dry ingredients of basic recipe add 125 mL (½ cup) grated cheese. Serve hot with salad.

Orange biscuits: Add grated rind of one orange to basic recipe. Dip a cube of sugar in orange juice and press into top of each biscuit. Bake quickly.

Lemon Biscuits: Make as orange biscuits except use lemon rind and lemon juice.

Shortcake: To basic recipe add 30 mL (2 tbsps.) sugar, 30 mL (2 tbsps.) fat, 1 egg. Roll out to 0.5 cm (¼ in.) thickness. Cut into desired shape. Spread with melted butter. Place an equal piece of biscuit dough on top. Bake till golden brown. Break apart and fill with fresh or canned fruit and whipped cream.

DATE AND NUT BREAD

Metric	Standard
1.5 L loaf pan (20 x 10 x 7 cm)	8 x 4 x 3 in. loaf pan
180°C	350°F
1 hour	

Ingredients:

Metric	Standard
250 mL chopped dates	1 cup chopped dates
5 mL baking soda	1 tsp. baking soda
175 mL boiling water	¾ cup boiling water
1 egg	1 egg
175 mL light brown sugar	¾ cup light brown sugar
5 mL salt	1 tsp. salt
5 mL vanilla	1 tsp. vanilla
375 mL flour	1½ cups flour
5 mL baking powder	1 tsp. baking powder
175 mL chopped walnuts	¾ cup chopped walnuts
50 mL melted shortening	¼ cup melted shortening

Grease loaf pan well. Sprinkle baking soda over chopped dates. Pour boiling water over top. Mix well and let cool. Beat egg until light. Add light brown sugar gradually, beating between additions. Add salt and vanilla. Combine creamed mixture with date mix. Sift flour and baking powder and add. Mix chopped walnuts with a little flour; mix in. Add melted (not hot) shortening, mix well. Pour into prepared loaf pan and bake. Loaf springs back at a light touch when done. Date and nut bread slices and tastes best when day old.

BEATEN BISCUITS

Metric	Standard
230°C	450°F
15 min.	
Yield: 2½ doz.	

Ingredients:

Metric	Standard
1000 mL flour	4 cups flour
20 mL baking powder	4 tsps. baking powder
5 mL salt	1 tsp. salt
125 mL butter	½ cup butter
2 eggs, beaten	2 eggs, beaten
250 mL milk	1 cup milk

Sift dry ingredients. Add butter and mix well. Add beaten eggs and milk, mix briefly. Drop onto ungreased cookie sheet and bake until golden. Serve hot with butter or margarine.

RAISED DOUGHNUTS

Metric	Standard
Yield: 5 doz. medium	

Ingredients:

Metric	Standard
5 mL sugar	1 tsp. sugar
125 mL lukewarm water	½ cup lukewarm water
1 pkg. (8 g) active dry yeast	1 pkg. active dry yeast
500 mL milk	2 cups milk
125 mL sugar	½ cup sugar
5 mL salt	1 tsp. salt
125 mL shortening	½ cup shortening
2 eggs	2 eggs
1750-1875 mL flour	7-7½ cups flour

Dissolve 5 mL (1 tsp.) sugar in lukewarm water. Sprinkle yeast over liquid. Let stand in warm place for 10 minutes. Scald milk. Add sugar, salt and shortening. Add yeast mixture and **eggs**. Gradually add remaining flour, mixing and kneading thoroughly. Place dough in lightly greased bowl and cover. Let rise for about 1½ hours or till double in bulk. Roll out dough about 1 cm (½ in.) thick. Cut with doughnut cutter. Place on cookie sheet and let rise for 30-45 minutes. Drop in hot fat (180°C or 350°F) with raised side down. Turn once and fry till golden brown. Remove and drain on absorbent paper. Shake doughnuts in bag with icing sugar.

Variation:

Dough may also be made into parkerhouse rolls. Let rise till double in bulk and bake at 190°C (375°F) for 15-20 minutes.

SOUR CREAM DOUGHNUTS

Metric	Standard
180°-190°C	350°-375°F
Yield: 2½ doz.	

Ingredients:

Metric	Standard
250 mL sour cream	1 cup sour cream
250 mL sugar	1 cup sugar
2 eggs	2 eggs
5 mL baking soda	1 tsp. baking soda
1 mL salt	¼ tsp. salt
750 mL flour	3 cups flour

Beat sour cream, sugar and eggs together. Mix dry ingredients and add. Roll out dough on lightly floured surface, about 2 cm (¾ in.) thick. Cut out with doughnut cutter and fry in hot, deep fat. Turn once to brown both sides. Place doughnuts on paper towel to drain.

DOUGHNUTS

Metric	Standard
180°-190°C	350°-375°F
Yield: 2½ doz.	

Ingredients:

2 eggs	2 eggs
30 mL butter	2 tbsps. butter
250 mL sugar	1 cup milk
2 mL baking soda	½ tsp. baking soda
250 mL milk	1 cup sugar
875-1000 mL flour	3½-4 cups flour
10 mL baking powder	2 tsp. baking powder
2 mL salt	½ tsp. salt
5 mL nutmeg	1 tsp. nutmeg

Beat eggs, butter and sugar together. Dissolve baking soda in milk and add. Sift flour, baking powder and salt together. Add to egg mixture and beat well. Add nutmeg. Roll out on floured surface, about 2 cm (¾ in.) thick. The softer the dough, the better. Cut with doughnut cutter and fry in deep fat until golden brown, turning once. Drain on paper towels and sprinkle with icing sugar before serving.

CAKE DOUGHNUTS

Metric	Standard
180°-190°C	350°-375°F
Yield: 2-3 doz.	

Ingredients:

125 mL sugar	½ cup sugar
5 mL salt	1 tsp. salt
1 egg	1 egg
125 mL Safflo **or** other salad oil	½ cup Safflo **or** other salad oil
250 mL buttermilk **or** sour milk	1 cup buttermilk **or** sour milk
2 mL vanilla	½ tsp. vanilla
900 mL sifted flour	3⅔ cups sifted flour
5 mL baking powder	1 tsp. baking powder
2 mL baking soda	½ tsp. baking soda

Combine sugar and salt in bowl. Stir in egg, Safflo oil, milk and vanilla. Sift remaining ingredients together and add in four or five portions to liquid. Mix and turn out on lightly floured surface. Dough should be soft. Roll out 1-2 cm (½ in.) thick. Cut with floured doughnut cutter. Deep fat fry in Safflo oil heated to brown a cube of bread in 60 seconds. Fry until golden brown, turning once during frying. Drain on absorbent paper. Cool and dust with icing sugar or cover with chocolate butter icing while warm.

BRAN MUFFINS

Metric	Standard
200°C	400°F

15 min.
Yield: 1 doz.

Ingredients:

250 mL sour cream	1 cup sour cream
5 mL baking soda	1 tsp. baking soda
50 mL sugar	¼ cup sugar
1 egg, beaten	1 egg, beaten
15-30 mL molasses	1-2 tbsps. molasses
375 mL bran	1½ cups bran
250 mL flour	1 cup flour
1 mL salt	¼ tsp. salt
250 mL raisins (optional)	1 cup raisins (optional)

Grease muffin tins lightly. Combine sour cream with baking soda. Add sugar, beaten egg and molasses; mix. Add bran, flour, salt and raisins. Fill prepared muffin tins ⅔ full and bake till brown.

REFRIGERATOR BRAN MUFFINS

Metric	Standard
180°C	350°F

25 min.
Yield: 5 doz.

Ingredients:

1000 mL flour	4 cups flour
1000 mL bran	4 cups bran
375-425 mL sugar	1½-1¾ cups sugar
15 mL baking soda	1 tbsp. baking soda
20 mL baking powder	4 tsps. baking powder
10 mL salt	2 tsps. salt
500 mL cold coffee	2 cups cold coffee
500 mL milk	2 cups milk
5 eggs	5 eggs
375 mL oil	1½ cups oil
10 mL vanilla	2 tsps. vanilla
500 mL raisins	2 cups raisins

Grease medium-sized muffin tins. Mix dry ingredients well. Make a well in center and add remaining ingredients. Mix well and refrigerate 8-10 hours. Spoon ⅔ full and bake. Dough keeps in refrigerator for several weeks.

BRAN MUFFIN VARIATIONS

Metric	Standard
200°C	400°F

Yield: 12 large

Ingredients:

500 mL pastry flour	2 cup pastry flour
2 mL salt	½ tsp. salt
15 mL baking powder	1 tbsp. baking powder
30 mL sugar	2 tbsps. sugar
200 mL milk	⅞ cup milk
2 eggs, beaten	2 eggs, beaten
50 mL oil	3 tbsps. oil.

Grease muffin tins. Sift dry ingredients and make well in center. Combine milk, beaten eggs and oil and pour into well. Blend just to moisten. Do not overmix. Fill greased muffin tins ¾ full and bake.

Variations:

1. Substitute 375 mL (1½ cups) Graham flour for 500 mL (2 cups) all-purpose flour.

2. Substitute 250 mL (1 cup) ALL BRAN for 125 mL (½ cup) pastry flour.

3. Substitute 250 mL (1 cup) corn meal for 250 mL (1 cup) pastry flour.

4. Add 30 mL (2 tbsps.) molasses instead of sugar.

5. Add 4 slices diced fried bacon instead of oil.

6. Add 50 mL (¼ cup) grated cheese instead of fat.

7. Add 50 mL (¼ cup) chopped dates, raisins or prunes.

8. Put preserved fruit in center of muffins before baking.

All variations are tasty, but muffins should be served warm.

BUTTERSCOTCH CURLS

Metric	Standard
3.5 L cake pan (33 x 21 x 5 cm)	13 x 9 x 2 in. cake pan
170°-180°C	350°F

Yield: 1½ doz.

Ingredients:

500 mL flour	2 cups flour
10 mL baking powder	2 tsps. baking powder
2 mL salt	½ tsp. salt
60 mL shortening	4 tbsps. shortening
150 mL milk	⅔ cup milk
50 mL butter	3 tbsps. butter
125 mL brown sugar	½ cup brown sugar

Grease baking pan. Sift flour, baking powder and salt together. Add shortening, mix with fork. Add milk, knead lightly. Roll out 0.5 cm (¼ in.) thick. Cream butter and spread on dough. Sprinkle with brown sugar. Roll up and cut in 2.5 cm (1 in.) slices. Stand rolls on end in a well greased pan or small muffin tins. Bake, till light brown. Centers curl up and glaze on edges

CHRUST
(Baby Slippers)

Metric	Standard
Yield: About 4 doz.	

Ingredients:

Metric	Standard
4 eggs **plus**	4 eggs **plus**
4 egg yolks **or**	4 egg yolks **or**
6 eggs	6 eggs
15 mL sugar	1 tbsp. sugar
750 mL sifted flour	3¼ cups sifted flour
8 mL butter	1½ tsps. butter
5 mL vanilla	1 tsp. vanilla
icing sugar	icing sugar

Beat eggs well and add sugar. Mix in flour and butter; add vanilla. Roll dough very thin 0.5 cm (⅛ in.) and cut in strips 3 cm by 10 cm (1 in. by 4 in.). Cut a slit along centre, twist one end through slit. Fry quickly in deep, hot 180°C (350°F) fat until light brown in color. Drain. Sprinkle with icing sugar and serve as snack.

Note: Fry as soon as cut as dough dries out quickly.

PLAIN PANCAKES

Metric	Standard
Yield: 9-25 cm pancakes	9-10 in. pancakes

Ingredients:

Metric	Standard
250 mL flour	1 cup flour
10 mL baking powder	2 tsps. baking powder
5 mL baking soda	1 tsp. baking soda
5 mL salt	1 tsp. salt
3 eggs, separated	3 eggs, separated
500 mL buttermilk	2 cups buttermilk

Sift dry ingredients together. Add beaten egg yolks to buttermilk. Combine dry ingredients and liquid. Stir only enough to moisten. Fold in stiffly beaten egg whites. Drop by spoonfuls in hot, greased frying pan. Turn as bubbles appear on surface. Serve hot with syrup, sausages or fruit preserve.

JAM BUNS

Metric	Standard
200°C	400°F
15 min.	
Yield: 4 doz.	

Ingredients:

500 mL flour	2 cups flour
15 mL baking powder	1 tbsp. baking powder
30 mL sugar	2 tbsps. sugar
1 mL salt	¼ tsp. salt
250 mL shortening	1 cup shortening
1 egg	1 egg
5 mL vanilla	1 tsp. vanilla
125 mL milk	½ cup milk
jam	jam

Mix dry ingredients. Cut in shortening till dough forms course crumbs. Add egg, vanilla and milk and mix well together. Roll out to about 0.5 cm (¼ in.) thickness. Cut in squares. Place dab of jam on each. Fold up corners and pinch edges together well. Place in small, ungreased muffin tins and bake.

GRIDDLE CAKES

Metric	Standard
Yield: About 14-8 cm cakes	12-3 in. cakes

Ingredients:

30 mL sugar	2 tbsps. sugar
250 mL sifted flour	1 cup sifted flour
25 mL baking powder	4 tsps. baking powder
3-5 mL salt	½-1 tsp. salt
250 mL milk	1 cup milk
1 egg, beaten	1 egg, beaten
75 mL Safflo **or** other	⅓ cup Safflo **or** other
salad oil	salad oil

Mix and sift dry ingredients. Mix milk, beaten egg and Safflo. Add liquid to dry ingredients and stir just enough to blend. Drop by spoonfuls into a hot, greased griddle or frying pan. Bake until bubbles appear all over surface. Turn and bake till golden brown. Serve hot with butter and syrup.

APPLE FRITTERS

Metric	*Standard*
180-190°C	350-375°F

Yield: 15 fritters

Ingredients:

250 mL flour	1 cup flour
1 mL salt	¼ tsp. salt
7 mL baking powder	1½ tsps. baking powder
75 mL milk	⅓ cup milk
50 mL sugar	3 tbsps. sugar
1 egg	1 egg
4 apples pared and thinly sliced	4 apples pared and thinly sliced

Mix dry ingredients. Beat egg; add milk. Make a well in the dry ingredients, add the liquid and mix just to moisten dry ingredients. Stir in apples. Drop batter by spoonfuls into hot deep fat. Fry, turning once, until golden brown.

Notes

YEAST BREADS AND ROLLS

RAISIN BREAD

Metric	Standard
Four 1.5 L loaf pans	Four loaf pans
(20 x 10 x 7 cm)	(8 x 4 x 3 in.)
180°C	350°F
45 min.	

Ingredients:

5 mL sugar	1 tsp. sugar
125 mL lukewarm water	½ cup lukewarm water
2 pkg. (8 g each) active dry yeast	2 pkg. active dry yeast
500 mL lukewarm milk	2 cups lukewarm milk
1 egg well beaten	1 egg well beaten
125 mL melted shortening	½ cup melted shortening
5 mL salt	1 tsp. salt
125 mL sugar (optional)	½ cup sugar (optional)
1000 mL flour	4 cups flour
5 mL cinnamon	1 tsp. cinnamon
500 mL washed raisins	2 cups washed raisins
125 mL peel (optional)	½ cup peel (optional)

Grease loaf pans. Dissolve sugar in lukewarm water. Sprinkle yeast over liquid and let rise five to ten minutes. Combine lukewarm milk, well beaten egg, melted shortening, salt and sugar. Stir yeast mixture and add. Add part of flour and beat well. Combine remaining flour and cinnamon. Gradually knead in flour along with washed raisins and peel. Knead for 10-15 minutes until dough is smooth. Shape into ball and place into lightly greased bowl. Cover and let rise in warm place till double in bulk. Shape into four equal loaves and place in greased loaf pans. Let rise till double in bulk and bake until loaf comes off sides of pan and sounds hollow. Turn out of pans and let cool on rack right side up.

WHOLE WHEAT BREAD

Metric	Standard
1.5 L loaf pans (20 x 10 x 7 cm)	8 x 4 x 3 in. loaf pans
180-190°C	350-375°F
1 hour	
Yield: 4 or 5 loaves	

Ingredients:

Metric	Standard
5 mL sugar	1 tsp. sugar
250 mL lukewarm water	1 cup lukewarm water
2 pkg. (8 g each) active dry yeast	2 pkg. active dry yeast
250 mL fat (oil, drippings)	1 cup fat (oil, drippings)
1 L liquid (potato water, cream, water)	4 cups liquid (potato water, cream, water)
30 mL molasses	2 tbsps. molasses
15 mL salt	1 tbsp. salt
3250 mL whole wheat flour	13 cups whole wheat flour

Dissolve sugar in lukewarm water. Sprinkle yeast over liquid and let rise in warm place for about 10 minutes. Mix fat, liquid molasses and salt. Add yeast mixture. Mix in part of flour with spoon, beating until smooth. Knead in remaining flour to form a soft not sticky dough. Shape into ball and place in greased bowl. Cover and let rise till double in size. Punch down. Let rise again for about 30 minutes. Shape into loaves and place into four or five greased loaf pans. Pans should not be more than half full. Let rise again till double in bulk. Bake till loaf sounds hollow when gently tapped.

"QUICK BUNS"

Metric	Standard
190°C	375°F
15-20 minutes	
Yield: 1½-2 doz.	

Ingredients:

Metric	Standard
5 mL sugar	1 tsp. sugar
75 mL lukewarm water	⅓ cup lukewarm water
2 pkg. (8 g each) active dry yeast	2 pkg. active dry yeast
250 mL milk	1 cup milk
2 mL salt	½ tsp. salt
50 mL butter	¼ cup butter
750-1000 mL flour	3-4 cups flour

Grease two cookie sheets. Dissolve sugar in warm water. Sprinkle yeast over liquid. Combine milk, salt and butter in saucepan and heat till warm. Add yeast and flour. Work and knead dough for about 10 minutes. Cover and let rise in warm place for about 30 minutes. Turn on floured surface and pat to 2 cm (¾ in.) thickness. Cut with round cookie cutter and place on greased cookie sheet. Let rise in warm place for about 45 minutes or until double in size. Bake and serve hot or cold.

WHITE BUNS

Metric	*Standard*
200°C	400°F
15-20 min.	
Yield: 5 doz.	

Ingredients:

10 mL sugar	2 tsps. sugar
125 mL lukewarm water	½ cup lukewa m water
2 pkg. (8 g each) active dry yeast	2 pkg. active dry yeast
500 mL scalded milk	2 cups scalded milk
125 mL lard	½ cup lard
125 mL butter	½ cup butter
500 mL potato water	2 cups potato water
10 mL salt	2 tsps. salt
2250 mL flour	9 cups flour

Dissolve sugar in lukewarm water. Sprinkle yeast over water and let rise in a warm place for about 10 minutes. Scald milk; add lard, butter, potato water and salt. Mix in the yeast. Add flour gradually. Knead in flour to make a soft dough. Dough should not be sticky. Place dough into greased pan, cover and let rise in warm place for about one hour. Punch down and let rise for another hour. Shape pieces of dough, the size of an egg into a small ball. Let rise in warm place till double in size. Allow ample time to rise. Bake till light brown.

Variation:

Part of the dough may be made into cinnamon buns. Roll out dough to 1 cm (½ in.) thickness. Brush with melted butter. Sprinkle with cinnamon and brown sugar, nuts and raisins. Roll up and cut into slices 2 cm (¾ in.) thick. Place on lightly greased cookie sheet and bake till golden brown.

AIR BUNS

Metric	*Standard*
180°C	350°F
20-25 min.	
Yield: 5-6 doz.	

Ingredients:

75 mL sugar	⅓ cup sugar
1 L warm water	4 cups warm water
15 mL active dry yeast	1 pkg. active dry yeast
125 mL shortening	½ cup shortening
10 mL salt	2 tsps. salt
30 mL vinegar	2 tbsps. vinegar
1750 mL flour	7 cups flour

Grease cookie sheet. Dissolve 5 mL (1 tsp.) of sugar in 125 mL (½ cup) of warm water. Sprinkle yeast over top and let rise for 10 minutes. Combine remaining sugar, shortening, salt vinegar and warm water in a large bowl and add yeast mixture. Add flour gradually, mixing well. Knead until dough is soft and easy to work with. Let rise in warm place for about 2 hours. Punch down and let rise again for 1 hour. Punch down, roll into balls, the size of a small orange. Place on a greased cookie sheet 5 cm (2½ in.) apart. Cover lightly with tea towel and let rise for 3 hours. Bake and serve warm or cold with cheese or jam.

BUTTER HORN ROLLS

Metric	*Standard*
200°C	400°F
15-20 min.	
Yield: 64	

Ingredients:

15 mL sugar	1 tbsp. sugar
250 mL lukewarm water	1 cup lukewarm water
2 pkg. (8 g each) active dry yeast	2 pkg. active dry yeast
750 mL lukewarm water	3 cups lukewarm water
175 mL butter and lard mixed **or**	¾ cup butter and lard mixed **or**
150 mL safflo oil	⅔ cup safflo oil
50 mL sugar (optional)	¼ cup sugar (optional)
2 well beaten eggs	2 well beaten eggs
5 mL salt	1 tsp. salt
2750 mL flour	11 cups flour

Dissolve sugar in lukewarm water. Sprinkle in yeast and let stand in warm place for about 10 minutes. Add and mix in remaining ingredients in order given. Knead for about 15 minutes. Shape dough into ball and place in greased bowl. Cover and let rise in warm place till double in bulk. Divide dough into eight parts. Roll out to size of pie crust, brush with butter. Cut in eight sections. Roll up from wide to narrow side. Place on lightly greased cookie sheet and let rise to double bulk. Bake till lightly browned.

PECAN ROLLS

Metric	Standard
180°C	350°F
20-25 minutes	
Yield: 3 doz.	

Ingredients:
Dough:

75 mL sugar	⅓ cup sugar
125 mL warm water	½ cup warm water
15 mL active dry yeast	1 pkg. active dry yeast
2 mL salt	½ tsp. salt
250 mL milk	1 cup milk
1625 mL flour	6½ cups flour
125 mL shortening melted	½ cup shortening melted
2 eggs	2 eggs

Base:

75 mL butter	⅓ cup butter
175 mL brown sugar	¾ cup brown sugar
125 mL whole pecans	½ cup whole pecans

Filling:

softened butter	softened butter
cinnamon	cinnamon
chopped pecan nuts	chopped pecan nuts

Dissolve 5 mL (1 tsp.) of sugar in warm water. Add yeast and let rise for 10 minutes. Add salt to milk, scald and cool to lukewarm. Add 375 mL (1½ cups) of flour and mix to make a thin sponge. Let rise 30 minutes. Add remaining sugar, flour, melted shortening, and eggs. Knead dough well for a few minutes. Let rise in covered greased bowl for 2½ hours. Combine butter and brown sugar; melt. Add whole pecans and place about 10 mL (2 tsps.) into bottom of each cup of muffin tins. Roll out dough to 0.5 cm (⅛ in.) thickness. Use desired amounts for filling. Spread dough with softened butter, cinnamon and chopped pecan nuts. Roll up and cut in 2 cm (¾ in.) slices. Place on pecan base, and cover with tea towel. Let rise until double in bulk. Bake and serve warm or cold.

CINNAMON BUNS

Metric	Standard
160°-180°C	325-350°F
20 min.	
Yield: 5 doz.	

Ingredients:

15 mL sugar	1 tbsp. sugar
250 mL lukewarm water	1 cup lukewarm water
2 pkg. (8 g. each) active dry yeast	2 pkg. active dry yeast
250 mL milk	1 cup milk
1500-1750 mL flour	6-7 cups flour
100 mL lard **or** butter	6 tbsps. lard **or** butter
125 mL sugar	½ cup sugar
3 eggs	3 eggs
2 mL salt	½ tsp. salt
melted butter	melted butter
sugar-cinnamon mixture	sugar-cinnamon mixture
currants	currants
chopped nuts	chopped nuts

Dissolve sugar in lukewarm water. Sprinkle yeast over liquid and let rise in warm place 10 minutes. Scald and cool milk to lukewarm. Add to yeast mixture. Add ½ amount of flour, beat until smooth. Add lard, sugar, salt, eggs and beat well. Mix adding remaining flour gradually to form a soft smooth dough. Knead lightly on floured board. Shape into ball and place in lightly greased bowl. Let rise in warm place for about two hours. Roll out dough to 1 cm (½ in.) thickness. Brush with melted butter. Sprinkle with sugar-cinnamon mixture, currants, and chopped nuts. Roll up and cut into 2 cm (1 in.) slices. Place on lightly greased cookie sheet. Let rise in warm place for about one hour. Bake and serve warm to enjoy the best flavor.

CINNAMON BRAID

Metric	Standard
Two 1.5 L loaf pans	Two 4½ x 8½ in. loaf pans
(20 x 10 x 7 cm)	
180°C	350°F
35 min.	

Ingredients:

1 pkg. (8 g) active dry yeast	1 pkg. active dry yeast
50 mL lukewarm water	¼ cup lukewarm water
250 mL milk scalded	1 cup milk scalded
125 mL granulated sugar	½ cup granulated sugar

5 mL salt	1 tsp. salt
50 mL shortening	¼ cup shortening
1 L flour	4½ cups flour
2 eggs	2 eggs

For Pans:

60 mL butter, melted	4 tbsps. butter, melted
15 mL sugar	1 tbsp. sugar
10 mL water	2 tsps. water

For Mixture:

15 mL cinnamon	1 tbsp. cinnamon
15 mL sugar	1 tbsp. sugar

Soften yeast in water, let stand 10 min. Scald milk, add sugar, salt, and shortening and cool to lukewarm. Add 250 mL (1 cup) flour; mix well to make a thick batter. Add yeast and eggs; beat well. Work in remaining flour to make a soft dough. Turn out on a lightly floured board and knead until smooth and satiny. Place dough in greased bowl, cover, and let rise until double in bulk (about 1½ hours). Punch down, divide dough in half and let rest 10 min. While dough is resting, pour melted butter into loaf pans; sprinkle in sugar and water. Divide each section of dough into 3 parts. Roll each into 50 cm (20 in.) strips, and roll in cinnamon-sugar mixture. Braid 3 strips together, place in pan and tuck ends under to fit the pan. Brush top with milk once, sprinkle with remaining cinnamon-sugar mixture. Let rise until double in bulk (about 45 min.) Bake.

JAM BUSTERS

Metric	*Standard*
Yield: 3½ doz.	

Ingredients:

Metric	Standard
5 mL sugar	1 tsp. sugar
125 mL lukewarm water	½ cup lukewarm water
1 pkg. (8 g) active dry yeast	1 pkg. active dry yeast
250 mL milk	1 cup milk
250 mL sugar	1 cup sugar
5 mL salt	1 tsp. salt
50 mL lard	¼ cup lard
50 mL butter	¼ cup butter
5 mL vanilla	1 tsp. vanilla
1500-1750 mL flour	6-7 cups flour

Dissolve 5 mL (1 tsp.) sugar in lukewarm water. Sprinkle yeast over liquid and let rise in warm place for about 10 minutes. Scald milk, add sugar, salt and cool slightly. Add lard, butter, yeast mixture and vanilla. Mix with part of flour beating well. Mix in remaining flour to make a soft dough. Knead till everything is well blended. Dough will be sticky. Place dough into greased bowl. Cover and let rise in warm place till double in bulk. Roll out dough on lightly floured board to about 1.5 cm (½ in.) thickness. Cut out with 12 cm (2 in.) cookie cutter. Place on lightly greased sheet and let rise till double in bulk and very light. Fry in hot deep fat (see deep fat frying chart). Remove, drain on paper towel. Slit with sharp knife and fill with jam. (Raspberry jam is suggested.)

CAKES

HONEY FRUIT CAKE

Metric	Standard
Two 2 L loaf pans (23 x 13 x 7 cm)	Two loaf pans (9 x 5 x 3 in.)
150°C	300°F
2½ hrs.	
Yield: 2 loaves	

Ingredients:

Metric	Standard
250 mL butter	1 cup butter
125 mL sugar	½ cup sugar
125 mL honey	½ cup honey
5 eggs	5 eggs
300 mL sifted flour	1¼ cups sifted flour
2 mL salt	½ tsp. salt
5 mL baking powder	1 tsp. baking powder
5 mL cinnamon	1 tsp. cinnamon
2 mL nutmeg	½ tsp. nutmeg
1 mL cloves	¼ tsp. cloves
75 mL pineapple juice	⅓ cup pineapple juice
5 mL brandy flavouring	1 tsp. brandy flavouring
375 mL seeded raisins	1½ cup seeded raisins
375 mL bleached sultana raisins	1½ cups bleached sultana raisins
300 mL candied cherries, halved	1¼ cup candied cherries, halved
300 mL chopped dates	1¼ cup chopped dates
500 mL cut, mixed peel	2 cups, mixed peel
500 mL walnuts	2 cups walnuts
125 mL flour	½ cup flour

Line 2 loaf pans with heavy, well greased paper. Cream butter thoroughly. Add sugar, then honey, beating well after each addition. Add eggs one at a time, beating well after each. Mix sifted flour with salt, baking powder and spices. Add to creamed mixture alternately with pineapple juice and brandy flavouring. Wash and dry raisins. Combine fruit and nuts and mix well. Add remaining flour and stir until mixed fruit is well coated. Add to batter. Pour batter into prepared pans. Place pan of hot water on lower oven rack. Bake for specified time or until cake is firm when pressed. Leave in pans for a few minutes. Remove and let cool on rack. Wrap in foil paper and store in closed container. Cake tastes best when aged a few weeks before serving.

WEDDING CAKE

Metric	Standard
Five 1.5 loaf pans	Five loaf pans
(20 x 10 x 7.5 cm) **or** a	(8 x 4 x 3 in.) **or**
1 set of 3 tiered, wedding	1 set of 3 tiered wedding
cake pans	cake pans
150°C, 160°C	300°F, 325°F
2½ hrs.	
Yield: 5-6 kg	11-12 lbs.

Ingredients:

Metric	Standard
2 L raisins	8 cups raisins
500 mL currants	2 cups currants
925 mL glace cherries **or**	3¾ cups glace cherries **or**
500 mL maraschino cherries	2 cups maraschino cherries
500 mL mixed peel	2 cups mixed peel
875 mL walnuts **or**	3½ cups walnuts **or**
other nuts	other nuts
300 mL flour	1¼ cups flour
500 mL butter **or**	2 cups butter **or**
half butter and	half butter and
shortening	shortening
500 mL sugar	2 cups sugar
12 eggs, separated	12 eggs, separated
675 mL flour	2¾ cups flour
5 mL baking soda	1 tsp. baking soda
5 mL salt	1 tsp. salt
125 mL juice (from	½ cup juice (from
maraschinos	maraschinos
or orange juice)	**or** orange juice)
10 mL flavoring	2 tsp. flavoring
2 mL cloves	½ tsp. cloves
2 mL nutmeg	½ tsp. nutmeg
5 mL cinnamon	1 tsp. cinnamon

Line pans with foil, shiny side down. Wash raisins and currants and dry well between towels. Candied cherries should be rinsed in warm water and dried. Maraschino cherries should be drained well. Mix all prepared fruit in large bowl. Add 300 mL (1¼ cup) flour and nuts and mix well. Cream butter and sugar. Add yolks to creamed mixture and beat well. Sift remaining flour, salt and spices. Add to creamed mixture and mix well. Add fruit and nuts and mix. Beat egg whites and fold in. Pour dough into pans about ⅔ full. Place pan of hot water on lower rack and cake on medium rack. Bake at lower temperature for 2 hours, then at higher temperature for ½ hour. Following baking, leave cakes in pans for a few minutes. Then remove and allow to cool on rack. Store in air-tight container.

MARINATED CHRISTMAS FRUIT CAKE

Metric	Standard
1.5 L loaf pans (20 x 10 x 7 cm)	8 x 4 x 3 in. loaf pans
140°C	275°F
3 hrs.	
Yield: 4 loaves	

Ingredients:

750 mL seedless raisins	1 lb. seedless raisins
750 mL currants	1 lb. currants
750 mL sultana raisins	1 lb. sultana raisins
375 mL figs, chopped	½ lb. figs, chopped
375 mL dates, chopped	½ lb. dates, chopped
300 mL glace cherries	½ lb. glace cherries
500 mL mixed peel	1 pkg. mixed peel
250 mL wine **or** some brandy	1 cup wine **or** some brandy
500 mL margarine **or** Crisco	2 cups margarine **or** Crisco
250 mL brown sugar	1 cup brown sugar
250 mL white sugar	1 cup white sugar
5 eggs	5 eggs
1000 mL flour	4 cups flour
10 mL allspice	2 tsp. allspice
5 mL baking powder	1 tsp. baking powder
5 mL baking soda	1 tsp. baking soda
2 mL salt	½ tsp. salt
75 mL molasses	⅓ cup molasses
juice and rind of 1 orange	juice and rind of 1 orange
250 mL fruit juice	1 cup fruit juice
10 mL almond flavoring	2 tsp. almond flavoring
250 mL almonds, chopped	1 cup almonds, chopped
250 mL walnuts, chopped	1 cup walnuts, chopped
juice and rind of 1 lemon	juice and rind of 1 lemon

Line four loaf pans with foil paper, shiny side down. Combine first eight ingredients and marinate for 8-10 hours in covered containers. Cream margarine, add sugars and beat well. Add eggs one at a time, beating after each. Sift flour and spices. Combine molasses, fruit juice, rind and almond flavoring. Add sifted ingredients and fruit juice mixture alternately to egg mixture. Beat well after each addition. Fold in marinated fruit and chopped nuts. Distribute dough evenly in pans. Bake till done when tested with toothpick.

Note:

Place pan of water on lowest rack to prevent excessive browning during long, slow baking time.

COCONUT CHRISTMAS CAKE

Metric	Standard
Three 1.5 L loaf pans	Three loaf pans
(20 x 10 x 7 cm)	(8 x 4 x 3 in.)
150°C-1 hr.	300°F
140°C-1 hr.	275°F
Yield: 2 loaves	

Ingredients:

750 mL raisins	1 lb. raisins
750 mL blanched almonds	1 lb. blanched almonds
375 mL glace cherries	½ lb. glace cherries
175 mL butter	¾ cup butter
500 mL sugar	2 cups sugar
6 eggs, beaten	6 eggs, beaten
250 mL milk	1 cup milk
5 mL vanilla	1 tsp. vanilla
10 mL almond extract	2 tsps. almond extract
1.5 L coconut	1 lb. coconut
125 mL citron peel	¼ lb. citron peel
500 mL flour	2 cups flour
7 mL baking powder	1½ tsp. baking powder

Line three loaf pans with well greased heavy paper or foil. Wash and dry raisins. Chop blanched almonds and glace cherries. Cream butter and sugar. Add beaten eggs, milk and flavouring. Mix fruit, nuts and flour. Gradually add to egg mixture, stirring well. Pour into prepared loaf pans. Place pan with water on lowest rack. Bake cakes at higher temperature for one hour, then at lower temperature for another hour. Remove cakes from pans and allow to cool a little. Remove greased paper and cool completely. Wrap in foil and allow to ripen at room temperature for a few weeks. Then serve or freeze to store.

GOLDEN FRUIT CAKE

Metric	Standard
1.5 L loaf pans (20 x 10 x 7 cm)	8 x 4 x 3 in. loaf pans
140°C-30 min.	275°F
150°C-2 hrs.	300°F
Yield: 2 loaves	

Ingredients:

375 mL blanched almonds	1½ cups blanched almonds
500 mL light seedless	2 cups light seedless
raisins	raisins
125 mL cut glace pineapple	½ cup cut glace pineapple
125 mL cut, mixed peel	½ cup cut, mixed peel
250 mL glace cherries	1 cup glace cherries

125 mL strained, crushed pineapple	½ cup strained, crushed pineapple
250 mL chopped fruitlets **or** gumdrops	1 cup chopped fruitlets **or** gumdrops
250 mL dried apricots	1 cup dried apricots
250 mL sugar	1 cup sugar
250 mL water	1 cup water
250 mL butter	1 cup butter
250 mL sugar	1 cup sugar
5 eggs	5 eggs
550 mL sifted all-purpose flour	2¼ cups sifted all-purpose flour
7 mL baking powder	1½ tsp. baking powder
5 mL salt	1 tsp. salt
5 mL vanilla	1 tsp. vanilla

Line two loaf pans with well greased brown paper. Chop almonds; wash and dry raisins. Combine almonds, raisins, pineapple (both), peel, cherries and gumdrops. Wash dried apricots, cover with water; bring to boil. Cook for 10 minutes; drain. Cool slightly, cut into slices. Combine 250 mL (1 cup) sugar and water. Heat and stir until sugar has dissolved. Add apricot strips and simmer for 25-30 minutes. Stir frequently to prevent sticking. Remove from heat and cool. Cream butter, add sugar gradually and cream. Beat eggs slightly and add. Sift dry ingredients together and add with vanilla. Add apricot slices, prepared fruit and nuts; mix well. Pour dough into pans and bake at lower temperature for 30 minutes, then at higher temperature for about two hours. Let set in pan for a few minutes. Remove and cool loaves on rack. Remove brown paper. Wrap in foil and let ripen at room temperature for about two weeks in a closed container. Freeze till time to be served.

WHITE CHRISTMAS CAKE

Metric	*Standard*
Two 2 L loaf pans (23 x 13 x 7 cm)	Two loaf pans (9 x 5 x 3 in.)
140-150°C	275-300°F
2 hrs.	
Yield: 2 loaves	

Ingredients:

250 mL butter	1 cup butter
375 mL sugar	1½ cup sugar
5 eggs, beaten separately	5 eggs, beaten separately
250 mL milk	1 cup milk
175 mL blanched almonds	¾ cup blanched almonds
250 mL mixed peel	1 cup mixed peel
300 mL glace cherries	1¼ cup glace cherries
750 mL white raisins	3 cups white raisins
750 mL flour	3 cups flour
1 mL salt	¼ tsp. salt
5 mL baking powder	1 tsp. baking powder
5 mL lemon extract	1 tsp. lemon extract

Line loaf pans with 2 layers well greased brown paper or foil with shiny side down. Cream butter and sugar well. Add well beaten egg yolks; stir in milk. Chop blanched almonds and fruit. Sift ⅓ of flour over nuts and fruit. Mix and add to batter. Sift remaining flour with salt and baking powder. Add to batter and mix well. Beat egg whites to stiff peaks (but not too dry). Fold egg whites and lemon extract into batter. Pour batter into pans. Bake till done when tested with a toothpick. Allow cakes to rest on rack for a few minutes before removing from pans.

PINEAPPLE FRUIT CAKE

Metric	*Standard*
Two 1.5 L loaf pans	Two loaf pans
(20 x 10 x 7 cm)	(8 x 4 x 3 in.)
150°C	300°F
1¾-2 hrs.	
Yield: 2 loaves	

Ingredients:

750 mL sultana raisins	1 lb. sultana raisins
175 mL glace cherries	¼ lb. glace cherries
175 mL blanched almonds	¼ lb. blanched almonds
1 can (398 mL) crushed pineapple	1 can (14 oz.) crushed pineapple
250 mL butter	1 cup butter
250 mL sugar	1 cup sugar

Metric	Standard
3 eggs	3 eggs
125 mL orange peel	¼ lb. orange peel
675 mL flour	2¾ cups flour
5 mL baking powder	1 tsp. baking powder
125 mL pineapple juice	½ cup pineapple juice
10 mL vanilla	2 tsps. vanilla

Grease loaf pans and line with heavy greased brown paper. Wash and dry sultana raisins. Chop glace cherries and sliver blanched almonds. Drain crushed pineapple and save juice. Cream butter and sugar. Add eggs; beat well. Dredge fruit in part of flour. Mix remaining flour and baking powder. Add to egg mixture. Mix in pineapple juice and vanilla. Lastly add fruit and mix well. Turn batter into loaf pans and bake. Place pan with water on low rack in oven for half the baking time. Cakes are done if firm when pressed with finger. Cool cakes on rack. Wrap in aluminum foil and store in airtight container.

SOUR CREAM CHOCOLATE CAKE

Metric	*Standard*
Two 1.2 L layer cake pans	Two 8 in. layer cake pans
(20 x 4 cm)	
180°C	350°F
20 min.	

Ingredients:

Metric	Standard
250 mL sugar	1 cup sugar
3 eggs	3 eggs
250 mL sour cream	1 cup sour cream
2 squares unsweetened chocolate	2 squares unsweetened chocolate
5 mL vanilla	1 tsp. vanilla
5 mL salt	1 tsp. salt
300 mL cake flour **or**	1¼ cups cake flour **or**
250 mL all-purpose flour	1 cup all-purpose flour
5 mL baking powder	1 tsp. baking powder
5 mL baking soda	1 tsp. baking soda
50 mL hot water	¼ cup hot water

Grease and flour cake pan. Beat sugar and eggs together. Add sour cream. Melt and cool unsweetened chocolate; add to sugar mixture. Add vanilla and mix well. Sift dry ingredients together and add; beating well. Add hot water and mix. Pour batter immediately into prepared cake pans. Bake till done when tested with toothpick. Cool and frost with desired icing.

CHOCOLATE CAKE

Metric	*Standard*
Two 1.5 L layer cake pans (20 x 4 cm)	Two 9 in. layer cake pans
180°C	350°F
35 min.	

Ingredients:

Metric	Standard
125 mL butter	½ cup butter
500 mL brown sugar	2 cups brown sugar
3 eggs, separated and beaten	3 eggs, separated and beaten
500 mL cake flour **or** 450 mL all-purpose flour	2 cups cake flour **or** 1¾ cups all-purpose flour
2 mL salt	½ tsp. salt
5 mL instant coffee powder	1 tsp. instant coffee powder
75 mL cocoa	⅓ cup cocoa
125 mL boiling water	½ cup boiling water
5 mL baking soda	1 tsp. baking soda
125 mL sour cream	½ cup sour cream
5 mL vanilla	1 tsp. vanilla

Grease and flour cake pans. Cream butter, brown sugar and egg yolks thoroughly. Sift flour and salt together. Dissolve instant coffee powder and cocoa in boiling water. (Perked coffee may be used in place of instant coffee and hot water.) Cool coffee-cocoa mixture slightly. Dissolve baking soda in sour cream. Add flour, coffee and sour cream mixture alternately to creamed ingredients, mixing well after each addition. Add vanilla. Beat egg whites to soft peaks and fold gently into batter. Pour into prepared layer pans and bake. Cool and spread with 500 mL (2 cups) date filling or slice layers and spread in between. Cover with glossy chocolate icing.

GLOSSY CHOCOLATE ICING

Metric	*Standard*
Yield: About 400 mL	2 cups

Ingredients:

Metric	Standard
3 squares unsweetened chocolate	3 squares unsweetened chocolate
50 mL shortening **or** butter	3 tbsps. shortening **or** butter
500 mL sifted icing sugar	2 cups sifted icing sugar
75 mL milk	⅓ cup milk
1 mL salt	¼ tsp. salt
5 mL vanilla	1 tsp. vanilla

Melt unsweetened chocolate and shortening over hot water. Cool slightly. Add remaining ingredients and beat until mixture is of spreading consistency. If icing is not used immediately, it may harden somewhat. Add a little milk and beat again to attain spreading consistency.

HONEY FUDGE CAKE

Metric	Standard
3.5 L cake pan (33 x 21 x 5 cm)	13 x 9 x 2 in. cake pan
180°C	350°F
40-45 min.	

Ingredients:

Metric	Standard
125 mL shortening	½ cup shortening
500 mL sifted cake flour **or**	2 cups sifted cake flour **or**
425 mL sifted all-purpose flour	1¾ cup sifted all-purpose flour
7 mL baking soda	1½ tsp. baking soda
5 mL salt	1 tsp. salt
275 mL honey	1⅛ cup honey
75 mL water	⅓ cup water
5 mL vanilla	1 tsp. vanilla
2 eggs	2 eggs
2.5 squares unsweetened, melted chocolate	2½ squares unsweetened, melted chocolate

Grease cake pan and dust with flour. Mix shortening just to soften. Sift in dry ingredients. Combine honey, water and vanilla. Add 250 mL (1 cup) of liquid and eggs to flour mixture. Mix until all flour is moistened. Beat 1 minute. Add remaining liquid and melted chocolate. Beat 2 minutes. Batter will be thin. Bake and frost with the following frosting.

EASY FLUFFY FROSTING

Metric	Standard
1 egg white	1 egg white
dash of salt	dash of salt
125 mL corn syrup **or** honey	½ cup corn syrup **or** honey
2 mL vanilla	½ tsp. vanilla

Beat egg white and salt to stiff peaks. Pour corn syrup over egg white, beating constantly till mixture holds its shape. Stir in vanilla. vanilla.

CRUMB CAKE

Metric	*Standard*
3.5 L cake pan (33 x 21 x 5 cm)	13 x 9 x 2 in. cake pan
190°C	375°F
30-35 min.	

Ingredients:

500 mL flour	2 cups flour
250 mL sugar	1 cup sugar
175 mL butter	¾ cup butter
5 mL baking soda	1 tsp. baking soda
175 mL sour milk	¾ cup sour milk
5 mL cloves	1 tsp. cloves
5 mL cinnamon	1 tsp. cinnamon
1 egg	1 egg
250 mL raisins	1 cup raisins
250 mL currants	1 cup currants.

Grease cake pan lightly. Mix flour, sugar and butter to consistency of crumbs. Measure and reserve 250 mL (1 cup) of crumbs. Dissolve baking soda in sour milk. Add to remaining crumbs with other ingredients. Mix and pour into prepared cake pan. Sprinkle top of batter with reserved crumbs. Bake.

SOFT MOLASSES CAKE

Metric	*Standard*
2 L cake pan (20 cm square)	8 x 8 x 2 in. cake pan
180°C	350°F
35-40 min.	

Ingredients:

125 mL shortening	½ cup shortening
125 mL brown sugar	½ cup brown sugar
1 egg	1 egg
75-125 mL molasses	⅓-½ cup molasses
500 mL flour	2 cups flour
15 mL baking powder	1 tbsp. baking powder
1 mL baking soda	¼ tsp. baking soda
2 mL salt	½ tsp. salt
2 mL allspice	½ tsp. allspice
5 mL cinnamon	1 tsp. cinnamon
125 mL milk	½ cup milk

Lightly grease cake pan. Cream shortening and brown sugar. Stir in egg and molasses. Sift dry ingredients together. Add alternately with milk to creamed mixture. Turn into greased cake pan. Bake and enjoy.

SPICE CAKE

Metric	Standard
2 L cake pan (20 cm square)	7 x 8 x 2 in. cake pan
180°C	350°F
35-45 min.	

Ingredients:

Metric	Standard
250 mL sugar	1 cup sugar
15 mL shortening	1 tbsp. shortening
1 egg	1 egg
250 mL sour milk	1 cup sour milk
500 mL flour	2 cups flour
7 mL baking soda	1½ tsps. baking soda
5 mL cinnamon	1 tsp. cinnamon
2 mL cloves	½ tsp. cloves
2 mL nutmeg	½ tsp. nutmeg
1 mL salt	¼ tsp. salt
250 mL raisins	1 cup raisins

Grease pan. Cream sugar and shortening. Add egg and sour milk; mix well. Sift dry ingredients together and gradually add to milk mixture, beating well. Roll raisins in flour and fold into batter. Pour into greased cake pan and bake on center rack. Test for doneness with toothpick.

CHOCOLATE FUDGE CAKE

Metric	Standard
2 L cake pan (20 cm square)	8 x 8 x 2 in. cake pan
180°C	350°C
20-25 min.	

Ingredients:

Metric	Standard
125 mL melted butter	½ cup melted butter
250 mL brown sugar	1 cup brown sugar
1 egg	1 egg
5 mL vanilla	1 tsp. vanilla
125 mL flour	½ cup flour
30 mL cocoa	2 tbsps. cocoa
175 mL chopped walnuts	¾ cup chopped walnuts

Lightly grease cake pan and dust with flour. Combine melted butter, sugar, egg and vanilla. Beat well. Sift flour and cocoa together and mix in chopped walnuts. Add dry ingredients and mix well. Pour into prepared cake pan. Bake until done when tested with toothpick. Frost cake while warm with Chocolate Butter Frosting.

CHOCOLATE BUTTER FROSTING

Metric	Standard
Yield: 250-400 mL	1-1½ cups

Ingredients:

375 mL icing sugar	1½ cups icing sugar
50 mL cocoa	3 tbsps. cocoa
30 mL butter	2 tbsps. butter
45-50 mL light cream **or** milk	3 tbsps. light cream **or** milk

Sift icing sugar and cocoa together. Mix in butter. Add light cream and mix to spreading consistency.

BOILED RAISIN CAKE

Metric	Standard
2.5 L cake pan (23 cm square)	9 x 9 x 2 in. cake pan
160°C	325°F
50-60 min.	

Ingredients:

250 mL raisins	1 cup raisins
2 mL cloves	½ tsp. cloves
2 mL cinnamon	½ tsp. cinnamon
375 mL flour	1½ cups flour
5 mL baking soda	1 tsp. baking soda
1 mL salt	¼ tsp. salt
125 mL butter	½ cup butter
250 mL brown sugar	1 cup brown sugar
1 egg	1 egg

Grease cake pan lightly. Cover raisins with water and boil for 20 minutes. Add spices and cook a few minutes longer. Drain raisins. Reserve and cool 125 mL (½ cup) liquid. Roll raisins in part of flour. Mix remaining flour with baking soda and salt. Cream butter, add sugar gradually. Add egg and beat. Add flour mixture and reserved liquid alternately to creamed mixture; blend after each addition. Fold in raisins. Pour into prepared cake pan and bake. Leave in pan to cool. Spread with butter icing and serve.

SNOW WHITE CAKE

Metric	Standard
Three 1.2 L layer cake pans (20 x 4 cm)	Three 8 in. layer cake pans
180°C	350°F
20 min.	

Ingredients:

Metric	Standard
125 mL Crisco shortening	½ cup Crisco shortening
500 mL sugar	2 cups sugar
750 mL flour	3 cups flour
10 mL baking powder	2 tsps. baking powder
2 mL salt	½ tsp. salt
250 mL milk	1 cup milk
2 mL lemon extract	½ tsp. lemon extract
2 mL almond extract	½ tsp. almond extract
4 egg whites	4 egg whites

Lightly grease and flour cake pans. In large bowl blend Crisco shortening and sugar. Sift dry ingredients. Add alternately with milk to first mixture. Add flavouring. Beat egg whites to stiff peaks and fold in. Pour into prepared cake pans. Bake till done when tested with toothpick. Cool and fill with lemon filling.

Variation:

Cake may also be baked in 25 cm (12 in.) round cake pan for 35 minutes, sliced into layers and finished as above.

LEMON FILLING

Metric	Standard
Yield: 250-400 mL	1-1½ cups

Ingredients:

Metric	Standard
250 mL sugar	1 cup sugar
1 mL salt	¼ tsp. salt
30 mL flour	2 tbsps. flour
4 egg yolks	4 egg yolks
50 mL cold water	¼ cup cold water
grated rind and juice of 1 lemon	grated rind and juice of 1 lemon
15 mL butter	1 tbsp. butter

Mix sugar, salt and flour in top of 1.5 L (1½ qts.) double boiler. Beat egg yolks and add. Add cold water, grated rind and lemon juice. Cook in double boiler until thick. Stir in butter. Cool and use with Snow White Cake.

STANDARD BUTTER CAKE

Metric	*Standard*
Two 1.2 L layer cake pans (20 x 4 cm)	Two 8 in. layer cake pans
180°C	350°F
30 min.	

Ingredients:

125 mL butter	½ cup butter
2 mL vanilla	½ tsp. vanilla
250 mL sugar	1 cup sugar
2 eggs, separated	2 eggs
500 mL sifted flour	2 cups sifted flour
20 mL baking powder	4 tsps. baking powder
2 mL salt	½ tsp. salt
250 mL milk	1 cup milk

Grease cake pans well and dust lightly with flour. Cream butter and vanilla thoroughly. Add sugar gradually, beating well until light and fluffy. Beat egg yolks until thick and light. Add to butter and sugar mixture. Sift flour twice; measure. Add baking powder and salt and sift twice more. Alternately, add dry ingredients and milk to mixture, beginning and ending with flour. Beat egg whites to stiff peaks and fold gently into mixture. Turn into prepared cake pans and bake till golden. Cool in pans for about 10 minutes. Run knife around edges of cakes. Place cooling rack over cake and turn upside down with cake. Cool on rack, then ice and decorate.

Note: Ingredients like butter, eggs and milk should be at room temperature for best results.

LAZY DAISY CAKE

Metric	*Standard*
2 L cake pan (20 cm square)	8 x 8 x 2 in. cake pan
180°C	350°F
40 min.	

Ingredients:
Cake:

2 eggs	2 eggs
5 mL vanilla	1 tsp. vanilla
250 mL sugar	1 cup sugar
250 mL sifted flour	1 cup sifted flour
5 mL baking powder	1 tsp. baking powder
1 mL salt	¼ tsp. salt
125 mL milk	½ cup milk
30 mL butter	2 tbsps. butter

Topping:

25 mL brown sugar	5 tsps. brown sugar
20 mL melted butter	4 tsps. melted butter
10 mL light cream	2 tsps. light cream
2 mL vanilla	½ tsp. vanilla
150 mL coconut	⅔ cup coconut

Grease cake pan.

For Cake:

Beat eggs with vanilla until thick and creamy. Gradually add sugar; continue beating. Sift together dry ingredients; add to egg mixture. Heat milk and butter to boiling point and mix in. Spread batter into greased cake pan.

For Topping:

Mix brown sugar and melted butter. Add light cream and vanilla and mix well. Add coconut, mix well and sprinkle over batter. Bake till golden brown.

DATE CAKE

Metric	*Standard*
2 L loaf pan (23 x 13 x 7 cm)	9 x 5 x 3 in. loaf pan
180°C	350°F
1 hr.	

Ingredients:

5 mL baking soda	1 tsp. baking soda
250 mL chopped dates	1 cup chopped dates
250 mL boiling water	1 cup boiling water
30 mL shortening	2 tbsps. shortening
200 mL brown sugar	⅞ cup brown sugar
1 egg	1 egg
250 mL sifted flour	1 cup sifted flour
5 mL baking powder	1 tsp. baking powder
5 mL salt	1 tsp. salt
125 mL bran	½ cup bran
125 mL nuts	½ cup nuts
15 mL grated orange rind	1 tbsp. grated orange rind

Lightly grease loaf pan. Sprinkle baking soda over chopped dates. Pour boiling water over top. Add shortening and cool. Add brown sugar and egg; beat well. Add sifted flour, baking powder and salt. Add bran, nuts and orange rind; mix well. Pour into greased loaf pan and bake.

BANANA CAKE

Metric	Standard
2.5 L cake pan (23 cm square)	9 x 9 x 2 in. cake pan
180°C	350°F
40 min.	

Ingredients:

Metric	Standard
125 mL butter	½ cup butter
125 mL white sugar	½ cup sugar
125 mL brown sugar	½ cup brown sugar
2 eggs	2 eggs
250 mL banana pulp	1 cup banana pulp
2 mL vanilla	½ tsp. vanilla
2 mL lemon extract	½ tsp. lemon extract
7 mL baking soda	1½ tsps. baking soda
50 mL boiling water	¼ cup boiling water
50 mL milk	¼ cup milk
500 mL flour	2 cups flour
7 mL baking powder	1½ tsps. baking powder
2 mL salt	½ tsp. salt
125 mL chopped walnuts (optional)	½ cup chopped walnuts (optional)

Grease pan and line with waxed paper. Cream butter, adding sugars gradually. Beat until light and fluffy. Add eggs, banana pulp, vanilla and lemon extract; blend. Dissolve baking soda in boiling water and add milk. Sift dry ingredients. Roll chopped nuts in part of dry ingredients. Add remaining dry ingredients and liquid alternately to the banana mixture. Fold in chopped nuts Pour into prepared cake pan. Bake and cool. Frost with butter icing and sprinkle with chopped nuts.

PRINCESS ELIZABETH CAKE

Metric	Standard
3 L cake pan (30 x 20 x 5 cm)	12 x 8 x 2 in. cake pan
180°C	350°F
35-40 min.	

Ingredients:
Cake:

Metric	Standard
250 mL chopped dates	1 cup chopped dates
5 mL baking soda	1 tsp. baking soda
250 mL boiling water	1 cup boiling water
50 mL shortening	¼ cup shortening
250 mL sugar	1 cup sugar
1 egg	1 egg
5 mL vanilla	1 tsp. vanilla

375 mL flour	1½ cups flour
5 mL baking powder	1 tsp. baking powder
1 mL salt	¼ tsp. salt
125 mL chopped walnuts	½ cup chopped walnuts

Grease cake pan. Sprinkle baking soda over chopped dates. Pour boiling water over this and allow to cool. Cream shortening, sugar, egg and vanilla. Add remaining ingredients, including cooled date mixture. Turn into greased cake pan and bake.

Topping:

75 mL brown sugar	5 tbsps. brown sugar
50 mL margarine	3 tbsps. margarine
30 mL light cream	2 tbsps. light cream
125 mL coconut	½ cup coconut

Mix all ingredients for topping. Cover hot cake with topping and return to oven. Broil for three minutes.

CHOCOLATE DATE CAKE

Metric	*Standard*
3 L cake pan (30 x 20 x 5 cm)	12 x 8 x 2 cake pan
180°C	350°F
30-35 min.	

Ingredients:
Cake:

5 mL soda	1 tsp. soda
250 mL chopped dates	1 cup chopped dates
125 mL boiling water	½ cup boiling water
375 mL shortening	1½ cups shortening
250 mL sugar	1 cup sugar
2 eggs, beaten	2 eggs, beaten
375 mL flour	1½ cups flour
1 mL salt	¼ tsp. salt
3 mL soda	¾ tsp. soda

Topping:

175 mL chocolate chips	6 oz. (1 pkg.) chocolate chips
125 mL brown sugar	½ cup brown sugar
125 mL walnuts	½ cup walnuts

Grease cake pan lightly. Combine soda, dates and boiling water; cool. Cream shortening and sugar until light and fluffy. Add beaten eggs. Combine salt, soda and flour. Add the date mixture to shortening, sugar and eggs, then mix in flour. Turn batter into prepared cake pan. Bake.

Note: Topping may be added before baking or about 10 minutes before cake is done.

ORANGE AND RAISIN CAKE

Metric	Standard
3.5 L cake pan (33 x 21 x 5 cm)	13 x 9 x 1 in. cake pan
160°C — 45 min.	325°F
180°C — 15 min.	350°F

Ingredients:

Metric	Standard
150 mL shortening **or** margarine	⅔ cup shortening **or** margarine
375 mL sugar	1½ cups sugar
3 eggs, beaten	3 eggs, beaten
5 mL salt	1 tsp. salt
7 mL baking soda	1½ tsps. baking soda
625 mL flour	2½ cups flour
250 mL nuts, chopped	1 cup nuts, chopped
375 seeded raisins	1½ cups seeded raisins
rind of 1½ oranges, chopped	rind of 1½ oranges, chopped
250 mL sour milk **or** buttermilk	1 cup sour milk **or** buttermilk
5 mL vanilla	1 tsp. vanilla

Grease cake pan. Cream shortening with sugar. Add beaten eggs. Sift dry ingredients together and add to creamed mixture. Add chopped nuts, seeded raisins and chopped orange rind; mix. Add sour milk and vanilla. Mix well and pour into greased cake pan. Bake and pour orange glaze over hot cake. Let stand for a day, then cut and serve.

ORANGE GLAZE

Metric	Standard
Yield: About 250 mL	1 cup

Ingredients:

Metric	Standard
juice of 1½ oranges	juice of 1½ oranges
175 mL sugar	¾ cup sugar

Combine and pour over hot cake, e.g.: Orange Raisin Cake.

RHUBARB CAKE

Metric	Standard
3.5 L cake pan (33 x 21 x 5 cm)	13 x 9 x 2 in. cake pan
180°C	350°F
35 min.	

Ingredients:
Cake:

375 mL brown sugar	1½ cups brown sugar
125 mL butter **or** margarine	½ butter **or** margarine
1 egg	1 egg
5 mL vanilla	1 tsp. vanilla
250 mL sour milk **or** buttermilk	1 cup sour milk **or** buttermilk
5 mL baking soda	1 tsp. baking soda
500 mL flour	2 cups flour
375 mL finely cut rhubarb	1½ cups finely cut rhubarb

Topping:

125 mL white sugar	½ cup white sugar
5 mL cinnamon	1 tsp. cinnamon
175 mL finely chopped nuts	¾ cup finely chopped nuts

Lightly grease cake pan.

For Cake:

Cream sugar and butter. Add egg and beat. Add remaining ingredients in order given; mix well. Turn batter into greased cake pan.

For Topping:

Combine ingredients and sprinkle over batter. Spread evenly over batter and bake. Cake should be fairly moist, but light when done.

QUICKER THAN QUICK CAKE

Metric	*Standard*
2 L cake pan (20 cm square)	8 x 8 x 2 in. cake pan
180°C	350°F
25 min.	

Ingredients:

375 mL sifted pastry flour	1½ cups sifted pastry flour
250 mL sugar	1 cup sugar
50 mL cocoa	¼ cup cocoa
5 mL baking powder	1 tsp. baking powder
5 mL baking soda	1 tsp. baking soda
1 mL salt	¼ tsp. salt
250 mL water	1 cup water
75 mL melted butter **or** oil	⅓ cup melted butter **or** oil
50 mL vinegar	¼ cup vinegar
5 mL vanilla	1 tsp. vanilla

Sift dry ingredients into ungreased cake pan. Make a well in center of mix and add remaining ingredients. Mix until blended and bake. Test with toothpick for doneness. Ice with favourite icing and serve.

COCONUT MACAROON CAKE

Metric	Standard
2.5 L cake pan (23 cm square)	9 x 9 x 2 in. cake pan
180°C	350°F
40 min.	

Ingredients:
Base:

Metric	Standard
125 mL butter	½ cup butter
125 mL sugar	½ cup sugar
2 egg yolks	2 egg yolks
250 mL flour	1 cup flour
5 mL baking powder	1 tsp. baking powder
15 mL milk	1 tbsp. milk

Topping:

Metric	Standard
2 egg whites	2 egg whites
125 mL fruit sugar **or** icing sugar	½ cup fruit sugar **or** icing sugar
250 mL fine coconut	1 cup fine coconut

Grease pan lightly.

For Base:

Cream butter, sugar and egg yolks. Mix flour and baking powder; add. Stir in milk. Spread evenly in lightly greased pan.

For Topping:

Beat egg whites to stiff peaks. Add fruit sugar and fine coconut. Spread on base and bake until nicely browned.

PINEAPPLE UP-SIDE-DOWN CAKE

Metric	Standard
2.5 L cake pan (23 cm square)	9 x 9 x 2 in. cake pan
180°C	350°F
30-40 min.	
Serves: 8	

Ingredients:
Topping:

Metric	Standard
50 mL Crisco shortening	¼ cup Crisco shortening
250 mL brown sugar	1 cup brown sugar
1 can (540 mL) pineapple slices	1 can (19 oz.) pineapple slices
8 maraschino cherries	8 maraschino cherries

Batter:

Metric	Standard
50 mL Crisco shortening	¼ cup Crisco shortening
175 mL sugar	¾ cup sugar
1 egg	1 egg
375 mL flour	1½ cups flour

10 mL baking powder	2 tsps. baking powder
2 mL salt	½ tsp. salt
125 mL milk **or** pineapple juice	½ cup milk **or** pineapple juice

For Topping:

Melt Crisco in cake pan. Add brown sugar and blend thoroughly; spread evenly. Arrange pineapple slices on mixture. Place a maraschino cherry in center of each slice.

For Batter:

Cream Crisco with sugar and egg until fluffy. Sift dry ingredients and add alternately with milk to Crisco mixture. Beat until smooth. Pour batter evenly over pineapple slices. Bake and turn out of cake pan up-side-down onto serving platter. Decorate with whipped cream and serve.

OATMEAL CAKE

Metric	Standard
3.5 L (33 x 21 x 5 cm) cake pan	13 x 9 x 2 in. cake pan
160°C	325°F
50-55 min.	

Ingredients:

500 mL oatmeal **plus**	2 cups oatmeal **plus**
500 mL hot water **or**	2 cups hot water **or**
625 mL leftover porridge	2½ cups leftover porridge
375 mL brown sugar	1½ cups brown sugar
125 mL margarine	½ cup margarine
4 eggs, beaten	4 eggs, beaten
500 mL raisins	2 cups raisins
500 mL flour	2 cups flour
12 mL baking soda	2½ tsps. baking soda
13 mL baking powder	2¾ tsps. baking powder
5 mL salt	1 tsp. salt
5 mL cinnamon	1 tsp. cinnamon

Grease cake pan. Pour hot water over porridge. Soak. Combine sugar, margarine, eggs and raisins. Sift dry ingredients together. Combine wet and dry ingredients. Mix briefly. Stir in oatmeal last. Pour into cake pan. Bake.

Variation:

Add 250 mL (1 cup) coconut to batter and decrease raisins to 250 mL (1 cup).

CARROT CAKE

Metric	Standard
3.5 L cake pan (33 x 21 x 5 cm)	13 x 9 x 2 in. cake pan
160°C	325°F
45 min.	

Ingredients:
Cake:

500 mL sugar	2 cups sugar
500 mL flour	2 cups flour
10 mL baking soda	2 tsps. baking soda
10 mL cinnamon	2 tsps. cinnamon
5 mL salt	1 tsp. salt
4 eggs, beaten	4 eggs, beaten
250 mL cooking oil	1 cup cooking oil
10 mL vanilla	2 tsps. vanilla
500 mL finely grated carrots	2 cups finely grated carrots
125 mL nuts	½ cup nuts

Icing:

500 mL icing sugar	2 cups icing sugar
50 mL soft butter	¼ cup soft butter
1 pkg. (113 g) Philadelphia cream cheese	1 pkg. (4 oz.) Philadelphia cream cheese
5 mL vanilla	1 tsp. vanilla

Grease cake pan.

For Cake:

Sift dry ingredients together. Make a well in center and add remaining ingredients. Mix well, and pour into prepared cake pan. Bake till toothpick comes out clean when tested in center of cake. Cake should be moist, however.

For Icing:

Cream ingredients together to spreading consistency. Ice cake when cool, and serve.

OLD FASHIONED POUND CAKE

Metric	Standard
3 L loaf pan (25 x 15 x 7 cm)	10 x 6 x 3 loaf pan
160°C	325°F
1 hr.	

Ingredients:

400 mL sugar	1⅔ cups sugar
250 mL soft butter	1 cup soft butter
500 mL cake flour **or**	2 cups cake flour **or**
425 mL all-purpose flour	1¾ cups all-purpose flour

pinch of salt	pinch of salt
1 mL mace	¼ tsp. mace
5 eggs	5 eggs
2 mL vanilla	½ tsp. vanilla

Grease loaf pan. Cream butter and sugar until sugar granules are dissolved. Sift flour and measure. Add salt and mace and sift again. Add eggs one at a time alternately with flour to creamed butter. Beat until light and fluffy. Add vanilla. Pour into prepared loaf pan; bake.

ALLEGRETTE CHIFFON CAKE

Metric	Standard
3 L tube pan (23 x 10 cm)	9 x 4 in. tube pan
160°C	325°F
55-60 min.	

Ingredients:

Metric	Standard
275 mL cake flour **or**	1⅛ cups cake flour **or**
225 mL all-purpose flour	1 cup all-purpose flour
200 mL sugar	⅞ cup sugar
7 mL baking powder	1½ tsps. baking powder
2 mL salt	½ tsp. salt
60 mL Safflo oil	¼ cup Safflo oil
2 eggs, separated	2 eggs, separated
60 mL cold water	¼ cup cold water
5 mL vanilla	1 tsp. vanilla
grated rind of one orange	grated rind of one orange
125 mL egg whites	½ cup egg whites
2 mL cream of tartar	¼ tsp. cream of tartar
1½ squares semi-sweet chocolate	1½ squares semi-sweet chocolate

Sift first four ingredients. Make well and add Safflo oil, egg yolks, cold water, vanilla and grated orange rind. Beat with spoon till smooth. Combine egg whites and cream of tartar and beat to very stiff peaks. Pour egg yolk mixture over beaten egg whites; fold in gently with rubber scraper till blended. Do not stir. Grate semi-sweet chocolate and sprinkle over batter, folding it in lightly. Pour into UNGREASED tube pan. Bake until top springs back when lightly touched. Place pan upside down on stand so that cake hangs free to cool. When cold, loosen carefully with knife from sides of pan. Remove, decorate and serve.

CHOCOLATE CHIFFON CAKE

Metric	*Standard*
4 L tube pan (25 x 10 cm)	10 in. tube pan
160°C	325°F
65-70 min.	

Ingredients:

250 mL egg whites (8 or 9)	1 cup egg whites (7 or 8)
125 mL sifted cocoa	½ cup sifted cocoa
175 mL boiling water	¾ cup boiling water
425 mL sifted cake flour	1¾ cups sifted cake flour
250 mL sugar	1 cup sugar
7 mL baking soda	1½ tsps. baking soda
5 mL salt	1 tsp. salt
125 mL salad oil	½ cup salad oil
8 egg yolks	8 egg yolks
10 mL vanilla	2 tsps. vanilla
2 mL cream of tartar	½ tsp. cream of tartar

In large bowl let egg whites come to room temperature, about 1 hour. Combine cocoa and boiling water, stirring until smooth. Let cool about 20 minutes. Sift together flour, sugar, baking soda and salt. Make a well in center of sifted ingredients and pour in salad oil, egg yolks, vanilla and cooled cocoa. Beat just until smooth. Sprinkle cream of tartar over egg whites. Beat at high speed until very stiff peaks form. Do not underbeat. Pour batter over egg whites. Gently fold in egg whites with rubber scraper or wire whisk, just until blended. Pour batter into ungreased tube pan. Bake for specified time or until cake tester comes out clean. Invert pan over cake holder or neck bottle. Let cool completely (about 1½ hours). With spatula, carefully loosen cake from pan; remove.

CHIFFON CAKE

Metric	*Standard*
4 L tube pan (25 x 10 cm)	10 in. tube pan
160°C 40-45 min.	325°F
180°C 10-15 min.	350°F

Ingredients:

550 mL sifted cake flour	2¼ cups sifted cake flour
375 mL sugar	1½ cups sugar
15 mL baking powder	1 tbsp. baking powder
5 mL salt	1 tsp. salt
125 mL Safflo **or** other cooking oil	½ cup Safflo **or** other cooking oil
5 egg yolks	5 egg yolks
175 mL cold water	¾ cup cold water
2 mL vanilla	½ tsp. vanilla

250 mL egg whites (8-9)	1 cup egg whites (7-8)
2 mL cream of tartar	½ tsp. cream of tartar

Sift together flour, sugar, baking powder and salt. Make a well and add in order Safflo oil, unbeaten egg yolks, cold water and vanilla. Beat with spoon until smooth. In large mixing bowl, combine egg whites and cream of tartar. Whip to very stiff peaks. Do not underbeat. Pour egg yolk mixture gradually over whipped egg whites. Gently fold into batter with rubber scraper just until blended. Do not stir. Immediately pour into ungreased tube pan. Bake at lower temperature for given time, then at higher temperature for remainder of time. When baked, immediately turn pan upside down placing tube part over neck of funnel or bottle. Let hang free until cool. Loosen from sides and tube with spatula. Turn pan over and hit edges sharply on table to loosen.

POPPY SEED CAKE

Metric	*Standard*
4 L tube pan (25 x 10 cm)	10 in. tube pan
180°C	350°F
65-70 min.	

Ingredients:

75 mL poppy seed	⅓ cup poppy seed
250 mL buttermilk	1 cup buttermilk
250 mL butter	1 cup butter
375 mL sugar	1½ cup sugar
5 eggs, separated	5 eggs, separated
600 mL flour	2½ cups flour
10 mL baking powder	2 tsp. baking powder
5 mL baking soda	1 tsp. baking soda
2 mL salt	½ tsp. salt
5 mL vanilla	1 tsp. vanilla
75 mL sugar	⅓ cup sugar
5 mL cinnamon	1 tsp. cinnamon

Mix poppy seed and buttermilk; refrigerate 8-10 hours. Cream butter and sugar. Add egg yolks one at a time, scraping bowl often. Sift flour, baking powder, baking soda and salt together. Add to creamed mixture alternately with buttermilk mixture and vanilla, starting and ending with dry. Beat egg whites to stiff peaks and fold into batter using a rubber spatula. Pour half the batter into buttered tube pan. Mix sugar and cinnamon; sprinkle over batter. Top with remaining batter. Bake. Dust with icing sugar before serving. A delicious cake.

FRESH ORANGE CHIFFON CAKE

Metric	Standard
2 L loaf pan (23 x 13 x 7 cm)	9 x 5 x 3 in. loaf pan
160°C	325°F
50-55 min.	

Ingredients:

Metric	Standard
275 mL sifted cake flour	1⅛ cups sifted cake flour
175 mL sugar	¾ cup sugar
7 mL baking powder	1½ tsps. baking powder
2 mL salt	½ tsp. salt
50 mL salad oil	¼ cup salad oil
2 egg yolks	2 egg yolks
juice of 1 medium orange plus water to make 90 mL liquid	juice of 1 medium orange plus water to make 6 tbsps. liquid
15 mL grated orange rind	1 tbsp. grated orange rind
125 mL egg whites	½ cup egg whites (4)
1 mL cream of tartar	¼ tsp. cream of tartar

Sift first four ingredients together in mixing bowl. Make a well and add salad oil, egg yolks, orange juice liquid and grated orange rind in order. Beat with spoon until smooth. In large mixing bowl, beat egg whites with cream of tartar until stiff peaks form. Do not underbeat. Pour egg yolk mixture gradually over whipped egg white, and gently fold in using rubber scraper just until blended. Do not stir. Immediately pour into ungreased loaf pan. Bake until top springs back when lightly touched. Immediately turn pan upside down, resting edges of pan on two other pans. Let hang free of table until cold. Loosen from sides with spatula. Turn pan over and hit edge sharply on table to loosen. Split cooled cake crosswise into three even layers. Spread orange filling and sweetened whipped cream between layers. Cover top with whipped cream. Chill in refrigerator for one to two hours. Garnish with orange slices if desired. To serve, slice in eight to ten pieces.

Note:

Use 250 mL (1 cup) heavy cream sweetened with 65 mL (¼ cup) sugar. Grated chocolate may be folded into the whipped cream.

SPONGE CAKE

Metric	Standard
3 L tube pan (23 x 10 cm)	9 in. tube pan
180°C	350°F
30-35 min.	

Ingredients:

Metric	Standard
3 eggs, separated	3 eggs, separated
250 mL sifted sugar	1 cup sifted sugar
45 mL warm water	3 tbsps. warm water
5 mL vinegar **or** lemon juice	1 tsp. vinegar **or** lemon juice
250 mL cake flour	1 cup cake flour
5 mL baking powder	1 tsp. baking powder
2 mL salt	½ tsp. salt

Beat egg whites until light. Gradually add about half of sifted sugar, beating until stiff peaks form. Beat egg yolks with remaining sugar until light and lemon coloured. Add warm water and flavouring and mix well. Fold into egg white mixture. Sift cake flour and measure. Add baking powder and salt. Sift again. Add 30 mL (2 tbsps.) at a time to egg mixture, folding in gently with a wire whisk. Pour into ungreased tube pan and cut with knife to destroy large air bubbles. Bake until cake springs back when pressed lightly with finger. Invert pan over funnel to cool. Do not leave cake in pan too long, since it may cause cake to stick. Loosen cake with knife around edges and remove. A very good and economical cake.

MATRIMONIAL CAKE

Metric	*Standard*
2 L cake pan (20 cm square)	8 x 8 x 2 in. cake pan
180-190°C	350°F
35 minutes	

Ingredients:

Metric	Standard
425 mL oatmeal	1¾ cups oatmeal
125 mL flour	½ cup flour
250 mL brown sugar	1 cup brown sugar
2 mL salt	½ tsp. salt
5 mL baking soda	1 tsp. baking soda
175 mL shortening	¾ cup shortening

Mix above ingredients and put half the mixture in bottom of pan.

Date Filling:

Metric	Standard
750 mL pitted dates	3 cups pitted dates
30 mL sugar	2 tbsps. sugar
175 mL water	¾ cup water
5 ml lemon juice **or** vanilla	1 tsp. lemon juice **or** vanilla

Combine date filling ingredients in saucepan. Simmer until slightly thick; cool. Spread filling over oatmeal mixture in pan. Top filling with remainder of oatmeal mixture. Bake till edges are light brown.

NUT TORTE

Metric	Standard
3 L tube pan (23 x 10 cm)	9 in. tube pan
180°C	350°F
40-45 min.	

Ingredients:

Metric	Standard
125 mL butter	½ cup butter
250 mL fine white sugar	1 cup fine white sugar
6 eggs, separated	6 eggs, separated
juice and grated rind of ½ lemon	juice and grated rind of ½ lemon
375 mL finely grated almonds **or** walnuts	1½ cups finely grated almonds **or** walnuts
175 mL fine dry bread crumbs	¾ cup fine dry bread crumbs
5 mL baking powder	1 tsp. baking powder

Cream butter and fine white sugar thoroughly. Add egg yolks one at a time and continue beating until thick and lemon coloured. Add lemon juice and grated rind. Mix together finely grated almonds, fine dry bread crumbs and baking powder. Add to egg yolk mixture one tablespoon at a time. Beat egg whites to stiff peaks and fold into egg yolk mixture. Turn into ungreased tube pan. Bake till cake springs back when lightly pressed. Turn immediately upside down and place tube over neck of funnel. Allow to cool. Cover with orange or chocolate butter icing.

WALNUT SLICE

Metric	Standard
3 L cake pan (30 x 20 x 5 cm)	12 x 8 x 2 in. cake pan
180°C	350°F
22-27 min.	
Yield: 24 slices	

Ingredients:

Base:

Metric	Standard
250 mL flour	1 cup flour
125 mL butter	½ cup butter
30 mL icing sugar	2 tbsps. icing sugar

Filling:

Metric	Standard
2 eggs	2 eggs
250 mL brown sugar	1 cup brown sugar
30 mL flour	2 tbsps. flour
7 mL baking powder	1½ tsps. baking powder
pinch of salt	pinch of salt
250 mL chopped walnuts	1 cup chopped walnuts
125 mL coconut	½ cup coconut
5 mL vanilla	1 tsp. vanilla

For Base:
Rub ingredients together to fine crumbs. Press into cake pan and bake for 12 minutes or until light brown.

For Filling:
Beat eggs well, add brown sugar and beat. Mix dry ingredients and fold in with chopped walnuts, coconut and vanilla. Pour onto baked base. Return to oven and bake for 12-15 minutes.

CHERRY AND NUT SLICE

Metric	*Standard*
2.5 L cake pan (20 cm square)	8 x 8 x 2 in. cake pan
200°C	400°F
10-12 min.; 25 min.	

Ingredients:

Base:

125 mL butter	½ cup butter
50 mL brown sugar	¼ cup brown sugar
125 mL nuts	½ cup nuts
250 mL flour	1 cup flour
2 mL baking powder	½ tsp. baking powder

Topping:

250 mL cut cherries	1 cup cut cherries
chopped nuts	chopped nuts
2 egg whites	2 egg whites
125 mL sugar	½ cup sugar
2 mL baking powder	½ tsp. baking powder
5 mL vanilla	1 tsp. vanilla

Rub base ingredients together to form crumbs. Pack firmly into cake pan and bake for 10-12 minutes. Spread base with cut cherries. Sprinkle with chopped nuts. Beat egg whites to stiff peaks. Beat in sugar, baking powder and vanilla. Spread over cherries and nuts. Bake for 25 minutes. Broil for a few minutes until golden.

DATE SLICES

Graham wafers
date jam or filling
white or chocolate icing
cake or dessert decorators

Sandwich four or five graham wafers with date jam. Cover each block with white icing and sprinkle with cake decorators. Let sit for a few hours. Just before serving, slice blocks to desired thickness.

CHOCOLATE SLICE

Metric	Standard
2 L cake pan (20 cm square)	8 x 8 x 2 in. cake pan

Ingredients:

Metric	Standard
125 mL soft butter	½ cup butter
75 mL sugar	⅓ cup sugar
75 mL cocoa	⅓ cup cocoa
5 mL vanilla	1 tsp. vanilla
1 egg	1 egg
500 mL Graham wafer crumbs	2 cups Graham wafer crumbs
250 mL coconut	1 cup coconut
125 mL chopped walnuts	½ cup chopped walnuts

Place first five ingredients in mixing bowl. Set in larger bowl with hot water. Stir mixture until butter has melted and mixture is consistency of custard. Mix remaining ingredients and add to cocoa mixture. Press into cake pan. Spread with Vanilla-Chocolate Icing. Allow to set, cut in small bars and serve.

VANILLA-CHOCOLATE ICING

Metric	Standard
Yield: about 250-375 mL	1-1½ cups

Ingredients:

Metric	Standard
60 mL butter	4 tbsps. butter
50 mL milk	3 tbsps. milk
30 mL vanilla instant pudding powder	2 tbsps. vanilla instant pudding powder
500 mL icing sugar	2 cups icing sugar
4 squares semi-sweet chocolate	4 squares semi-sweet chocolate
15 mL butter	1 tbsp. butter

Cream 50 mL (3 tbsps.) butter. Combine milk and vanilla instant pudding powder. Add to creamed butter. Mix in icing sugar. Spread over base or cake. Allow to harden a bit. Melt semi-sweet chocolate. Mix in remaining butter. Spread evenly over icing mixture. Allow to set, then cut squares or cake.

CHOCOLATE CREAM ROLL

Metric	Standard
2 L jelly roll pan (40 x 25 x 2 cm)	15 x 10 x ¾ in. jelly roll pan
190°C	375°F
15 min.	

Ingredients:

90 mL sifted cake flour	6 tbsps. sifted cake flour
or	**or**
75 mL sifted all-purpose flour	5 tbsps. sifted all-purpose flour
90 mL cocoa	6 tbsps. cocoa
1 mL salt	¼ tsp. salt
2 mL baking powder	½ tsp. baking powder
4 eggs, separated	4 eggs, separated
175 mL sugar	¾ cup sugar
5 mL vanilla	1 tsp. vanilla
1 carton (289 mL) whipping cream	1 carton (10 oz.) whipping cream
icing sugar	icing sugar

Line pan with wax paper. Sift flour, cocoa, salt and baking powder together. Beat egg whites to stiff peaks. Fold in sugar. Beat egg yolks till thick, fold into beaten egg whites. Add vanilla. Fold in sifted dry ingredients. Spread batter into prepared pan and bake. Prepare coarse, damp towel, sprinkled with icing sugar. With sharp knife, cut thin strip from edges of cake. Turn warm cake on towel, roll up gently, let cool. Bake whipping cream with vanilla and sugar to taste. Unroll cake and spread with whipped cream. Roll up and serve. Keep refrigerated or frozen if to be used at a later time. An excellent dessert.

JELLY ROLL

Metric	Standard
2 L jelly roll pan (40 x 25 x 2 cm)	15 x 10 x ¾ in. jelly roll pan
200°C	400°F
12 min.	

Ingredients:

Metric	Standard
4 eggs, separated	4 eggs, separated
250 mL sugar	1 cup sugar
2 mL vanilla	½ tsp. vanilla
250 mL flour	1 cup flour
5 mL baking powder	1 tsp. baking powder
1 mL salt	¼ tsp. salt
15 mL cold water	1 tbsp. cold water
icing sugar	icing sugar

Line pan with well greased paper. Beat egg yolks until thick, adding sugar gradually. Add vanilla. Beat egg whites to stiff peaks and fold in. Sift together flour, baking powder, salt and fold in alternately with cold water. Turn batter into pan and bake. While jelly roll bakes, prepare a clean, coarse, damp towel sprinkled with icing sugar. Remove jelly roll from oven and turn immediately onto prepared towel. With a sharp knife cut a thin strip from sides and ends of cake to prevent cracking when rolled. Spread with jam, roll quickly and wrap in waxed paper to keep shape. Place on rack to cool.

LEMON CRUMBLE

Metric	Standard
3.5 L cake pan (33 x 21 x 5 cm)	13 x 9 x 2 in. cake pan
180°C	350°F
25-30 min.	

Ingredients:

Base:

Metric	Standard
500 mL rolled unsalted soda crackers	2 cups rolled unsalted soda crackers
300 mL flour	1¼ cups flour
7 mL baking powder	1½ tsps. baking powder
250 mL coconut	1 cup coconut
250 mL butter	1 cup butter
50 mL milk	¼ cup milk

Lemon Filling:

Metric	Standard
1 egg	1 egg
juice and grated rind of 1 lemon	juice and grated rind of 1 lemon

250 mL sugar	1 cup sugar
65 mL butter	¼ cup butter
175 mL boiling water	¾ cup boiling water
15 mL cornstarch	1 tbsp. cornstarch

For Base:

Mix dry ingredients and butter until crumbly. Add milk and mix. Pat ⅔ of mixture into cake pan.

For Lemon Filling:

Beat egg; add remaining ingredients in order given. Bring to boil in 1 L (1 qt.) saucepan. Cook until thick; pour over base. Sprinkle on remaining crumbs. Press lightly with spoon. Bake and serve.

COCONUT BARS

Metric	*Standard*
2.5 L Cake pan (23 cm square)	9 x 9 x 2 in. cake pan
160°C	325°F
30 min.	
Yield: 27 2.5 x 7.5 cm bars	27 1'' x 3'' bars

Ingredients:

Base:

125 mL butter **or** margarine	½ cup butter **or** margarine
125 mL brown sugar	½ cup brown sugar
250 mL sifted flour	1 cup sifted flour

Filling:

2 eggs	2 eggs
1 mL salt	⅛ tsp. salt
250 mL brown sugar	1 cup brown sugar
5 mL vanilla	1 tsp. vanilla
30 mL flour	2 tbsp. flour
2 mL baking powder	½ tsp. baking powder
250 mL chopped nuts	1 cup chopped nuts
250 mL coconut	1 cup coconut

For Base: Grease cake pan. Mix butter, sugar and flour well. Press into cake pan. Bake till very lightly browned.

Filling: Combine and beat eggs, salt, sugar, vanilla, flour and baking powder. Fold in chopped nuts and coconut. Spread over partially baked batter and bake till browned. Cool, cut and serve.

Notes

CONFECTIONS AND FROSTINGS

BUTTER ICING

Metric	*Standard*
Yield: 300 mL	1¼ cups

Ingredients:

45 mL soft margarine	3 tbsps. soft margarine
500 mL icing sugar	2 cups icing sugar
5 mL vanilla	1 tsp. vanilla
30-45 mL cream **or** milk	2-3 tbsps. cream **or** milk

Cream margarine, add some icing sugar and continue whipping. Add vanilla and some cream. Whip. Add remaining cream if icing seems too thick. Whip until light and fluffy.

Variation:

Chocolate butter icing. Melt 1 square unsweetened chocolate with margarine, or sift 50 mL (½ cup) cocoa with icing sugar and increase margarine to 75 mL (5 tbsps.). Follow above method.

CHOCOLATE FLUFF TOPPING

Metric	*Standard*
Yield: 1 L	Yield: 1 qt.

Ingredients:

500 mL whipping cream	2 cups whipping cream
250 mL icing sugar, sifted	1 cup icing sugar, sifted
125 mL cocoa	½ cup cocoa
dash of salt	dash of salt

Combine all ingredients and beat until stiff peaks form.

MARSHMALLOW TOPPING

Metric	*Standard*
1 L double boiler	1 qt. double boiler
Yield: 375 mL	1½ cups

Ingredients:

16 large marshmallows	16 large marshmallows
125 mL milk	½ cup milk
5 mL vanilla **or**	1 tsp. vanilla **or**
peppermint extract	peppermint extract

Place marshmallows and milk in top of double boiler. Heat to melt marshmallows. Remove from heat; add flavoring. Beat well. Serve warm as a sauce over cake or ice cream.

BOILED CHOCOLATE ICING

Metric	*Standard*
Yield: approx. 375 mL	1½ cups

Ingredients:

175 mL sugar	¾ cup sugar
50 mL cornstarch	¼ cup cornstarch
30 mL cocoa	2 tbsps. cocoa
30 mL butter	2 tbsps. butter
2 mL vanilla	½ tsp. vanilla
1 mL salt	¼ tsp. salt
250 mL water	1 cup water

In 1.5 L (1½ qt.) saucepan combine all ingredients except water. Add water, a little at a time; mix. Boil until icing thickens.

FLUFFY WHITE ICING

Metric	*Standard*
Yield: about 625-750 mL	2½-3 cups

Ingredients:

375 mL brown **or** white sugar	1½ cups brown **or** white sugar
75 mL water	⅓ cup water
1 mL cream of tartar	¼ tsp. cream of tartar
2 egg whites (unbeaten)	2 eggs whites (unbeaten)

Place all ingredients in top of 2 L (2 qt.) double boiler. Cook over boiling water beating constantly with beater until icing stands in peaks, about seven minutes. Remove from heat and add any flavouring. Beat thoroughly to spreading consistency and ice cake.

BUTTERSCOTCH ICING

Metric	*Standard*
Yield: approx. 250 mL	1 cup

Ingredients:

250 mL brown sugar	1 cup brown sugar
125 mL heavy cream	½ cup heavy cream
5 mL vanilla	1 tsp. vanilla

Combine brown sugar and heavy cream in 2 L (2 qt.) saucepan. Bring to boil and cook to 115°C (236°F) (when dropped into very cold water forms a soft pliable ball). Add vanilla and beat well. When icing begins to thicken pour immediately on cake and ice.

Note: If icing has been boiled too long, add a little cream while beating.

SEA FOAM ICING

Metric	Standard
Yield: 750 mL	3 cups

Ingredients:

250 mL brown sugar	1 cup brown sugar
50 mL water	¼ cup water
2 beaten egg whites	2 beaten egg whites
250 mL chopped walnuts (optional)	1 cup chopped walnuts (optional)

Combine brown sugar and water in 1 L (1 qt.) saucepan. Boil till syrup reaches 110°-112°C (225°F) (spins a thread when dropped from spoon). Pour syrup onto beaten egg whites and beat till the stiff peak stage. Add chopped walnuts and spread on cake.

CHOCOLATE CREAM FILLING

Metric	Standard
1 L saucepan	1 qt. saucepan
Yield: 500-750 mL	2-3 cups

Ingredients:

2 squares unsweetened chocolate	2 squares unsweetened chocolate
175 mL sugar	¾ cup sugar
dash of salt	dash of salt
45 mL water	3 tbsps. water
2 egg yolks well beaten	2 egg yolks well beaten
375 mL whipping cream	1½ cups whipping cream
5 mL vanilla	1 tsp. vanilla

Combine unsweetened chocolate, sugar, salt and water. Boil gently for 3 minutes stirring constantly. Gradually add well beaten egg yolks. Beat until well blended. Cool. Whip cream with vanilla. Fold cooled chocolate mixture into whipped cream. Chill in refrigerator about ½ hour or until thick enough to spread. Makes a delicious cake filling.

FRESH ORANGE FILLING

Metric	Standard
1 L saucepan	1 qt. saucepan
Yield: about 400 mL	1¾ cups

Ingredients:

Metric	Standard
250 mL sugar	1 cup sugar
2 mL salt	½ tsp. salt
50 mL cornstarch	¼ cup cornstarch
250 mL orange juice and pulp	1 cup orange juice and pulp
15-30 mL grated orange rind	1-2 tbsps. grated orange rind
7 mL lemon juice	1½ tsps. lemon juice
30 mL butter	2 tbsps. butter

In saucepan mix sugar, salt and cornstarch. Slowly stir in orange juice and pulp. Cook over moderate heat. Stir constantly until mixture thickens and boils. Boil one minute. Remove from heat. Blend in remaining ingredients and cool. Good with chiffon cake.

CHOCOLATE FUDGE

Metric	Standard
2 L cake pan (20 cm square)	8 x 8 x 2 in. cake pan
Yield: 600 g	1¼ lbs.

Ingredients:

Metric	Standard
250 mL white sugar	1 cup white sugar
250 mL brown sugar	1 cup brown sugar
150 mL milk	⅔ cup milk
30 mL light corn syrup	2 tbsps. corn syrup
2 squares unsweetened chocolate	2 squares unsweetened chocolate
50 mL butter **or** margarine	¼ cup butter **or** margarine
5 mL vanilla	1 tsp. vanilla

Combine sugars, milk, corn syrup and chocolate. Heat gradually stirring constantly until mixture boils. Boil slowly, stirring till mixture reaches 113°C (236°F) (forms a soft ball when dropped into very cold water). Remove from heat, add butter without stirring. Cool to lukewarm, 45°C (110°F). Add vanilla and beat until fairly thick. Pour into greased pan. Cut before fudge hardens.

Variation: Spread chopped pitted dates, 75 mL (⅓ cup) and chopped walnut meats, 75 mL (⅓ cup) in pan. Pour fudge over. Immediately mark in diamonds. Press half walnut on each. Cool; cut in diamonds. A delicious fudge.

FUDGE RECIPE

Metric	Standard
2 L cake pan (20 cm square)	8 x 8 x 2 in. cake pan
Yield: about 700 g	1½ lbs.

Ingredients:

Metric	Standard
250 mL white sugar	1 cup white sugar
250 mL brown sugar	1 cup brown sugar
pinch of salt	pinch of salt
30 mL cocoa	2 tbsps. cocoa
20 mL syrup	4 tsps. syrup
125 mL sour cream	½ cup sour cream
5 mL butter	1 tsp. butter
5 mL vanilla	1 tsp. vanilla
250 mL chopped nuts	1 cup chopped nuts

Mix sugars, salt, cocoa, syrup and sour cream together. Cook slowly without stirring until the mixture reaches 113°C — (235°F) (forms a soft ball when dropped into very cold water). Add butter and stir just to blend in. Remove from heat and stir in vanilla. Let cool. Add chopped nuts, beat until creamy. Pour into greased pan. Cut in squares before fudge hardens.

Tip:

If fudge turns sugary during the process, add 15 mL (1 tbsp.) cream or milk and boil once more, briefly.

FUDGE RECIPE

Metric	Standard
Yield: 700-800 g	24-26 oz.

Ingredients:

Metric	Standard
250 mL white sugar	1 cup white sugar
250 mL brown sugar	1 cup brown sugar
125 mL sour cream	½ cup sour cream
30 mL cocoa	2 tbsps. cocoa
25 mL corn syrup	1½ tbsps. corn syrup
pinch of salt	pinch of salt
5 mL butter	1 tsp. butter
5 mL vanilla	1 tsp. vanilla
125 mL chopped nuts	½ cup chopped nuts

Mix first six ingredients in 2 L (2 qt.) saucepan. Simmer without stirring until mixture reaches 113°C (235°F) (forms a soft ball when dropped in cold water). Add butter, remove from heat. Stir in vanilla and let cool. Add chopped nuts and beat until the shiny appearance dulls. Pour into buttered pan. Cut in squares before fudge hardens.

MARSHMALLOWS

Metric	Standard
Yield: 16 5 x 5 cm marshmallows	16 2 x 2 in. marshmallows

Ingredients:

20 mL unflavored gelatine dissolved in	2 tbsps. (2 pkg) unflavored gelatine dissolved in
50 mL cold water	¼ cup cold water
500 mL sugar	2 cups sugar
425 mL water	1⅔ cups water
2 mL white vanilla concentrate **or**	½ tsp. vanilla concentrate **or**
4 mL vanilla extract	1 tsp. vanilla extract

Dissolve gelatine in water in a large bowl. Boil water and sugar in 1 L (1 qt.) saucepan until syrupy. Pour syrup slowly into gelatine mixture, stirring until dissolved. Cool a few minutes and beat until stiff peaks form. Add flavoring and pour into a mold or pan that has been rinsed in cold water. When set, cut into squares. (dip knife in hot water occasionally) and roll in chopped toasted nuts, coconut or crushed corn flakes. Store in cold place.

PEANUT BRITTLE

Metric	Standard
3 L cake pan (30 x 20 x 5 cm)	12 x 8 x 2 in. cake pan
Yield: Approx. 600 g	20-22 oz.

Ingredients:

500 mL sugar	2 cups sugar
1 mL salt	¼ tsp. salt
1 mL baking soda	¼ tsp. baking soda
5 mL vanilla	1 tsp. vanilla
250 mL shelled peanuts	1 cup shelled peanuts

Grease cake pan. Heat sugar gradually in a frying pan 180°C (350°F). Stir constantly with bowl of spoon until sugar is melted. Remove from heat and stir in quickly salt, baking soda and vanilla. Sprinkle shelled peanuts into greased pan. Pour syrup over peanuts. Cool and break.

CHOCOLATES

Metric	Standard
Yield: 700-800 g	26-28 oz.

Ingredients:

8 squares semi-sweet chocolate chocolate	8 squares semi-sweet chocolate

½ cake (12.5 x 6 x 4 cm) parawax	½ cake (5 x 2½ x 1½ in.) parawax
1500 mL icing sugar	6 cups icing sugar
50 mL melted butter	¼ cup melted butter
90 mL heavy cream **or** condensed milk	6 tbsps. heavy cream **or** condensed milk
125 mL cornstarch	½ cup cornstarch
15 mL corn syrup	1 tbsp. corn syrup
flavouring to taste	flavouring to taste

Melt chocolate and parawax in top of 1 L (1 qt.) double boiler over hot water. Combine remaining ingredients in 2.5 L (2½ qt.) pot. Boil until ingredients are well blended and mixture begins to thicken. Drop by teaspoonfuls on to waxed paper. Allow to set. Pick with toothpicks and dip into melted chocolate-wax mixture. Dry and serve.

Variation:
Chopped nuts or coconut may be added before dropping mixture on wax paper.

DIVINITY FUDGE

Metric	*Standard*
2 L cake pan (20 cm square)	8 x 8 x 2 in. cake pan
Yield: 1 kg	2 lbs.

Ingredients:

750 mL sugar	3 cups sugar
150 mL corn syrup	⅔ cup corn syrup
1 mL salt	¼ tsp. salt
75 mL water	⅓ cup water
2 egg whites	2 egg whites
5 mL vanilla	1 tsp. vanilla
125 mL chopped nuts	½ cup chopped nuts

Combine and bring to a boil sugar, syrup, salt and water. Continue boiling until mixture reaches 127°C (260°F) (or forms a hard ball when dropped into very cold water). Beat egg whites to stiff peak. Add the sugar mixture gradually in a thin trickle, beating constantly. When mixture begins to stiffen add vanilla and nuts. Pour into buttered cake pan.

Variation:
Cherries, raisins or candied pineapple may be used in place of nuts.

MAPLE CREAM CANDY

Metric	*Standard*
3.5 L cake pan (33 x 4 x 5 cm)	13 x 9 x 2 in. cake pan
Yield: 1.25-1.5 kg	2¼-3 lbs.

Ingredients:

1000 mL brown sugar	4 cups brown sugar
30 mL flour	2 tbsps. flour
250 mL whole milk **or**	1 cup whole milk **or**
light cream	light cream
50 mL butter	¼ cup butter
10 mL baking powder	2 tsps. baking powder
few grains of salt	few grains of salt
5 mL vanilla	1 tsp. vanilla
500 mL chopped nuts	2 cups chopped nuts

Lightly grease cake pan. Mix first six ingredients in 2 L (2 qt.) saucepan. Cook, stirring constantly until mixture reaches 113°C (235°F) (or forms a soft ball in cold water). Add vanilla and chopped nuts. Beat two to five minutes or until candy begins to thicken. Quickly pour into greased cake pan. Spread out evenly and cut while soft.

POPCORN OR PUFFED WHEAT BALLS

Metric	*Standard*
Yield: about 2 doz.	

Ingredients:

125 mL white sugar	½ cup white sugar
125 mL brown sugar	½ cup brown sugar
15 mL molasses	1 tbsp. molasses
125 mL light corn syrup	½ cup light corn syrup
30 mL water	2 tbsps. water
50 mL cocoa	¼ cup cocoa
15 mL butter	1 tbsp. butter
2 L popcorn **or** puffed wheat	2 qt. popcorn **or** puffed wheat

Cook sugars, molasses, syrup, until the mixture reaches 150°C (300°F) (separates into hard, brittle threads when dropped into cold water). Add butter and stir in. Remove from heat and pour over popcorn. Stir well and cool slightly. Roll in balls and set apart to cool completely.

Variation: Popcorn and syrup mixture may also be pressed in 3.5 L cake pan (33 x 21 x 5 cm) or 13 x 9 x 2 in. cake pan and cut into squares when cool.

POPCORN BALLS

Metric	Standard
Yield: 30 large or 60 small	

Ingredients:

Metric	Standard
250 mL sugar	1 cup sugar
250 mL corn syrup	1 cup corn syrup
15 mL butter **or** margarine	1 tbsp. butter **or** margarine
7 mL vinegar	1½ tsps. vinegar
1 mL baking soda	¼ tsp. baking soda
10 mL water	2 tsp. water
2 L freshly popped corn	2 qts. freshly popped corn

Combine first four ingredients in 1 L (1 qt.) saucepan. Cook, stirring frequently until syrup reaches 127°C (260°F) (forms a hard ball when dropped into cold water). Dissolve baking soda in water. Remove syrup from heat, add soda mixture. Pour syrup over freshly popped corn. Stir till each kernel is coated. Quickly roll into balls and place separately on cookie sheet to cool and dry.

CHOCOLATE MARSHMALLOW BALLS

Metric	Standard
Yield: 2 doz.	

Ingredients:

Metric	Standard
1 egg	1 egg
250 mL icing sugar	1 cup icing sugar
15 large marshmallows	15 large marshmallows
2 squares unsweetened chocolate	2 squares unsweetened chocolate
coconut	coconut

Beat egg and gradually add icing sugar. Quarter marshmallows; add to mixture. Let stand 20 minutes. Melt unsweetened chocolate; add to mixture. Let stand at least 20 minutes longer or until set. Form small (2 cm or 1½ in.) balls and roll in coconut, or place by teaspoonfuls on wax paper.

PEANUT BUTTER BALLS

Metric	Standard
Yield: about 3½ doz.	

Ingredients:

Metric	Standard
250 mL peanut butter	1 cup peanut butter
250 mL finely chopped dates	1 cup finely chopped dates

250 mL chopped walnuts	1 cup chopped walnuts
250 mL icing sugar	1 cup icing sugar
25 mL butter	1 tbsp. butter
6 squares semi-sweet chocolate	6 squares semi-sweet chocolate
1 square (about 3 x 3 x 1 cm) Parawax	1 square (about 2 x 2 x ½ in.) Parawax

Combine peanut butter, dates, nuts, sugar and butter; mix well. Form balls, 2 cm. (1 in.) in diameter. Melt semi-sweet chocolate and parawax together. Dip balls into hot liquid. Place on wax paper, let harden.

CHOCOLATE CLUSTERS

Metric	*Standard*
Yield: 2½-3 doz.	

Ingredients:

1 square unsweetened chocolate	1 square unsweetened chocolate
75 mL butter **or** margarine	⅓ cup butter **or** margarine
20 large fresh marshmallows	20 large fresh marshmallows
500 mL quick cooking rolled oats	2 cups quick cooking rolled oats
125 mL coconut	½ cup coconut

Melt unsweetened chocolate, butter and large fresh marshmallows in top of 2 L (2 qt.) double boiler, over boiling water. Stir until smooth. Remove from heat and stir in rolled oats, then coconut. Drop from teaspoon or roll into small balls. Cool on wax paper. A quick and easy dainty.

ALMOND CRUNCH

Metric	*Standard*
2.5 L cake pan (23 cm square)	9 x 9 x 2 in. cake pan

Ingredients:

125 mL margarine	½ cup margarine
250 mL sugar	1 cup sugar
375 mL slivered almonds	1½ cup slivered almonds
1125-250 ml chocolate chips	½-1 cup chocolate chips

Melt margarine; add sugar and almonds and cook, stirring until mixture is golden brown (10-15 min.). Spread in cake pan. While mixture is still hot, sprinkle with chocolate chips. As they melt, spread evenly to form a glaze. Cool. When hardened, break into pieces and store in a covered container in the refrigerator.

Notes

COOKIES

SOUR CREAM COOKIES

Metric	Standard
190°C	375°F

10-15 mins.
Yield: 7½-8 doz. large cookies

Ingredients:

Metric	Standard
250 mL shortening	1 cup shortening
500 mL brown sugar	2 cups brown sugar
2 mL salt	½ tsp. salt
2 eggs beaten	2 eggs beaten
250 mL nuts	1 cup nuts
250 mL raisins	1 cup raisins
250 mL sour cream	1 cup sour cream
1125 mL flour	4½ cups flour
20 mL baking powder	4 tsps. baking powder
5 mL baking soda	1 tsp. baking soda
2 mL nutmeg	½ tsp. nutmeg

Grease cookie sheet. Cream first three ingredients together. Add beaten eggs, nuts and raisins, mix well. Stir in sour cream. Sift remaining ingredients together. Add gradually and mix well. Drop by spoonfuls on prepared cookie sheet. Bake till golden brown.

CHOCOLATE CHIP COOKIES

Metric	Standard
180°C	350°F

10 min.
Yield: 3-3½ doz.

Ingredients:

Metric	Standard
125 mL soft butter	½ cup soft butter
175 mL brown sugar	¾ cup brown sugar
1 egg	1 egg
1 mL vanilla	¼ tsp. vanilla
250 mL flour	1 cup flour
1 mL salt	¼ tsp. salt
1 mL baking soda	¼ tsp. baking soda
30 mL cornstarch	2 tbsps. cornstarch
125 mL chocolate chips	½ cup chocolate chips

Grease cookie sheet. Mix above ingredients well. Drop by teaspoonfuls on well-greased cookie sheet and bake.

SNO-CAPS

Metric	Standard
180°C	350°F
12-15 mins.	
Yield: 4-5 doz.	

Ingredients:

Dough:

Metric	Standard
500 mL sifted flour	2 cups sifted flour
10 mL baking powder	2 tsps. baking powder
2 mL baking soda	½ tsp. baking soda
5 mL salt	1 tsp. salt
125 mL cocoa	½ cup cocoa
125 mL shortening	½ cup shortening
250 mL white sugar	1 cup white sugar
2 eggs beaten	2 eggs beaten
2 mL vanilla	½ tsp. vanilla
125 mL fine coconut	½ cup fine coconut
or walnuts	or walnuts
125 mL sour milk	½ cup sour milk

Icing:

Metric	Standard
500 mL icing sugar	2 cups icing sugar
50 mL cocoa	¼ cup cocoa
50 mL butter	3 tbsps. butter
30 mL shortening	2 tbsps. shortening
90 mL light cream	6 tbsps. light cream
2 mL vanilla	½ tsp. vanilla
fine coconut	fine coconut

Grease cookie sheets.

For Dough: sift first five ingredients together. Cream shortening and white sugar. Add beaten eggs and vanilla to creamed mixture. Add coconut, sour milk and sifted ingredients to creamed mixture. Drop by spoonfuls into greased cookie sheet. Bake. While still warm, cover with the following:

Icing: Sift icing sugar and cocoa together. Mix in butter and shortening. Add light cream and vanilla, mix well. Spread over cookies and sprinkle with fine coconut.

OATMEAL COOKIES

Metric	Standard
180°C	350°F
15 mins.	
Yield: 4 doz.	

Ingredients:

Metric	Standard
250 mL brown sugar	1 cup brown sugar

Metric	Standard
125 mL shortening (half lard and half butter)	½ cup shortening (half lard and half butter)
2 eggs slightly beaten	2 eggs slightly beaten
250 mL chopped raisins	1 cup chopped raisins
125 mL chopped nuts	½ cup chopped nuts
5 mL baking soda	1 tsp. baking soda
45 mL sour milk	3 tbsps. sour milk
250 mL flour	1 cup flour
5 mL cinnamon	1 tsp. cinnamon
500 mL quick cooking oatmeal	2 cups cooking oatmeal

Grease cookie sheet lightly. Cream sugar and shortening together. Add slightly beaten eggs, chopped raisins and nuts, mix. Dissolve baking soda in sour milk and add. Sift flour with cinnamon and mix with quick cooking oatmeal. Add dry ingredients to batter, mix. Drop by spoonfuls on cookie sheet about 3 cm (2 ins.) apart. Bake till golden.

Variation: Replace raisins and nuts with coconut, chopped dates or semisweet chocolate pieces.

MARSHMALLOW ROLL

Metric	Standard

Yield: 4 doz. slices

Ingredients:

Metric	Standard
4 squares semi-sweet chocolate	4 squares semi-sweet chocolate
60 mL butter	4 tbsps. butter
250 mL icing sugar	1 cup icing sugar
500 mL miniature marshmallows	2 cups miniature marshmallows
1 egg beaten	1 egg beaten
125 mL chopped walnuts (optional)	½ cup chopped walnuts (optional)
5 mL vanilla	1 tsp. vanilla
coconut	coconut

In top of 2 L (2 qt.) double boiler melt semi-sweet chocolate and butter over boiling water. Remove from heat. Add remaining ingredients except coconut, mix. Spread coconut thinly on waxed paper. Place half of the mashmallow-chocolate mixture on half of the coconut. Roll to coat well. Shape into roll and wrap in waxed paper. Repeat with remaining mixture. Place in refrigerator to set. Slice and serve.

RAGGED ROBINS

Metric	Standard
160-180°C	325-350°F
10 mins.	
Yield: 3-3½ doz.	

Ingredients:

2 eggs	2 eggs
125 mL sugar	½ cup sugar
5 mL vanilla	1 tsp. vanilla
250 mL walnuts	1 cup walnuts
375 mL chopped pitted dates	1½ cups chopped pitted dates
500 mL cornflakes	2 cups cornflakes

Grease cookie sheet. Beat eggs well. Gradually add sugar, beating well. Mix in vanilla, walnuts and chopped dates. Add cornflakes, last, mix. Drop on greased cookie sheet and bake until brown.

ALMOND MACAROONS

Metric	Standard
120°C	250°F
25 mins.	
Yield: 1½ doz.	

Ingredients:

1 egg white	1 egg white
1 mL salt	¼ tsp. salt
175 mL fruit sugar **or** icing sugar	¾ cup fruit sugar **or** icing sugar
250 mL finely minced almonds **or** fine coconut	1 cup finely minced almonds **or** fine coconut
2 mL almond extract	½ tsp. almond extract

Grease cookie sheet lightly. Beat egg white with salt until stiff. Gradually add ⅔ of sugar, beating in well. Fold in remaining sugar, fine nuts and flavouring; beat well. Drop with dessert spoon on cookie sheet and bake. Store in covered container for a week to develop best flavour.

PEANUT BUTTER - OATMEAL COOKIES

Metric	Standard
190°C	375°F
12 mins.	
Yield: 3½-4 doz.	

Ingredients:

Metric	Standard
250 mL flour	1 cup flour
10 mL baking powder	2 tsps. baking powder
2 mL salt	½ tsp. salt
125 mL shortening	½ cup shortening
125 mL peanut butter	½ cup peanut butter
75 mL brown sugar	⅓ cup brown sugar
1 egg	1 egg
5 mL vanilla	1 tsp. vanilla
125 mL dark corn syrup	½ cup dark corn syrup
375 mL quick cooking rolled oats	1½ cups quick cooking rolled oats
50 mL chopped peanuts	¼ cup chopped peanuts

Grease cookie sheet. Sift flour, baking powder and salt together. Blend shortening, peanut butter, brown sugar, egg, vanilla, and half of dark corn syrup. Add sifted ingredients and blend well for about two minutes. Fold in remaining syrup and quick cooking oats. Drop from teaspoon onto greased cookie sheet. Sprinkle with chipped peanuts. Bake and enjoy.

CHOCOLATE NUT DROP COOKIES

Metric	Standard
190°C	375°F
10-12 mins.	
Yield: 4½-5 doz.	

Ingredients:

Metric	Standard
125 mL shortening	½ cup shortening
300 mL brown sugar	1¼ cups brown sugar
2 eggs	2 eggs
2 squares unsweetened chocolate	2 squares unsweetened chocolate
500 mL sifted flour	2 cups sifted flour
5 mL baking powder	1 tsp. baking powder
1 mL baking soda	¼ tsp. baking soda
1 mL salt	¼ tsp. salt
30 mL milk	2 tbsps. milk
2 mL vanilla	½ tsp. vanilla
250 mL finely chopped nuts	1 cup finely chopped nuts

Lightly grease cookie sheets. Cream shortening and sugar. Add eggs and beat. Melt unsweetened chocolate and add. Sift dry ingredients together and add. Mix in milk. Add vanilla and finely chopped nuts. Drop by teaspoonfuls in lightly greased cookie sheet and bake.

COCONUT KISSES

Metric	Standard
140°C	275°F
20 mins.	
Yield: 3½ doz.	

Ingredients:

3 egg whites	3 egg whites
250 mL finely granulated sugar	1 cup finely granulated sugar
15 mL cornstarch	1 tbsp. cornstarch
450-500 mL coconut	1¾-2 cups coconut
5 mL baking powder	1 tsp. baking powder
5 mL vanilla	1 tsp. vanilla

Grease cookie sheets. Beat egg whites to stiff peak. Add finely granulated sugar and cornstarch. Transfer to top of double boiler. Place over boiling water and beat till crust forms on edges of pot. Add remaining ingredients. Drop by spoonfuls on greased cookie sheet and bake.

Variation:

Dates or walnuts may be substituted for coconut.

BARBARA'S BOUNTIES

Metric	Standard
190°C	375°F
15 min.	
Yield: 10 doz. small	

Ingredients:

150 mL butter	⅔ cup butter
150 mL shortening	⅔ cup shortening
2 eggs beaten	2 eggs beaten
500 mL sugar	2 cups sugar
125 mL molasses	½ cup molasses
10 mL cloves	2 tsps. cloves
10 mL cinnamon	2 tsps. cinnamon
10 mL ginger	2 tsps. ginger
10 mL baking soda	2 tsps. baking soda
1000 mL flour	4 cups flour

Grease cookie sheets. Cream butter, shortening, eggs and sugar together. Add molasses and spices, mix well. Combine baking soda and flour to mixture. Roll dough into balls. (If too soft add a little more flour.) Roll balls in white sugar and place on greased cookie sheet. Do not flatten, bake.

PECAN PUFFS

Metric	Standard
160°C	325°F
20-25 mins.	
Yield: 4 doz.	

Ingredients:

250 mL butter	1 cup butter
500 mL sifted flour	2 cups sifted flour
50 mL fruit sugar **or**	¼ cup fruit sugar **or**
icing sugar	icing sugar
2 mL salt	½ tsp. salt
45 mL milk	3 tbsps. milk
10 mL vanilla	2 tsps. vanilla
500 mL chopped pecans	2 cups chopped pecans

Grease cookie sheet. Cream butter. Sift dry ingredients. Add to butter and mix well. Add milk, vanilla and nuts, and mix thoroughly. Roll into small balls, size of a walnut. Place on greased cookie sheet and bake. While still warm roll in fruit sugar or icing sugar.

OATMEAL COOKIES

Metric	Standard
190°C	375°F
10 mins.	
Yield: 6-7 doz.	

Ingredients:

250 mL shortening	1 cup shortening
125 mL white sugar	½ cup white sugar
125 mL brown sugar	½ cup brown sugar
2 eggs	2 eggs
5 mL vanilla	1 tsp. vanilla
375 mL flour	1½ cups flour
2 mL salt	½ tsp. salt
5 mL baking soda	1 tsp. baking soda
750 mL quick cooking oats	3 cups quick cooking oats

Cream together shortening and sugars. Add eggs, vanilla and beat well. Sift together dry ingredients and add to shortening mixture. Put quick cooking oats through food chopper, add. Shape dough into rolls 4 cm (1½ in.) in diameter. Chill 8-10 hours. Grease several cookie sheets. Slice rolls and place on greased cookie sheet. Bake until golden brown.

Variation: Dough may also be rolled out and cut with cookie cutters. Bake and place some date filling between two cookies and serve.

BUTTERSCOTCH COOKIES

Metric	Standard
190°C	375°F
10-12 min.	
Yield: 5 doz.	

Ingredients:

175 mL butterscotch chips	¾ cup butterscotch chips
125 mL soft margarine	½ cup soft margarine
150 mL brown sugar	⅔ cup brown sugar
1 egg	1 egg
5 mL vanilla	1 tsp. vanilla
300 mL sifted flour	1⅓ cups sifted flour
3 mL baking soda	¾ tsp. baking soda
1 mL salt	¼ tsp. salt
500 mL slightly crushed corn flakes	2 cups slightly crushed corn flakes
75 mL slivered almonds	⅓ cup slivered almonds

Place half of butterscotch chips in small saucepan. Melt over low heat, stirring occasionally. Combine melted butterscotch chips, soft margarine, brown sugar, egg and vanilla. Beat well. Combine sifted flour, baking soda, and salt sifting this into beaten mixture. Stir in remaining chips, crushed corn flakes and slivered almonds. Shape into small balls. Place on ungreased cookie sheet. Flatten slightly with fork. Bake until nicely brown. Remove from cookie sheet while warm.

CRISPY OATMEAL COOKIES

Metric	Standard
160°C	325°F
15 min.	
Yield: 6 doz.	

Ingredients:

250 mL butter **or** shortening	1 cup butter **or** shortening
250 mL brown sugar	1 cup brown sugar
1 egg well beaten	1 egg well beaten
125 mL crushed cornflakes	½ cup crushed cornflakes
250 mL quick cooking oats	1 cup quick cooking oats
375 mL flour	1½ cups flour
1 mL baking powder	¼ tsp. baking powder
1 mL baking soda	¼ tsp. baking soda
250 mL finely chopped peanuts	1 cup finely chopped peanuts
5 mL milk (optional)	1 tsp. milk (optional

Grease cookie sheets. Cream butter and brown sugar, add well beaten egg. Add crushed cornflakes and mix. Add quick cooking oats and mix. Sift flour, baking powder and baking soda and add to butter mixture. Add finely chopped peanuts. If dough is too hard add milk. Roll into small balls and place on greased cookie sheet. Flatten with fork and bake until delicately brown. Makes a crisp pleasant tasting cookie.

GINGER CREAM COOKIES

Metric	Standard
180-190°C	350°F
12-15 min.	
Yield: about 7 doz.	

Ingredients:

250 mL shortening	1 cup shortening
250 mL sugar	1 cup sugar
2 eggs	2 eggs
225 mL molasses	⅞ cup molasses
250 mL buttermilk	1 cup buttermilk
10 mL ginger	2 tsps. ginger
5 mL cinnamon	1 tsp. cinnamon
7 mL baking soda	1½ tsps. baking soda
5 mL baking powder	1 tsp. baking powder
pinch of salt	pinch of salt
1250 mL flour	5 cups flour

Grease cookie sheet. Cream shortening adding sugar gradually. Add eggs, continue beating. Combine molasses and buttermilk. Sift dry ingredients. Add dry ingredients and liquid alternately to shortening mixture, mixing well after each addition. Chill 1 hour. Roll out dough on floured board about 1.5 cm (½ inch) thick and cut out with cookie cutter. Bake on greased cookie sheet. Spread with following frosting.

Frosting:

350 mL sugar	1½ cups sugar
350 mL water	1½ cups water
5 mL syrup	1 tsp. syrup
5 mL vinegar	1 tsp. vinegar
2 beaten egg whites	2 beaten egg whites
12 large marshmallows cut	12 large marshmallows cut

Boil sugar, water, syrup, vinegar until mixture spins a thread. Pour into beaten egg whites. Add cut up marshmallows. Beat until thick enough to spread on cookies. Coconut may be sprinkled over frosting.

GINGER SNAPS

Metric	Standard
190°C	375°F
10-12 min.	
Yield: 5-6 doz.	

Ingredients:

250 mL sugar	1 cup sugar
250 mL shortening	1 cup shortening
250 mL molasses	1 cup molasses
5 mL baking soda	1 tsp. baking soda
5 mL salt	1 tsp. salt
7 mL ginger	1½ tsps. ginger
875 mL flour	3½ cups flour
125 mL boiling water	½ cup boiling water

Grease cookie sheets. Cream sugar and shortening. Add molasses and beat well. Sift dry ingredients together and add to creamed mixture. Add boiling water and mix well. Dough should be very soft. Pinch off pieces the size of a walnut or small egg and roll with slightly floured hands into ball. Place on greased cookie sheet about 2 cm. (1 in.) apart. Bake until dark brown and firm when lightly touched. Cookies should flatten and crack to have the right appearance.

SOFT GINGER COOKIES

Metric	Standard
180°C	350°F
15 min.	
Yield: 5½ doz.	

Ingredients:

175 mL shortening	⅔ cup shortening
2 eggs	2 eggs
175 mL brown sugar	⅔ cup brown sugar
1 L flour	4 cups flour
5 mL salt	1 tsp. salt
5 mL ginger	1 tsp. ginger
3 mL soda	¾ tsp. soda
5 mL baking powder	1 tsp. baking powder
175 mL molasses	¾ cup molasses
175 mL sour cream	¾ cup sour cream

Cream shortening and sugar. Add eggs, beat well. Sift dry ingredients together. Add to creamed mixture alternately with molasses and sour cream. Make small balls (more flour may be needed) and place on greased cookie sheet. Press down with a fork and bake.

PEANUT BUTTER COOKIES

Metric	*Standard*
180°C	350°F
10-12 min.	
Yield: 3 doz.	

Ingredients:

325 mL flour	1⅓ cups flour
10 mL baking powder	2 tsps. baking powder
2 mL salt	1 tsp. salt
125 mL lard **or** shortening	½ cup lard **or** shortening
125 mL peanut butter	½ cup peanut butter
125 mL brown sugar	½ cup brown sugar
90 mL fine white sugar	6 tbsps. fine white sugar
2 eggs	2 eggs
2 mL vanilla	½ tsp. vanilla

Sift flour, measure. Mix and sift flour, salt and baking powder twice. Cream lard and peanut butter together, blend well. Add sugars, beating in well. Beat eggs slightly, add vanilla. Mix into sugar mixture. Add dry ingredients a little at a time, mixing well after each addition. Form into balls (size of walnuts). Place on ungreased cookie sheet 2 cm (1 in.) apart. Press crosswise with fork and bake.

HONEY COOKIES

Metric	*Standard*
160°C	325°F
10-15 min.	
Yield: 4-5 doz.	

Ingredients:

250 mL brown sugar	1 cup brown sugar
125 mL shortening	½ cup shortening
125 mL butter	½ cup butter
45 mL honey	3 tbsps. honey
2 eggs	2 eggs
30 mL milk	2 tbsps. milk
1000 mL flour	4 cups flour

Cream sugar, shortening and butter. Add honey and mix. Add eggs and mix well. Add milk and flour alternately, mixing well after each addition. Roll into balls the size of a walnut. Place on ungreased cookie sheet and press with floured fork. Bake until lightly browned.

QUICK-MIX OATMEAL COOKIES

Metric	Standard
180°C	350°F
10-12 min.	
Yield: 3½-4 doz.	

Ingredients:

250 mL flour	1 cup flour
2 mL salt	½ tsp. salt
2 mL baking powder	½ tsp. baking powder
2 mL baking soda	½ tsp. baking soda
125 mL brown sugar	½ cup brown sugar
125 mL white sugar	½ cup white sugar
125 mL shortening	½ cup shortening
1 egg	1 egg
30 mL water	2 tbsps. water
5 mL vanilla	1 tsp. vanilla
375 mL quick cooking oats	1½ cup quick cooking oats

Grease cookie sheets. Sift flour, salt, baking powder and baking soda. Add remaining ingredients except quick cooking oats. Beat until dough is smooth (about 2 minutes). Fold in quick cooking oats. Shape into balls size of a walnut. Place 5 cm (2 in.) apart on greased cookie sheet. Bake on upper rack in oven.

BUTTER BUDS

Metric	Standard
200°C	400°F
10-15 min.	
Yield: 6-7 doz.	

Ingredients:

250 mL butter **or** shortening	1 cup butter **or** shortening
250 mL brown sugar	1 cup brown sugar
2 eggs well beaten	2 eggs well beaten
625 mL flour	2½ cups flour
20 mL baking powder	4 tsp. baking powder
1 mL salt	¼ tsp. salt
10 mL vanilla	2 tsp. vanilla

Grease cookie sheets lightly. Cream butter, add sugar, then well beaten eggs. Sift 500 mL (2 cups) flour with baking powder and salt. Add dry ingredients to creamed mixture, blend. Add flavoring and mix to a soft dough. Add remaining flour if necessary. Roll dough into balls, the size of a walnut. Place on lightly greased cookie sheet. Press with floured fork and bake.

TEA CAKES

Metric	Standard
190-200°C	375-400°F
10-12 min.	
Yield: 6-7 doz.	

Ingredients:

750 mL flour	3 cups flour
5 mL salt	1 tsp. salt
20 mL baking powder	4 tsps. baking powder
250 mL butter **or** shortening	1 cup butter **or** shortening
250 mL sugar	1 cup sugar
2 eggs	2 eggs
75 mL milk	⅓ cup milk
250 mL raisins	1 cup raisins

Grease cookie sheet lightly. Mix flour, salt and baking powder. Cream butter and sugar with electric mixer. Add eggs and milk and mix well. Gradually add dry ingredients. Mix in raisins. Roll dough in balls and place on lightly greased cookie sheet. Bake until golden.

Variation:

Cookies may be topped with part of maraschino cherry, nut or coconuts.

ICE BOX OATMEAL COOKIES

Metric	Standard
190-200°C	375-400°F
5 min.	
Yield: 10 doz.	

Ingredients:

750 mL rolled oats	3 cups rolled oats
250 mL brown sugar	1 cup brown sugar
250 mL flour	1 cup flour
2 mL salt	½ tsp. salt
250 mL butter	1 cup butter
5 mL baking soda	1 tsp. baking soda
50 mL boiling water	¼ cup boiling water

Grease cookie sheet lightly. Mix rolled oats with sugar, flour and salt. Add butter and mix well. Dissolve baking soda in boiling water and add to mixture. Shape dough into rolls of about 5 cm (2 in.) diameter. Freeze slightly. Slice thin and bake on lightly greased cookie sheet.

BUTTERSCOTCH COOKIES

Metric	Standard
190-200°C	375-400°F
8-10 min.	
Yield: 10 doz.	

Ingredients:

250 mL butter **or** margarine	1 cup butter **or** margarine
500 mL brown sugar	2 cups brown sugar
2 eggs	2 eggs
5 mL vanilla	1 tsp. vanilla
850 mL flour	3½ cups flour
2 mL salt	½ tsp. salt
2 mL baking powder	½ tsp. baking powder
5 mL baking soda	1 tsp. baking soda
125 mL finely chopped glace cherries	½ cup finely chopped glace cherries
walnuts **or** raisins	walnuts **or** raisins

Grease cookie sheet lightly. Cream butter and sugar. Add eggs and vanilla; beat. Mix dry ingredients and stir into creamed mixture. Mix until well blended. Add finely chopped glace cherries, walnuts or raisins. Shape into rolls 4 cm (1½ in.) in diameter. Chill for several hours. Slice rolls into 0.5 cm (¼ in.) slices. Place about 2 cm (1 in.) apart on cookie sheet. Bake and remove from cookie sheet immediately.

CHOCOLATE REFRIGERATOR COOKIES

Metric	Standard
190°C	375°F
10 min.	
Yield: 4 doz.	

Ingredients:

250 mL shortening	1 cup shortening
5 mL vanilla	1 tsp. vanilla
125 mL brown sugar	½ cup brown sugar
125 mL white sugar	½ cup white sugar
2 eggs beaten	2 eggs beaten
3 squares unsweetened chocolate melted **or** 50 mL cocoa dissolved in 15 mL boiling water	3 squares unsweetened chocolate melted **or** 3 tbsps. cocoa dissolved in 1 tbsp. boiling water
625 mL sifted flour	2½ cups sifted flour
5 mL baking powder	1 tsp. baking powder
2 mL baking soda	½ tsp. baking soda
1 mL salt	¼ tsp. salt
125 mL finely chopped nuts	½ cup finely chopped nuts

Cream shortening until fluffy. Add vanilla, sugars and beat till creamy. Add eggs; beat well. Add melted chocolate; mix well. Combine remaining ingredients and add mixing well. Chill, shape into rolls 5 cm (2 in.) diameter. Chill for several hours. Cut rolls in 0.5 cm (⅛ in.) slices. Bake on ungreased cookie sheet.

JAM-JAMS

Metric	Standard
190°C	375°F
12-15 min.	
Yield: 3 doz. 3″ cookies	

Ingredients:

2 eggs	2 eggs
250 mL brown sugar	1 cup brown sugar
90 mL syrup	6 tbsps. syrup
250 mL shortening	1 cup shortening
10 mL soda	2 tsps. soda
5 mL lemon or vanilla flavoring	1 tsp. lemon or vanilla flavoring
1-1.5 L flour to roll thin	4-5 cups flour to roll thin

Mix all ingredients adding enough flour to roll thin. Cut with round cookie cutters and bake on lightly greased cookie sheets. While warm, put together with jam. Especially good with raspberry or gooseberry jam.

RED SUGAR COOKIES

Metric	Standard
190°C	375°F
12-15 min.	
Yield: 4-5 doz.	

Ingredients:

2 eggs	2 eggs
250 mL butter	1 cup butter
125 mL milk	½ cup milk
500 mL granulated sugar	2 cups granulated sugar
5 mL baking soda	1 tsp. baking soda
10 mL cream of tartar	2 tsps. cream of tartar
5 mL vanilla	1 tsp. vanilla
1250 mL flour	5-6 cups flour

Cream sugar and butter, add remaining ingredients. Roll dough for cutting cookies. Cut with cookie cutter and place on lightly greased baking sheet. Brush tops with water and sprinkle with red decorating sugar. Bake.

CHOCOLATE-OATMEAL REFRIGERATOR COOKIES

Metric	Standard
180°C	350°F

10-12 min.
Yield: 5 doz.

Ingredients:

2 squares unsweetened chocolate	2 squares unsweetened chocolate
250 mL flour	1 cup flour
2 mL salt	½ tsp. salt
2 mL baking soda	½ tsp. baking soda
125 mL shortening	½ cup shortening
250 mL brown sugar	1 cup brown sugar
1 egg	1 egg
2 mL almond extract	½ tsp. almond extract
250 mL quick cooking oats	1 cup quick cooking oats
125 mL chopped walnuts	½ cup chopped walnuts

Melt and cool chocolate. Sift dry ingredients together into mixing bowl. Add shortening, sugar, egg, flavorings, and chocolate. Beat until smooth, about 2 minutes. Fold in quick cooking oats and chopped nuts. Shape into rolls about 4 cm (1½ in.) in diameter. Wrap in wax paper and chill thoroughly. Slice 0.5 cm (¼ in.) thick. Bake on ungreased cookie sheet.

BACHELOR BUTTONS

Metric	Standard
190°C	375°F

10-12 min.
Yield: 2 doz.

Ingredients:

125 mL shortening	½ cup shortening
175 mL brown sugar	¾ cup brown sugar
1 egg	1 egg
375 mL flour	1½ cups flour
2 mL baking soda	½ tsp. baking soda
2 mL cream of tartar	½ tsp. cream of tartar
2 mL vanilla	½ tsp. vanilla
jam	jam

Lightly grease two cookie sheets. Cream shortening and sugar. Add egg and mix. Sift dry ingredients and add along with vanilla. On floured surface roll out dough fairly thin. Cut out with 5 cm (2 in.) cookie cutter. Place dab of jam in centre of cookie; on sheet. Place another cookie on top and press down firmly all around. Bake till brown. A tasty snack.

AMMONIA COOKIES

Metric	Standard
180°C	350°F

10-15 min.

Yield: 5½ doz. large cookies

Ingredients:

Metric	Standard
250 mL shortening	1 cup shortening
500 mL sugar	2 cups sugar
125 mL light cream	½ cup light cream
375 mL milk	1½ cups milk
10 mL peppermint extract	2 tsps. peppermint extract
1675 mL flour	6¾ cups flour
50 mL baking ammonia	¼ cup baking ammonia

Grease cookie sheet lightly. Cream shortening and sugar. Add cream, milk and peppermint extract. Sift flour and baking ammonia together; Add gradually to mixture. Roll out dough to about 1 cm (½ in.) thickness on well floured surface. Cut out with 5 cm (2 in.) cookie cutter. Place on prepared cookie sheet and bake. Cookies should look white when finished and are done if they spring back when lightly touched. A typical cookie is large and thick and has a pleasant flavor of ammonia and peppermint. Store in closed container.

CHEERY ALMOND CRESCENTS

Metric	Standard
160°C	325°F

10 min.

Yield: 7 doz.

Ingredients:

Metric	Standard
250 mL soft butter	1 cup soft butter
75 mL icing sugar	⅓ cup icing sugar
60 mL corn starch	¼ cup corn starch
375 mL flour	1½ cups flour
1 mL salt	¼ tsp. salt
125 mL chopped glace red and green cherries	½ cup chopped glace red and green cherries
125 mL finely chopped blanched almonds	½ cup finely chopped blanched almonds

Cream butter, sugar and corn starch. Mix remaining ingredients and add to creamed mixture. Turn on floured board. Form into 1 cm (½ in.) rolls. Cut into 5 cm (2 inch) lengths and pinch ends. Shape into crescents on ungreased cookie sheet. Bake. Roll in sifted icing sugar while still warm.

DATE-FILLED COOKIES

Metric	Standard
180°C	350°F
10 min.	
Yield: 3 doz.	

Ingredients:

125 mL shortening	½ cup shortening
125 mL butter	½ cup butter
250 mL brown sugar	1 cup brown sugar
125 mL milk	½ cup milk
500 mL quick cooking oats	2 cups quick cooking oats
425 mL sifted flour	1¾ cups sifted flour
15 mL baking powder	1 tbsp. baking powder
2 mL salt	½ tsp. salt

Grease cookie sheets well. Cream shortening and butter. Gradually add brown sugar creaming until very light. Add milk and mix. Add quick cooking oats and mix. To sifted flour, add baking powder and salt and sift again. Add to first mixture. Dough should be very soft. Chill dough thoroughly. On floured board roll out to about 0.5 cm (¼ in.) thickness. Cut out with cookie cutter. Place on well greased cookie sheet and bake. When cooled put cookies together with following date filling:

Filling:

750 mL pitted dates	3 cups pitted dates
150 mL water	⅔ cup water
125 mL sugar	½ cup sugar
5 mL lemon juice (optional)	1 tsp. lemon juice (optional)

Combine pitted dates, water and sugar. Cook until thick, stirring well. Cool and add lemon juice.

DATE FILLING

Metric	Standard
Yield: 500-600 mL	2-2¼ cups

Ingredients:

750 mL pitted dates	3 cups pitted dates
150 mL water	⅔ cup water
125 mL sugar	½ cup sugar
5 mL lemon juice	1 tsp. lemon juice.

Chop pitted dates. Combine with water and sugar in 1 L (1 qt.) saucepan. Cook until thick, stirring well. Add lemon juice. Cool and use to fill cookies or cakes.

PIN WHEEL COOKIES

Metric	Standard
190°C	375°F
12 min.	
Yield: 6-7 doz.	

Ingredients:

500 mL brown sugar	2 cups brown sugar
250 mL shortening	1 cup shortening
3 eggs beaten	3 eggs beaten
1000 mL flour	4 cups flour
5 mL cinnamon	1 tsp. cinnamon
5 mL baking soda	1 tsp. baking soda
pinch of salt	pinch of salt
250 mL finely chopped nuts	1 cup finely chopped nuts

Filling:

750 mL chopped pitted dates **or** raisins	3 cups chopped pitted dates **or** raisins
30 mL sugar	2 tbsps. sugar
175 mL water	¾ cup water

Grease cookie sheets lightly. Combine ingredients for filling. Boil for 2 minutes. Allow filling to cool, while preparing dough. Cream brown sugar, shortening and beaten eggs. Mix flour, cinnamon, baking soda and salt. Add gradually to creamed mixture. Roll out dough on wax paper. Spread with filling and chopped nuts. Roll up and chill for a few hours. Cut in 2 cm (½ in.) slices and bake on lightly greased cookie sheet.

WHIPPED SHORTBREAD

Metric	Standard
140°C	275°F
12-15 min.	
Yield: 5-6 doz.	

Ingredients:

500 mL soft margarine	1 lb. soft margarine
125 mL cornstarch	½ cup cornstarch
250 mL sifted icing sugar	1 cup sifted icing sugar
750 mL flour	3 cups flour
6 mL vanilla (optional)	1¼ tsps. vanilla (optional)

Cream margarine with electric beater. Add cornstarch and icing sugar a little at a time. Add flour and continue beating until mixture has the appearance of whipped cream. Drop by spoonfuls on ungreased cookie sheet. Bake until golden, but not brown. A delicious shortbread which melts in your mouth.

SHORTBREAD

Metric	Standard
180°C	350°F
15 min.	
Yield: 3 doz.	

Ingredients:

Metric	Standard
250 mL butter	1 cup butter
125 mL brown sugar	½ cup brown sugar
500 mL sifted flour	2 cups sifted flour

Cream butter thoroughly until light and fluffy and is the consistency of whipped cream. (This is most important.) Add brown sugar gradually 5 mL (1 tsp.) at a time, beating after each addition. Add flour gradually 15-30 mL (1-2 tbsps.) at a time. Beating after each addition. If necessary add more flour to give a smooth but not cracked dough. Gently pat dough into oblong or round piece about 0.5 cm (¼ in.) thick. Gently smooth top with lightly floured rolling pin. Cut out desired shapes. Place on ungreased cookie sheet. Bake till golden, not brown.

FIG BARS

Metric	Standard
190°C	375°F
12 min.	
Yield: 4-5 doz.	

Ingredients:

Metric	Standard
250 mL brown sugar	1 cup brown sugar
250 mL butter **or** shortening	1 cup butter **or** shortening
5 mL vanilla	1 tsp. vanilla
2 eggs beaten	2 eggs beaten
750 mL sifted flour	3 cups sifted flour
5 mL cream of tartar	1 tsp. cream of tartar
3 mL salt (if using shortening)	¾ tsp. salt (if using shortening)
2 mL baking soda	½ tsp. baking soda
15 mL hot water	1 tbsp. hot water

Cream sugar and butter. Add vanilla, beaten eggs and beat until fluffy. Mix sifted flour with cream of tartar and salt. Dissolve baking soda in hot water. Add dry ingredients alternately with water mixture. Beat after each addition. Chill over night.

Filling:

Metric	Standard
250 mL chopped figs	1 cup chopped figs
175 mL water	¾ cup water
75 mL sugar	⅓ cup sugar

Combine all ingredients and cook till thick, stirring frequently. On floured board roll out dough to 0.5 cm (½ in.) thickness. Cut with 5 cm (2½ in.) cookie cutter. Place on greased cookie sheet 5 cm (2½ in.) apart. Put a dab of filling on each cookie. Cover each with another cookie and press edges together securely. Bake until golden brown.

Variation: Fig bars may also be shaped as follows. Roll out dough, cut in 10 cm (4 in.) wide strips. Place filling along center of strip and fold edges over, pressing dough together. Cut in 4 cm (1½ in.) slices. Place on lightly greased cookie sheet and bake.

CHRISTMAS DROP COOKIES

Metric	*Standard*
180-190°C	350°F
12-15 min.	
Yield: 5-6 doz.	

Ingredients:

125 mL butter **or** margarine	½ cup butter **or** margarine
250 mL brown sugar	1 cup brown sugar
3 eggs well beaten	3 eggs well beaten
425 mL sifted flour	1¾ cups sifted flour
5 mL baking soda	1 tsp. baking soda
5 mL nutmeg	1 tsp. nutmeg
150 mL sour cream	⅔ cup sour cream
125 mL sultana raisins	½ cup sultana raisins
75 mL finely cut citron peel	⅓ cup finely cut citron peel
125 mL chopped pitted dates	½ cup chopped pitted dates
45 mL chopped gum drops	3 tbsps. chopped gum drops
125 mL red and green maraschino cherries, halved	½ cup red and green maraschino cherries, halved
125 mL chopped walnuts	½ cup chopped walnuts
175 mL shredded coconut	¾ cup shredded coconut

Grease cookie sheet. Cream butter. (If margarine is used, add a bit of salt to the recipe.) Gradually add sugar, creaming thoroughly after each addition. Add well beaten eggs. Combine sifted flour, baking soda, nutmeg and sift. Add dry ingredients alternately with sour cream to beaten mixture. Mix remaining ingredients, except coconut and stir well into mixture. Stir in coconut. Drop by spoonfuls onto greased cookie sheet, 4 cm (1½ in.) apart and bake.

CHRISTMAS ALMOND COOKIES

Metric	Standard
180°C	350°F
15 min.	
Yield: 3-4 doz.	

Ingredients:

150 mL blanched almonds	⅔ cup blanched almonds
125 mL Safflo **or** other salad oil	½ cup Safflo **or** other salad oil
45 mL milk	3 tbsps. milk
1 egg	1 egg
5 mL almond extract	1 tsp. almond extract
500 mL sifted flour	2 cups sifted flour
125 mL white sugar	½ cup white sugar
15 mL baking powder	1 tbsp. baking powder
2 mL salt	½ tsp. salt
125 mL brown sugar	½ cup brown sugar
glace cherries, halved	glace cherries, halved

Chop almonds fine, saving a few whole nuts for decoration. Mix Safflo oil, milk, egg and almond extract. Sift dry ingredients together and add along with brown sugar. Blend well. Stir in chopped blanched almonds. Roll dough into small balls and place 6 cm (2½ in.) apart on ungreased cookie sheet. Decorate with whole amonds or glace cherry halves. Bake till light brown.

BIRD'S NESTS

Metric	Standard
160°C	325°F
10 min.	
Yield: 3 doz.	

Ingredients:

125 mL butter **or** margarine	½ cup butter **or** margarine
50 mL brown sugar	¼ cup brown sugar
1 egg separated	1 egg separated
250 mL flour	1 cup flour
5 mL baking powder	1 tsp. baking powder
Jam **or** Jelly	Jam **or** Jelly

Grease cookie sheet lightly. Cream butter and sugar. Add egg yolk and continue creaming. Sift in flour and baking powder, mix well. Roll into small balls, size of walnuts and place on greased cookie sheet. With thimble dipped in flour make deep impressions into each ball. Bake. Remove from oven and fill centre with jam. Drop a spoonful of meringue on top of each. Return to oven and bake until meringue is a delicate brown.

Meringue:

1 egg white	1 egg white
50 mL white fruit sugar **or** icing sugar	¼ cup white fruit sugar **or** icing sugar
1 mL almond flavoring	¼ tsp. almond flavoring

Beat egg white, adding sugar and almond flavoring gradually until mixture stands in stiff peaks.

FOOD FOR THE GODS

Metric	*Standard*
2.5 L cake pan (2.3 x 5 cm)	9 x 9 x 2 in. cake pan
190°C	
25-30 min.	
Yield: 27 2.5 x 7.5 cm fingers	27 1″ x 3″ fingers

Ingredients:

175 mL crushed graham wafers	¾ cup crushed graham wafers
250 mL brown sugar	1 cup brown sugar
250 mL nuts	1 cup nuts
250 mL dates **or** dates and cherries	1 cup dates **or** dates and cherries
2 eggs	2 eggs

Grease pan lightly. Mix all ingredients with electric mixer. Put in pan. Bake and cut into fingers.

CRAZY CAKE

Metric	*Standard*
3.5 L cake pan (33 x 21 x 5 cm)	13 x 9 x 2 in. cake pan

Ingredients:

50 mL butter	¼ cup butter
125 mL syrup **or** honey	½ cup syrup **or** honey
30-45 mL cocoa	2-3 tbsps. cocoa
250 mL brown **or** white sugar	1 cup brown **or** white sugar
2.25-2.5 L puffed wheat	9-10 cups puffed wheat

Grease cake pan with butter. Combine first four ingredients in 3L (3 qt.) saucepan. Boil for two to three minutes. Add puffed wheat, mix well. Turn into prepared cake pan. Pat down a little. Set aside to cool for about 15 minutes. Cut into squares and serve.

MELTING MOMENTS

Metric	Standard
190°C	375°F
14-15 min.	
Yield: 4 doz.	

Ingredients:

175 mL brown sugar	¾ cup brown sugar
250 mL soft butter	1 cup soft butter
1 egg	1 egg
425 mL flour	1¾ cups flour
2 mL cream of tartar	½ tsp. cream of tartar
2 mL baking soda	½ tsp. baking soda
5 mL vanilla	1 tsp. vanilla
125 mL finely chopped nuts	½ cup finely chopped nuts
24 glacé cherries	24 glacé cherries

Cream brown sugar, butter and egg. Sift dry ingredients together and add along with vanilla. Mix well. Roll into small balls the size of a walnut. Dip into finely chopped nuts. Flatten slightly and place on greased cookie sheet. Halve glacé cherries and place a half in centre of each cookie. Press in slightly. Bake until golden brown. DO NOT OVERBAKE. A lovely Christmas cookie.

MARSHMALLOW SQUARES

Metric	Standard
2.5 L cake pan (23 x 5 cm)	9 x 9 x 2 in. cake pan

Ingredients:

30 large marshmallows	30 large marshmallows
375 mL graham wafer crumbs	1½ cups graham wafer crumbs
75 mL chopped maraschino cherries	⅓ cup chopped maraschino cherries
1 can (397 g) sweetened condensed milk	1 can (14 oz.) sweetened condensed milk
5 mL vanilla	1 tsp. vanilla
few grains of salt	few grains of salt
375 mL fine coconut	1½ cups fine coconut

Cut marshmallows in quarters. Combine all ingredients **except** coconut. Line cake pan with ⅔ of the coconut. Press marshmallow mixture into pan. Sprinkle with remaining coconut; press. Store in refrigerator for 24 hours to ripen. Cut in squares and serve. Stored in refrigerator, marshmallow squares keep for several days.

CARMEL SQUARES

Metric	Standard
2 L cake pan (20 x 5 cm)	8 x 8 x 2 in. cake pan
170-180°C	350°F
20 min.	

Ingredients:

50 mL butter	¼ cup butter
250 mL brown sugar	1 cup brown sugar
1 egg	1 egg
125 mL flour	½ cup flour
1 mL salt	¼ tsp. salt
5 mL baking powder	1 tsp. baking powder
250 mL coconut	1 cup coconut
125 mL walnuts	½ cup walnuts
2 mL vanilla	½ tsp. vanilla

Melt butter and sugar together; cool. Add egg and beat well. Add remaining ingredients and mix well. Spread into pan, bake and cool. Ice with chocolate or white icing (optional). Cut in squares and serve.

ALMOND CHERRY SQUARES

Metric	Standard
2 L cake pan (20 x 5 cm)	8 x 8 x 2 in. cake pan

Ingredients:

45 mL honey	3 tbsps. honey
30 mL soft butter	2 tbsps. soft butter
1 mL almond flavoring	¼ tsp. almond flavoring
375 mL unblanched ground almonds	1½ cups unblanched ground almonds
125 mL chopped glace cherries	½ cup chopped glace cherries
125 mL fine coconut toasted	½ cup fine coconut toasted
8 squares semi-sweet chocolate	8 squares semi-sweet chocolate

Line cake pan with wax paper. Blend honey, butter and almond flavoring. Work in unblanched ground almonds, chopped glace cherries and fine toasted coconut. Pat mixture into pan and chill. Melt semi-sweet chocolate over hot water. Spread over almond mixture. Let harden, cut in squares and serve.

PINEAPPLE CHERRY SLICE

Metric	Standard
3.5 L cake pan (33 x 21 x 5 cm)	13″ x 9″ x 2″ cake pan
190°C, 20 min.	350°F, 20 min.
200°C, 5 min.	400°F, 5 min.

Ingredients:
Crust:

500 mL flour	2 cups flour
30 mL sugar	2 tbsps. sugar
125 mL margarine	½ cup margarine
dash of salt	dash of salt

Combine all ingredients and press into pan. Bake.

Filling:

250 mL crushed pineapple, drained	1 cup crushed pineapple, drained
50 mL sugar	¼ cup sugar
30 mL cornstarch	2 tbsps. cornstarch
50 mL cold water	¼ cup cold water
150 mL maraschino cherries, cut	⅔ cup maraschino cherries, cut

Combine all ingredients except cherries in a 1 L (1 qt.) saucepan. Cook until mixture thickens. Add cherries, cool, and spread over crust.

Topping:

2 egg whites	2 egg whites
30 mL water	2 tbsps. water
1 mL cream of tartar	¼ tsp. cream of tartar
20 mL sugar	1 tbsp. and 1 tsp. sugar
almond flavoring	almond flavoring
coconut to sprinkle over top	coconut to sprinkle over top

Beat egg whites to stiff peaks. Add sugar and flavoring. Spread over filling and sprinkle with coconut. Bake until golden brown.

PINEAPPLE COCONUT BARS

Metric	Standard
2 L cake pan (20 x 5 cm)	8 x 8 x 2 in. cake pan
180°C	350°F
30 min.	
Yield: 16 5 x 5 cm bars	16 2 x 2″ bars

Ingredients:

15 mL sugar	1 tbsp. sugar
15 mL butter	1 tbsp. butter
15 mL baking powder	1 tbsp. baking powder

1 mL salt	¼ tsp. salt
250 mL pastry flour	1 cup pastry flour
3 eggs well beaten	3 eggs well beaten
1 can (540 mL) crushed pineapple	1 can (19 oz.) crushed pineapple
175 mL sugar	¾ cup sugar
15 mL melted butter	1 tbsp. melted butter
500 mL unsweetened shredded coconut	2 cups unsweetened shredded coconut

Grease cake pan. Cream first two ingredients. Sift baking powder, salt and pastry flour. Blend into creamed mixture. Add half of well beaten eggs; mix thoroughly. Mixture will be quite thick. Spread into greased cake pan. Drain crushed pineapple and spread over batter. Mix remaining sugar, melted butter and unsweetened coconut. Mix in remainder of beaten eggs. Spread over pineapple. Bake and cut in squares to serve.

OH HENRY BARS

Metric	*Standard*
2 L cake pan (20 cm square)	8 x 8 x 2 in. cake pan
Yield: 36 bars	

Ingredients:
Base:

25 graham wafers	25 graham wafers
125 mL butter **or** margarine	½ cup butter **or** margarine
125 mL milk	½ cup milk
250 mL brown sugar	1 cup brown sugar
250 mL chopped nuts	1 cup chopped nuts

Icing:

375 mL icing sugar	1½ cups icing sugar
30 mL melted butter	2 tbsps. melted butter
30 mL cocoa	2 tbsps. cocoa
30 mL milk	2 tbsps. milk
5 mL vanilla	1 tsp. vanilla

For base:
Line cake pan with 10 graham wafers. Melt butter, milk and brown sugar. Bring to a boil and cook for 2 minutes. Crush and add remaining wafers and chopped nuts. Mix well and pour into wafer lined pan. Chill.

For icing:
Beat all ingredients together to smooth consistency and spread on chilled base. Cut in bars to serve. To store, refrigerate or freeze.

OH HENRY CHOCOLATE BARS

Metric	*Standard*
3.5 L cake pan	13 x 9 x 2 in. cake pan
(33 x 21 x 5 cm)	
Yield: Approx. 4 doz.	

Ingredients:

250 mL corn syrup	1 cup corn syrup
125 mL sugar	½ cup sugar
250 mL peanut butter	1 cup peanut butter
5 mL vanilla	1 tsp. vanilla
500 mL Corn Flakes	2 cups Corn Flakes
500 mL Rice Krispies	2 cups Rice Krispies
250 mL shelled peanuts	1 cup shelled peanuts
5-6 squares semi-sweet	5-6 squares semi-sweet
chocolate	chocolate
3 x 3 x 1 cm square parawax	2 in. square parawax

Combine corn syrup and sugar in 1 L (1 qt.) saucepan. Heat to melt. Add peanut butter and vanilla, mix. Combine Corn Flakes, Rice Krispies and shelled peanuts. Pour melted syrup over Corn Flake mixture. Press into cake pan. Cool and cut into rectangles. Melt semi-sweet chocolate and parawax in double boiler over hot water. Dip rectangles into warm melted chocolate. Let cool and serve.

PINEAPPLE MALLOW SQUARES

Metric	*Standard*
2 L cake pan (20 cm square)	8 x 8 x 2 in. cake pan
Serves: 6-8	

Ingredients:

250 mL diced pineapple, drained	1 cup diced pineapple, drained
500 mL diced marshmallows	2 cups diced marshmallows
pinch of salt	pinch of salt
500 mL crushed graham wafers	2 cups crushed graham wafers
125 mL chopped nuts	½ cup chopped nuts
flavoring to taste	flavoring to taste

Grease cake pan. Combine all ingredients and mix thoroughly. Pack into greased pans. Chill 12 hours. Spread with butter icing and cut in squares.

Variation: Pack combined ingredients into jello mold. Chill and cover with whipped cream.

JOHNNIES

Metric	Standard
3 L cake pan	12 x 8 x 2 in. cake pan
(30 x 20 x 5 cm)	
180°C	350°F
40 min.	
Yield: 24 pieces	

Ingredients:

Base:

125 mL butter	½ cup butter
250 mL sugar	1 cup sugar
3 egg yolks	3 egg yolks
125 mL flour	½ cup flour
45 mL cocoa	3 tbsps. cocoa
1 mL salt	¼ tsp. salt
5 mL vanilla	1 tsp. vanilla
250 mL chopped walnuts	1 cup chopped walnuts

Topping:

3 egg whites	3 egg whites
125 mL sugar	½ cup sugar
250 mL coconut	1 cup coconut

For Base:

Cream butter, add sugar, then egg yolks; mix well. Sift dry ingredients together and fold in. Add vanilla and walnuts. Spread in greased cake pan. Bake for 15 minutes.

Topping:

Beat egg whites to stiff peak but not dry. Gradually beat in sugar, then coconut. Spread on baked base. Return to oven and bake for another 25 minutes. When cool spread with chocolate icing. Cut in squares and serve.

KRUNCHIES

Metric	Standard
Yield: 7 doz.	

Ingredients:

454 g sweet chocolate **or**	1 lb. sweet chocolate **or**
16 squares semi-sweet	16 squares semi-sweet
chocolate	chocolate
1.15 L crushed corn flakes	5 cups crushed corn flakes
125 mL chopped nuts	½ cup chopped nuts

Melt chocolate in top of double boiler. Stir in crushed corn flakes and chopped nuts. Mix well and drop on wax paper. Let set in cool place.

SCOTTISH FANCIES

Metric	Standard
180°C	350°F
15 min.	
Yield: 2 doz.	

Ingredients:

1 egg	1 egg
125 mL sugar	½ cup sugar
1 mL salt	⅛ tsp. salt
250 mL coconut	1 cup coconut
125 mL quick cooking oats	½ cup quick cooking oats
15 mL melted butter	1 tbsp. melted butter
1 mL vanilla	¼ tsp. vanilla

Beat egg, add sugar and salt, beat well. Add remaining ingredients. Drop by spoonfuls on greased cookie sheet and bake.

CORN FLAKES FANCIES

Metric	Standard
180°C	350°F
15 min.	
Yield: 3 doz.	

Ingredients:

1 L corn flakes	4 cups corn flakes
500 mL coconut	2 cups coconut
250 mL sugar	1 cup sugar
4 egg whites	4 egg whites

Combine corn flakes, coconut and sugar; mix well. Beat egg whites to stiff peaks. Fold in cornflake mixture. Shape into desired size. Place on lightly greased cookie sheet. Bake until delicate brown in color.

PORCUPINES

Metric	Standard
180°C	350°F
8-10 min.	
Yield: 3 doz. 5 cm logs	3 doz. 2 in. logs

Ingredients:

Metric	Standard
250 mL brown sugar	1 cup brown sugar
15 mL butter	1 tbsp. butter
2 eggs	2 eggs
250 mL chopped walnuts	1 cup chopped walnuts
250 mL chopped dates	1 cup chopped dates
1000 mL shredded coconut	4 cups shredded coconut

Cream butter and brown sugar; add eggs and beat well. Add nuts and dates, mix thoroughly. Drop by spoonful into a dish of shredded coconut. Roll into oblong shape. Bake on greased cookie sheet until a delicate brown.

Notes

DESSERTS, PUDDINGS, SAUCES

CHEESE CAKE

Metric	Standard
3 L cake pan (30 x 20 x 5 cm)	12 x 8 x 2 in. cake pan

Serves: 9-12

Ingredients:

Base:

500 mL Graham wafer crumbs	2 cups Graham wafer crumbs
125 mL butter	½ cup butter
50 mL sugar	¼ cup sugar

Cheese Filling:

1 pkg (85 g) lemon jello powder	1 pkg (3 oz.) lemon jello powder
250 mL boiling water	1 cup boiling water
1 pkg (42.5 g) Dream Whip	1 pkg Dream Whip
1 pkg (227 g) Philadelphia Cream Cheese	1 pkg. (8 oz.) Philadelphia Cream Cheese
125 mL milk	½ cup milk
250 mL sugar	1 cup sugar

Topping:

1 can (540 mL) cherry **or** strawberry pie filling	1 can (19 oz.) cherry **or** strawberry pie filling

For Base:

Mix ingredients and save 50 mL (¼ cup). Put remainder into cake pan. Bake at 180°C (350°F) for 8-10 minutes. Cool.

For Cheese Filling:

Dissolve lemon jello powder in boiling water. Cool, but DO NOT LET SET. Combine Dream Whip, cream cheese (at room temperature), milk and sugar. Beat all together. Add cooled lemon jello. Pour over cooled base.

For Topping:

Spread cherry pie filling over cheese filling. (If cheese filling is somewhat liquid, allow to set before spreading on fruit). Sprinkle with remaining crumbs. Refrigerate for a day before serving. This gives better flavour and consistency.

CREAM CHEESE CAKE

Metric	*Standard*
2 L cake pan (20 x 5 cm)	8 x 8 x 2 in. cake pan
150°C	300°F
15 mins.	
Yield: 16 pieces	

Ingredients:

500 mL crushed Graham wafers	2 cups crushed Graham wafers
50 mL soft butter	¼ cup soft butter
1 pkg (227 g) Philadelphia Cream Cheese	1 pkg. (8 oz.) Philadelphia Cream Cheese
250 mL milk	1 cup milk
100 mL instant vanilla pudding powder	3¼ oz. instant vanilla pudding powder
10 maraschino cherries, chopped	10 maraschino cherries, chopped

Mix crushed Graham wafers and soft butter. Press ¾ of mixture into cake pan (reserve remainder for topping). Bake until golden brown. Cool. Beat remaining ingredients thoroughly; pour on baked base. Sprinkle remaining crumbs over as topping. Chill in refrigerator. DO NOT BAKE!

CREAM PUFFS

Metric	*Standard*
220°C for 10 mins.	425°F
180°C for 20-25 mins.	350°F
Yield: 3 doz. medium	

Ingredients:

125 mL butter	½ cup butter
250 mL boiling water	1 cup boiling water
375 mL flour	1¼ cups flour
1 mL salt	¼ tsp. salt
4 eggs	4 eggs

Grease cookie sheet. Place butter and boiling water in saucepan over low heat until butter is melted. Sift flour and salt together. Add all at once to hot mixture. Stir vigorously until mixture leaves side of pan. Remove from heat. Add unbeaten eggs one at a time, beating thoroughly after each addition. Drop batter by spoonfuls on greased cookie sheet, about 5 cm (2 ins.) apart. Bake at higher temperature for 10 minutes. Reduce heat and bake at lower temperature for 20-25 minutes or until beads of moisture no longer appear on surface. Cool and slit side of each puff. Fill with whipped cream, pudding or fruit pie filling.

SCHNEEFLOCKEN
(Floating Islands)

Metric	Standard
Serves: 6	

Ingredients:

Metric	Standard
2 eggs, separated	2 eggs, separated
75 mL sugar	⅓ cup sugar
625 mL milk	2½ cups milk
30 mL cornstarch	2 tbsps. cornstarch
pinch of salt	pinch of salt
2 mL vanilla	½ tsp. vanilla

Beat egg whites, gradually adding 15 mL (1 tbsp.) of sugar, to stiff peaks. Scald 500 mL (2 cups) of milk in 2 L (2 qt.) saucepan. Place stiffly beaten egg whites by spoonfuls into scalding milk. Turn once after two minutes. Remove after an additional two minutes. Set on dry surface. Combine egg yolks, remaining sugar, cornstarch and salt. Mix well and add to boiling milk. Stir continuously till mixture comes to full boil and thickens. If mixture tastes starchy, cook a little longer. Remove from heat and add vanilla. Pour into dessert dishes. Top with cooked meringue. Chill and top with jelly or nuts; serve. A nice light dessert.

FRUIT COCKTAIL DESSERT

Metric	Standard
2 L jelly roll pan	15 x 10 x ¾ in.
(40 x 25 x 2 cm)	jelly roll pan
180°C	350°F
40-45 mins.	

Ingredients:

Metric	Standard
1 can (540 mL) fruit cocktail	1 can (19 oz.) fruit cocktail
375 mL flour	1½ cups flour
5 mL baking soda	1 tsp. baking soda
5 mL baking powder	1 tsp. baking powder
1 mL salt	¼ tsp. salt
250 mL sugar	1 cup sugar
1 egg, slightly beaten	1 egg, slightly beaten

Topping:

Metric	Standard
250 mL brown sugar	1 cup brown sugar
175 mL chopped nuts	¾ cup chopped nuts

Drain fruit cocktail and save juice. Mix dry ingredients, beaten egg and juice of fruit cocktail. Mix in the fruit and pour into greased pan. Mix brown sugar and chopped nuts and sprinkle on top. Bake and serve with lemon sauce or whipped cream.

GINGERBREAD WITH ORANGE SAUCE

Metric	Standard
2.5 L cake pan (23 x 5 cm)	9 x 9 x 2 in. cake pan
180°C	350°F
45 mins.	

Ingredients:

Metric	Standard
125 mL butter	½ cup butter
125 mL sugar	½ cup sugar
1 egg, well beaten	1 egg, well beaten
625 mL flour	2½ cups flour
7 mL soda	1½ tsps. soda
5 mL cinnamon	1 tsp. cinnamon
5 mL ginger	1 tsp. ginger
5 mL cloves	1 tsp. cloves
2 mL salt	½ tsp. salt
250 mL molasses	1 cup molasses
250 mL hot water	1 cup hot water

Line cake pan with paper. Cream butter and sugar. Add beaten egg. Measure and sift together dry ingredients. Combine molasses and hot water. Add dry ingredients and molasses mixture alternately to butter mixture, beating until smooth after each addition. Bake in paper lined pan. Serve with:

ORANGE SAUCE

250 mL sugar	1 cup sugar
juice of 2 oranges	juice of 2 oranges

Blend together. Pour over hot gingerbread and serve at once.

APPLE ROLL

Metric	Standard
2.5 L cake pans (23 x 5 cm)	9 x 9 x 2 in. cake pan
190°C	375°F
45 mins.	
Yield: about 15 rolls	

Ingredients:

Metric	Standard
375 mL sugar	1½ cups sugar
500 mL water	2 cups water
500 mL flour	2 cups flour
20 mL baking powder	4 tsps. baking powder
5 mL salt	1 tsp. salt
90 mL shortening	6 tbsps. shortening
175 mL milk	¾ cup milk
250 mL shredded apples	1 cup shredded apples

butter
cinnamon and sugar mixture

butter
sugar and cinnamon
mixture

Dissolve sugar and water in small saucepan. Simmer for five minutes and pour into cake pan. Make biscuit dough as follows: Mix dry ingredients. Cut in shortening. Add milk just to moisten. Roll out dough on floured surface. Sprinkle with shredded apples. Roll as for jelly roll and cut into slices 3 cm (2 in.) thick. Place slice in syrup in cake pan. Dot with butter and sprinkle with cinnamon/sugar mixture. Bake until crust is brown.

Variation: Prune Plums or other fruit may be used in place of apples.

APRICOT WHIP

Metric	*Standard*
Serves: 4	

Ingredients:

125 mL dried apricots	½ cup dried apricots
1 egg white	1 egg white
25 mL sugar	1½ tbsps. sugar

Barely cover dried apricots with cold water in 1 L (1 qt.) saucepan. Boil until soft; put through sieve. Beat egg white with sugar to stiff peak. Fold into sieved apricots. Chill and serve with custard sauce.

FROZEN WHIPPED CREAM DESSERT

Metric	*Standard*
Serves: 6-8	

Ingredients:

250 mL whipping cream **or**	1 cup whipping cream **or**
1 pkg (42.5 g) Dream Whip **plus** 100 mL milk and 30 mL sugar	1 pkg Dream Whip **plus** ½ cup milk and 2 tbsps. sugar
1 L finely chopped marshmallows	4 cups finely chopped marshmallows
125 mL chopped walnuts	½ cup chopped walnuts
50 mL chopped maraschino cherries	¼ cup chopped maraschino cherries

Beat whipping cream. Mix all ingredients together and freeze. Scoop into sherbet glasses to serve. Top with half of maraschino cherry syrup.

LEMON RICE

Metric	Standard
2 L casserole dish	2 qt. casserole dish
160°C	325°F
20 mins.	
Serves: 6	

Ingredients:

125 mL rice	½ cup rice
750 mL milk	3 cups milk
2 eggs, separated	2 eggs, separated
125 mL sugar	½ cup sugar
1 mL salt	¼ tsp. salt
grated rind of ½ lemon	grated rind of ½ lemon
7 mL lemon juice	1½ tsps. lemon juice

Grease casserole dish. Wash rice and cook with milk in top of 2 L (2 qt.) double boiler over boiling water until rice is tender. Beat egg yolks and mix with sugar, salt, grated rind of lemon and lemon juice. Add to hot rice and cook for five minutes. Transfer into greased casserole dish. Beat egg whites to stiff peaks, scoop over rice and bake until golden brown.

Note: Egg whites may also be folded into rice mixture, then baked.

KISS PUDDING

Metric	Standard
1.5 L casserole dish	1½ qt. casserole dish
190°C	375°F
10 min.	
Serves: 6	

Ingredients:

3 eggs, separated	3 eggs, separated
125 mL granulated sugar	½ cup granulated sugar
25 mL butter **or** margarine	1½ tbsps. butter **or** margarine
25 mL cornstarch	1½ tbsps. cornstarch
500 mL milk	2 cups milk
5 mL vanilla	1 tsp. vanilla
75 mL icing sugar	5 tbsps. icing sugar

Butter casserole dish. Beat egg yolks with granulated sugar until light. Add butter and cornstarch. Stir in milk and transfer to top of 2 L (2 qt.) double boiler. Heat over boiling water stirring constantly until thick. Flavour and pour into buttered casserole dish or oven-proof pudding dish. Beat egg whites to stiff dry peaks with icing sugar. Cover pudding with egg whites. Place in oven to brown slightly. Serve with whipped cream and fruit.

RICE SURPRISE

Metric	*Standard*
Serves: 4-6	

Ingredients:

Metric	Standard
75 mL rice	⅓ cup rice
375 mL whipped cream **or**	1½ cups whipped cream **or**
1 pkg (42.5 g)	1 pkg Dream Whip **plus**
Dream Whip **plus**	½ cup milk
100 mL milk	
75 mL sugar	⅓ cup sugar
250 mL crushed pineapple,	1 cup crushed pineapple,
drained	drained

Cook rice, rinse, drain and chill. Whip cream, adding sugar. Fold whipped cream and drained pineapple into rice. Pile into dessert dishes. Decorate with your favourite topping and serve.

CHOCOLATE RICE PUDDING

Metric	*Standard*
1 L casserole dish	1 qt. casserole dish
180°C	350°F
20-30 mins.	
Serves: about 6	

Ingredients:

Metric	Standard
125 mL uncooked rice	½ cup uncooked rice
1 mL salt	¼ cup salt
750 mL boiling water	3 cups boiling water
150 mL sugar	⅔ cup sugar
50 mL cocoa	¼ cup cocoa
2 eggs, separated	2 eggs, separated
300 mL warm milk	1¼ cups warm milk
30 mL butter	2 tbsps. butter

Wash rice and cook with salt and boiling water until tender. Drain through sieve and rinse with hot water. Drain again. Combine sugar, cocoa and egg yolks. Add warm milk and butter. Add to well drained rice. Beat egg whites, fold into rice mixture. Bake and serve.

Optional:

Rice mixture may be cooked in double boiler over hot water 20-30 minutes, then fold in egg whites and serve.

GLORIFIED RICE

Metric	Standard
Serves: 8	

Ingredients:

Metric	Standard
1 can (398 mL) pineapple tidbit or fruit cocktail	1 can (14 oz.) pineapple tidbit or fruit cocktail
250 mL cooked rice	2 cups cooked rice
3 mL salt	¾ tsp. salt
6 marashino cherries, diced	6 maraschino cherries, diced
250 mL miniature marshmallows	1 cup miniature marshmallows
500 mL prepared whipped topping **or** 1 pkg. (150 mL) Dream Whip **plus** 125 mL milk	2 cups prepared whipped topping **or** 1 pkg. Dream Whip **plus** ½ cup milk

Drain fruit. Measure syrup and add water to make 300 mL. Bring syrup to a boil over high heat in a 1 L (1 qt.) saucepan. Stir in cooked rice, salt and cover. Reduce heat and simmer 5 min. Remove from heat, add fruit and chill thoroughly. When chilled, stir in whipped topping. Serve.

LEMON PUDDING

Metric	Standard
2 L Pyrex casserole dish	2 qt. Pyrex casserole dish
190°C	375°F
30-45 min.	
Serves: 5-6	

Ingredients:

Metric	Standard
2 eggs, separated	2 eggs, separated
1 lemon	1 lemon
250 mL sugar	1 cup sugar
125 mL flour	½ cup flour
250 mL milk	1 cup milk
30 mL melted butter	2 tsps. melted butter

Beat egg yolks, adding juice and a little grated rind of lemon, sugar, flour, milk and butter. Beat egg whites to stiff peaks and fold in. Pour into lightly greased Pyrex casserole dish. Place casserole in pan with hot water. Bake. Top should be light brown when done.

LEMON SPONGE OR SNOW PUDDING

Metric	Standard
Serves: 4-6	

Ingredients:

1 pkg. (15 mL) gelatin	1 pkg. (1 tbsp.) gelatin
50 mL cold water	¼ cup cold water
175 mL sugar	¾ cup sugar
1 mL salt	¼ tsp. salt
250 mL hot water	1 cup hot water
25 mL lemon juice	1½ tbsps. lemon juice
grated rind of ½ lemon	grated rind of ½ lemon
2 egg whites	2 egg whites

Soften gelatin in cold water. Add sugar, salt, and hot water; stir until dissolved. Add lemon juice and grated rind. Cool till quite thick. Beat until frothy. Beat egg whites to stiff peaks. Add to frothy gelatin and continue beating till sponge holds its shape. Spoon into dishes; chill. Serve plain or with custard sauce.

BREAD OR CAKE PUDDING

Metric	Standard
2 L casserole dish	2 qt. casserole dish
180°C	350°F
30 min.	
Serves: 5	

Ingredients:

500 mL milk	2 cups milk
15 mL butter	1 tbsp. butter
125 mL raisins	½ cup raisins
250 mL fine bread **or**	1 cup fine bread **or**
cake crumbs	cake crumbs
5 mL vanilla	1 tsp. vanilla
75 mL sugar	⅓ cup sugar
1 egg, beaten	1 egg, beaten

Grease casserole dish. Scald milk; add butter. Wash and dry raisins; add to milk. Add fine bread crumbs, vanilla and sugar. Fold beaten eggs into mixture. Pour into greased casserole dish and bake until knife comes out clean when inserted.

Variation:

Fine bread crumbs may be substituted by 500 mL (2 cups) bread or cake cubes. Raisins may be replaced by 15 mL (1 tbsp.) cocoa.

PERFECT FOOD

Metric	Standard
Serves: 2	

Ingredients:

Metric	Standard
15 mL honey	1 tbsp. honey
15 mL hot water	1 tbsp. hot water
15 mL light cream **or** milk	1 tbsp. light cream **or** milk
15 mL chopped hazelnuts	1 tbsp. chopped hazelnuts
15 mL quick cooking oats	1 tbsp. quick cooking oats
10 mL lemon juice	2 tsps. lemon juice
2 grated apples	2 grated apples

Dissolve honey in hot water. Add light cream, chopped hazelnuts and quick cooking oats. Sprinkle lemon juice over grated apples and mix with above ingredients. Serve as a dessert.

CARAMEL PUDDING

Metric	Standard
Serves: 4	

Ingredients:

Metric	Standard
50 mL white sugar	3 tbsps. white sugar
125 mL brown sugar	½ cup brown sugar
60 mL cornstarch	4 tbsps. cornstarch
50 mL cold water	¼ cup cold water
500 mL boiling water	2 cups boiling water
30 mL butter	2 tbsps. butter
2 mL vanilla	½ tsp. vanilla

Melt sugars in frying pan. Mix cornstarch with cold water and add to boiling water. Add caramelized sugar. Cook until thick, stirring constantly. Add butter and vanilla. Cook a few minutes longer. Pour into dessert dishes. Chill and serve with whipped cream.

COFFEE CREAM

Metric	Standard
Serves: 4	

Ingredients:

Metric	Standard
8 large marshmallows	8 large marshmallows
125 mL whipping cream **or**	½ pint whipping cream **or**
75 mL Dream Whip **plus**	⅓ Dream Whip **plus**
50 mL milk	¼ cup milk
125 mL hot strong coffee	½ cup hot strong coffee
(4 mL instant coffee with	(1 tsp. instant coffee,
50 mL water)	¼ c. water)

Whip cream or Dream Whip. Dissolve marshmallows in hot coffee. Allow to partly set, then mix with whipped cream. Pile into sherbet glasses and serve.

MANNAGRÜTZE
(Cream of Wheat Pudding)

Metric	Standard

Serves: 6-8

Ingredients:

Metric	Standard
750 mL milk	3 cups milk
125 mL cream of wheat	½ cup cream of wheat
2 eggs, separated	2 eggs, separated
125 mL sugar	½ cup sugar
1 mL salt	¼ tsp. salt
5 mL vanilla	1 tsp. vanilla

Heat milk to boiling point in 2 L (2 qt.) saucepan. Slowly sprinkle in cream of wheat, stirring constantly while mixture thickens. Beat and mix egg yolks, sugar, salt and vanilla. Add to milk mixture. Stir and cook over low heat for a few minutes. Remove from heat. Beat egg whites to stiff peaks and fold into pudding. Chill and serve. A pudding traditionally eaten with Pluma Moos or any fruit preserve.

APPLE OR RHUBARB CRISP

Metric	Standard
2.5 L cake pan (23 x 5 cm)	9 x 9 x 2 in. cake pan
180°C	350°F
25-35 min.	

Ingredients:

Metric	Standard
500-750 mL diced apples	2-3 cups diced apples
few drops lemon juice	few drops lemon juice
125 mL flour	½ cup flour
75 mL butter **or**	⅓ cup butter **or**
margarine	margarine
250 mL brown sugar	1 cup brown sugar
1 mL salt	⅛ tsp. salt

Place diced apples in greased baking dish. Sprinkle with lemon juice. Combine flour, butter, brown sugar and salt into crumbs. Sprinkle over apples. Bake till nicely browned.

Variation: Apples may be replaced with rhubarb. Mix rhubarb with 50 mL (¼ cup) or more sugar, if desired, before placing in greased baking dish. For remainder follow recipe as above.

APPLE CRUNCH

Metric	Standard
3.5 L cake pan	13 x 9 x 2 in. cake pan
(33 x 21 x 5 cm)	
190°C	375°F
30-40 min.	
Serves: 8	

Ingredients:

1 L thinly sliced apples	4 cups thinly sliced apples
175 mL quick cooking oats	¾ cup quick cooking oats
175 mL brown sugar	¾ cup brown sugar
250 mL white sugar	1 cup white sugar
15 mL flour	1 tbsp. flour
50 mL melted butter **or** margarine	¼ cup melted butter **or** margarine

Grease cake pan. Place thinly sliced apples in greased pan. Combine and mix dry ingredients. Add melted butter and work into crumbs. Sprinkle crumbs over apples and press them down. Bake until apples are tender. Serve warm with milk, ice cream or whipped cream.

CHERRY DELIGHT DESSERT

Metric	Standard
3.5 L cake pan	13 x 9 x 2 in. cake pan
(33 x 21 x 5 cm)	
190°C	375°F
10-15 min.	
Serves: 12-15	

Ingredients:

28 Graham wafers	28 Graham wafers
125 mL melted margarine	½ cup melted margarine
500 mL whipping cream	2 cups whipping cream
1 pkg. (283 g) miniature marshmallows	1 pkg. (10 oz.) miniature marshmallows
1 can (540 mL) cherry pie filling	1 can (10 oz.) cherry pie filling

Crush Graham wafers. Add melted margarine and mix well. Pat into cake pan and bake till delicately brown. Cool. Whip cream till thick. Add miniature marshmallows and mix. Spread ½ of mixture on baked crust. Spread cherry pie filling over this. Cover with remaining marshmallow mixture. Sprinkle with a few Graham wafer crumbs. Refrigerate to set and serve a delicious dessert.

Variation:

Any other pie filling may be used or make your own as follows:

2 cans (398 mL each) fruit	2 cans (14 oz. each) fruit
50-75 mL sugar	¼-⅓ cup sugar
75 mL drained juice	⅓ cup drained juice
25 mL cornstarch	1½ tbsps. cornstarch

Drain fruit and reserve juice. Cut fruit in small pieces. Combine sugar and 50 mL (¼ cup) drained juice. Bring to a boil. Combine 25 mL (1½ tbsps.) drained juice and cornstarch. Add to boiling liquid and stir until liquid thickens. Add drained fruit, stir and bring mixture to a boil. Cool and use as pie filling.

RAISIN DELIGHT

Metric	*Standard*
2.5 L cake pan (23 cm square)	9 x 9 x 2 in. cake pan
180°C	350°F
25 min.	
Serves: 8-10	

Ingredients:

Syrup:

250 mL brown sugar	1 cup brown sugar
15 mL butter	1 tbsp. butter
125 mL raisins	½ cup raisins
5 mL vanilla	1 tsp. vanilla
500 mL boiling water	2 cups boiling water

Batter:

15 mL soft butter	1 tbsp. soft butter
125 mL white sugar	½ cup white sugar
175 mL flour	¾ cup flour
10 mL baking powder	2 tsps. baking powder
125 mL milk	½ cup milk

For Syrup:

Combine ingredients in 2 L (2 qt.) saucepan. Boil together until it is of syrup consistency.

For Batter:

Grease cake pan. Cream butter and white sugar together. Sift flour and baking powder together. Add alternately with milk to creamed mixture, beginning and ending with flour mixture. Pour batter into greased cake pan and bake. Serve syrup over top of cake.

CHOCOLATE SAUCE

Metric	Standard
1 L saucepan	1 qt. saucepan
Yield: 400 mL	1½ cups
Ingredients:	
375 mL sugar	1½ cups sugar
125 mL cocoa	½ cup cocoa
pinch of salt	pinch of salt
250 mL water	1 cup water
2 mL vanilla	½ tsp. vanilla

Combine sugar, cocoa, salt and mix well. Add water and stir. Bring to boil and cook for three minutes, stirring. Remove from heat, add vanilla. Store in refrigerator. Use as sauce oven pudding, ice cream or as base for chocolate milk.

CRANBERRY SAUCE

Metric	Standard
2 L saucepan	2 qt. saucepan
Yield: about 1 L	1 quart
Ingredients:	
500 mL sugar	2 cups sugar
500 mL water	2 cups water
1 L cranberries	4 cups cranberries

Combine sugar and water and boil for 5 minutes. Add cranberries and cook for another 5 minutes. Serve hot or cold with poultry. An excellent sauce.

CUSTARD SAUCE

Metric	Standard
2 L saucepan	2 qt. saucepan
Yield: about 1 L	1 qt.
Ingredients:	
750 mL milk	3 cups milk
3 eggs	3 eggs
125 mL sugar	½ cup sugar
5 mL vanilla	1 tsp. vanilla

Bring milk to boil. Beat eggs and sugar. Add egg mixture to boiling milk, stir. Bring just to boiling point but do not let come to full rolling boil. Remove from heat. Add vanilla, stir. Serve hot or cold over puddings, cakes or fruit.

WAFFLE SAUCE

Metric	*Standard*
1 L saucepan	1 qt. saucepan
Yield: about 500 mL	2 cups

Ingredients:

50 mL sugar	¼ cup sugar
30 mL cornstarch	2 tbsps. cornstarch
dash of salt	dash of salt
500 mL milk	2 cups milk
5 mL vanilla	1 tsp. vanilla

Combine dry ingredients. Stir in milk and cook till thick, stirring constantly. Add vanilla and serve with waffles.

Notes

JAMS, PICKLES, CANNING

RHUBARB JAM

Metric	Standard
Yield: 1.5 L	6 cups

Ingredients:

1.25 L diced rhubarb	5 cups diced rhubarb
1.25 L sugar	5 cups sugar
125 mL orange juice	½ cup orange juice
15 mL grated orange rind	1 tbsp. grated orange rind
1 pkg. (85 g) strawberry jellow powder	1 pkg. (3 oz.) strawberry jello powder

Combine rhubarb, sugar, orange juice and orange rind and boil for three to five minutes. Remove from heat and add strawberry jello powder. Stir till jello crystals are dissolved. Pour into hot sterilized jars. Seal with melted wax or cover with lids and seal in steamer for 10-15 minutes. Store in cool, dark, dry place.

BLUEBERRY RHUBARB JAM

Metric	Standard
Yield: 2 L	2 qts.

Ingredients:

2 L blueberries mashed	2 qts. blueberries mashed
1 L finely cut rhubarb	1 qt. finely cut rhubarb
1.5 L sugar	1½ qts. sugar
1 pkg. (85 g) strawberry jello	1 pkg. (3 oz.) strawberry jello

Stir fruit and sugar together. Boil for about 15 minutes. Remove from heat and add strawberry jello, stir thoroughly. Pour into sterilized jars; cover with lids. Let cool and freeze. A tasty jam of good consistency.

QUICK STRAWBERRY JAM

Metric	Standard
Yield: 1.25 L	5 cups

Ingredients:

1 L mashed strawberries	4 cups mashed strawberries
1 L sugar	4 cups sugar

Combine mashed strawberries and sugar in 3 L (3 qt.) saucepot. Bring to boil and cook for 15 minutes. Stir occasionally. Pour into hot sterilized jars and close. Let stand in cool place for two days, then freeze.

BLUEBERRY OR STRAWBERRY JAM

Metric	Standard
Yield: about 2 L	2 qts.

Ingredients:

1.5 L mashed blueberries	6 cups mashed blueberries
125 mL water	½ cup water
½ lemon and juice	½ lemon and juice
1.5 L sugar	6 cups sugar
½ bottle (85 mL) Certo	½ bottle Certo

Combine mashed blueberries and water. Squeeze ½ lemon, add peel and juice. Cook for about 15 minutes. Add sugar and stir well. Boil till sugar is dissolved, about one minute. Remove from heat, add Certo. Stir and skim foam. Pour into hot sterilized jars, close. Let cool and freeze or seal with melted wax and store in cool dark dry place.

CHOKECHERRY JAM

Metric	Standard
Yield: 1.75-2 L	7-8 cups

Ingredients:

2 L chokecherries	2 qts. chokecherries
500 mL water	2 cups water
2000 mL sugar	8 cups sugar
125 mL liquid Certo	½ cup liquid Certo

Clean and wash chokecherries. Add water and bring to boil. Simmer until cherries pop and flesh comes easily off from pits. Strain through sieve washing chokecherries thoroughly. Rinse leftover pits and skins with water. Add some rinsed water to strained juice to make 1 L (1 qt.) liquid. Combine liquid and sugar. Stir thoroughly bringing juice to boil. Add liquid Certo and bring to boil stirring constantly. Cook at full boil for 60 seconds. Skim off foam. Pour into hot sterilized jars. Seal with melted paraffin wax or cool and freeze. Store in cool dark dry place.

RHUBARB STRAWBERRY JAM

Metric	Standard
Yield: about 2 L	2 qts.

Ingredients:

1.25 L diced rhubarb	5 cups diced rhubarb
1 can (540 mL) crushed pineapple	1 can (19 oz.) crushed pineapple
1250 mL sugar	5 cups sugar

| 2 pkg. (85 g ea.) strawberry jello powder | 2 pkg. (3 oz. ea.) strawberry jello powder |

Combine rhubarb, pineapple and sugar in 4 L (4 qt.) saucepan. Bring to boil and cook for about 15 minutes or until rhubarb is tender. Remove from heat and stir in strawberry jello powder. Stir well till jello crystals are dissolved. Pour into hot sterilized jars. Seal with melted wax or cool and freeze.

STRAWBERRY JAM

Metric	Standard
Yield: 1 L	1 qt.

Ingredients:

1 L strawberries	1 qt. strawberries
boiling water	boiling water
cold water	cold water
750 mL sugar	3 cups sugar
juice of ½ lemon	juice of ½ lemon

Pour boiling water over strawberries for a second, drain. Repeat with cold water, drain. Add ⅓ of sugar. Bring fruit and sugar to a boil and cook for four minutes. Stir to prevent burning. Remove from heat. Add lemon juice and remaining sugar. Return to heat, bring to rolling boil and cook for six minutes. Skim, pour into bowl and let stand 8 to 10 hours. Pour into sterilized jars and seal with wax or freeze (leave 1.5 cm ½'' head space for expansion).

SUPPSEL

Metric	Standard
Yield: 2-2.5 L	2-2.5 qts.

Ingredients:

4 L chokecherries	4 qts. chokecherries
750 mL water	3 cups water
1500-1750 mL sugar	6-7 cups sugar

Combine chokecherries and water. Cook till cherries have popped (15-30 minutes), stirring occasionally. Strain through sieve. Measure and add equal amount of sugar to liquid. Combine and cook for 30 minutes or until mixture slightly thickens, stirring frequently. Pour into hot sterilized jars and close. Store in dry cool dark place.

To Serve:

Pour a little suppsel into plate, dip in bread and enjoy, or serve over cereal. A typical southern Manitoba custom familiar to many.

SUPPSEL

Ingredients:
chokecherries
water
sugar

Wash and clean chokecherries. Just barely cover with water. Bring to boil and simmer until cherries are well cooked, about one hour. Strain cherries and mash to get as much flesh out as possible, leaving pits in strainer. Measure juice; and add equal amount of sugar. Bring to boil and cook for ¾-1 hour. Stir frequently. Pour into hot sterilized jars. Cover with saran wrap and place elastic around it. Store in cool dark, dry place or freeze. Suppsel should have runny consistency like syrup. Pour into plate and dip bread into it. A traditional southern Manitoba jam.

PEACH AND ORANGE MARMALADE

Metric	*Standard*
Yield: about 3.5 L	3.5 qts.

Ingredients:

20 peaches	20 peaches
3 oranges	3 oranges
12 maraschino cherries	12 maraschino cherries
sugar	sugar
10 mL almond flavoring	2 tsps. almond flavoring

Wash, but do not peel fruit. Cut in quarters, remove pits and seeds. Put through food chopper. Measure pulp into preserving bottle. Add equal amount of sugar. Boil for about 20 minutes or until jam-like consistency. Do not overcook. Add almond flavoring. Pour into hot sterilized jars and seal with wax or cool and freeze. An excellent marmalade.

PINEAPPLE APRICOT MARMALADE

Metric	*Standard*
Yield: 4 L	4 qts.

Ingredients:

1 kg dried apricots	2 lbs. dried apricots
2 oranges	2 oranges
1 lemon	1 lemon
2 cans (398 mL each) crushed pineapple	2 cans (14 oz. each) crushed pineapple

| 875 mL sugar | 3½ cups sugar |
| water | water |

Pour boiling water over dried apricots and let stand 8-10 hours. Drain and save juice. Squeeze juice from oranges and lemon and save. Put drained apricots, orange and lemon peels through food chopper. Add crushed pineapple and sugar. Combine drained juices and add water up to 875 mL (3½ cups). Add liquid to fruit pulp and bring to boil. Simmer for about 15 minutes or until thickened. Stir occasionally. Pour into hot sterilized jars and seal with melted wax. Jars may also be sealed by steaming 15-20 minutes in canner.

HEAVENLY MARMALADE

| *Metric* | *Standard* |
| Yield: 3 L | 3 qts. |

Ingredients:

3 lemons	3 lemons
3 oranges	3 oranges
8 peaches	8 peaches
4 pears	4 pears
6 apples	6 apples
2750 mL sugar	11 cups sugar

Wash fruit. Remove outer thin rind from lemons; cut into strips or grate. Remove edible fruit meats from lemons and oranges. Discard seeds and membranes. Place meat of citrus fruits and prepared rind in bowl and cover with water. Let soak for 8-10 hours. Bring to boil and simmer gently until tender. Remove peel and pits from peaches, pears and apples. Cut in cubes and add to first mixture. Bring to boil adding sugar gradually. Stir until dissolved. Simmer gently for about 15 minutes until mixture thickens as for jam. Pour into hot sterilized jars. Seal with melted wax. Let cool, cover and store in cool, dark, dry place.

PEAR MARMALADE

Metric	*Standard*
Yield: 6 jars (approx. 455 mL ea.)	6 pts.

Ingredients:

1.5 kg unpeeled pears, (cut fine)	3 lbs. unpeeled pears, (cut fine)
3 medium oranges	3 medium oranges
1 can (398 mL) crushed pineapple, drained	1 can (14 oz.) crushed pineapple, drained

Squeeze oranges, remove seeds from juice. Put through a food chopper. Measure 175 mL (²⁄₃ cup) sugar to each 250 mL (1 cup) fruit. Place in saucepan and cook until mixture thickens (15 min.) Pour into hot jars and seal immediately with a layer of melted wax. Let cool and pour another layer of wax over top to seal completely. Cover with a lid and store in a cool dark place **or** close jars and store in freezer. If freezing, leave 2.5 cm (1 in.) head space for expansion.

PEAR MARMALADE

Metric	*Standard*
Yield: about 4 L	4 qts.

Ingredients:

6 oranges	6 oranges
2.5 L pears cut up (not peeled)	10½ cups pears cut up (not peeled)
1 can (398 mL) crushed pineapple	1 can (14 oz.) crushed pineapple
1.75 L sugar (approx.)	7-8 cups sugar (approx.)

Squeeze juice from oranges. Remove pits and put oranges through food chopper. Combine and measure fruit into 6 L (6 qt.) pot. Add 175 mL (²⁄₃ cup) sugar for each 250 mL (1 cup) of fruit. Cook for about one hour or until thickened. Stir occasionally. Cool and stir occasionally to mix fruit throughout. Pour into jars and seal with melted wax.

Note:

Hot marmalade may also be poured into hot sterilized jars and sealed in canner for 15-20 minutes.

RHUBARB MARMALADE

Metric	*Standard*
Yield: About 2 L	2 qts.

Ingredients:

2 oranges	2 oranges
1 lemon	1 lemon
1.5 L diced rhubarb	6 cups diced rhubarb
1.5 L sugar	6 cups sugar
pinch of salt	pinch of salt
250 mL raisins	1 cup raisins

Squeeze juice from oranges and lemon. Peel rind thinly from fruit. Discard white membrane and pulp. Sliver rind and combine with juice in 3 L (3 qt.) saucepan. Add diced rhubarb, sugar and salt. Stir over medium heat until sugar is dissolved. Add raisins and bring to boil. Cook over medium heat until thick, about four to five minutes. Skim and pour into hot sterilized jars. Seal with melted wax, let cool. Cover and store in cool, dark, dry place. Marmalade may also be sealed by steaming closed jars in canner for a few minutes.

APRICOT JAM

Metric	*Standard*
Yield: 1.75-2 L	7-8 cups

Ingredients:

1.5 L quartered pitted apricots	6 cups quartered pitted apricots
875 mL sugar	3½ cups sugar
30 mL lemon juice	2 tbsps. lemon juice
6 peeled chopped apricot pits	6 peeled chopped apricot pits

Combine all ingredients. Let stand for one hour. Boil for 10 minutes, stirring occasionally. If jam is fairly thin add 15 mL (1 tbsp.) liquid Certo. Boil for two more minutes. Pour into hot sterilized jars. Seal with melted wax or cool and freeze.

APRICOT JAM

Metric	*Standard*

Ingredients:

any amount apricots
sugar

Pit and cook apricots until soft. Stir frequently. Measure apricot pulp and add sugar, half the amount of apricot pulp. Cook for 10 minutes, stirring frequently. Pour hot into sterilized jars. Seal with melted wax or cool and freeze.

Variation:

Peaches may be substituted but should be peeled and mashed before cooking. For sweeter jam add equal amount of sugar to fruit.

WILD PLUM JAM

Metric	Standard
Yield: 2-2.5 L	Approx. 16-17 cups

Ingredients:

4 L wild plums	4 qts. wild plums
250 mL water	1 cup water
sugar	sugar

Boil plums in water till plums are all broken. Remove most pits as they rise to top. As soon as plums are broken measure pulp and add equal amount of sugar. Boil for another half hour, stirring frequently. Do not overcook — destroys colour and flavour. Pour into hot sterilized jars. Cover jars with lids or seal with melted wax. Store in cool place.

Note:

Less sugar may be used if a tart jam is desired.

WILD PLUM JAM

Metric	Standard
Yield: 5 jars (455 mL each)	5 pt. jars

Ingredients:

1.25 L wild plums	5 cups wild plums
1 L water	1 qt. water
10 mL baking soda	2 tsp. baking soda
125 mL water	½ cup water
1000 mL sugar	4 cups sugar

Combine plums, water and baking soda in 4 L (4 qt.) pot. Bring to boil and cook for two to three minutes. Pour off water and rinse fruit well. Return fruit and 125 mL (½ cup) water to pot. Cook until very tender. Remove pits as they rise to the surface. Add sugar and cook, stirring almost constantly until jam is thick and clear (about 20 minutes). Pour into hot sterilized jars. Seal with melted wax. When cooled and sealed, close with lid and store in cool, dark, dry place.

CHOW CHOW

Metric	Standard
Yield: Approx. 12 jars (455 mL each)	12 pt. jars

Ingredients:

3.5 kg green tomatoes (25 medium sized)	8 lbs. green tomatoes (25 medium sized)

2000 mL sugar	8 cups sugar
1 L white vinegar	4 cups white vinegar
50 mL pickling salt	3 tbsps. pickling salt
50 mL ground cloves	3 tbsps. ground cloves
50 mL cinnamon (optional)	3 tbsps. cinnamon (optional)
5 mL mace	1 tsp. mace

Put tomatoes through food chopper. Add sugar, white vinegar and pickling salt. Bring to boil and simmer for three hours in open kettle. (Mixture should be fairly thick.) Add ground spices and boil for 15 minutes. Pour into hot sterilized jars. Close immediately to seal.

CARROT SWEET PICKLES

Metric	*Standard*
Yield: 2 jars (909 mL each)	2 qt. jars

Ingredients:

2 L small carrots	2 qts. small carrots
1 L water	4 cups water
15 mL pickling salt	1 tbsp. pickling salt
500 mL white vinegar	2 cups white vinegar
1000 mL sugar	4 cups sugar
7 mL pickling spice	1½ tsps. pickling spice

Scrape small carrots. Combine with water and pickling salt in 4 L (4 qt.) saucepan. Boil for 10 minutes till not quite tender. Combine remaining ingredients and boil briefly. Drain carrots and place in hot sterilized jars. Pour boiling brine over carrots and close jars immediately to seal.

WATERMELON PICKLES

Metric	*Standard*
Yield: 6 jars (909 mL ea.)	6 qts.

Ingredients:

Watermelon chunks to fill 6 jars	Watermelon chunks to fill 6 qt. jars
500 mL sugar	2 cups sugar
250 mL white vinegar	1 cup white vinegar
125 mL pickling salt	½ cup pickling salt
1-2 sprigs dill/jar	1-2 sprigs dill/qt.

Cut watermelon and place in clean sterilized jars; add dill. Combine ingredients for brine and bring to a boil. Cook 5 mins. Pour over watermelon. Close and steam 10-15 min. in hot water bath canner to seal.

BEET PICKLES

Metric	Standard
Yield: 4 jars (455 mL each)	4 pts.

Ingredients:

2 L beets	2 qts. beets
375 mL white vinegar	1½ cups white vinegar
375 mL white **or** brown sugar	1½ cups white **or** brown sugar
375 mL water	1½ cups water
(from cooked beets)	(from cooked beets)
50 mL pickling spice	¼ cup pickling or
or whole cloves	or whole cloves

Wash beets. Cut off leaves and roots leaving 2.5 cm (1 in.) at each end. Cover with water and boil until soft, (but not overcooked), when tested with fork. Drain, reserving water. Pour cold water over beets to cool. Peel and cut off ends. Cube or slice. Place into clean sterilized jars. Combine remaining ingredients, bring to a boil, and pour over beets. Close jars and seal in water bath canner for 5 min. at a full boil.

EIGHT DAY PICKLED ONIONS

Metric	Standard
Yield: 6-7 jars (455 mL each)	6-7 pts.

Ingredients:

4 L small pickling onions	4 qts. small pickling onions
125 mL pickling salt	½ cup pickling salt
1 L sugar	4 cups sugar
50 mL pickling spices	¼ cup pickling spices
(tied in bag)	(tied in bag)
1 L white cider vinegar	4 cups white cider vinegar
5 mL alum	1 tsp. alum

Peel onions and place in crock. Sprinkle with ½ cup (125 mL) pickling salt and cover with boiling water. Let stand 24 hours. Drain. Repeat for 6 days using ½ cup salt every day.

Day 7: Wash onions in water. Return to crock and sprinkle with alum. Cover with boiling water.

Day 8: Wash onions in water, pack into clean sterilized 500 mL (1 pt.) sealers. Combine remaining ingredients, bring to a boil and pour over onions. Seal.

DILL PICKLES

Metric	*Standard*
100-110°C	200-250°F
11-15 min.	
Yield: 4-5 jars	4-5 2 qt. jars
(1818 mL each)	

Ingredients:

8 kg small fresh cucumbers	16-17 lbs. small fresh cucumbers
1 bunch of dill	1 bunch of dill
4-5 hot peppers	4-5 hot peppers
4-5 pieces horseradish	4-5 pieces horseradish
4-5 cloves garlic (optional)	4-5 cloves garlic (optional)
4 L cold water	4 qts. cold water
250 or 500 mL white vinegar	1 or 2 cups white vinegar
250 mL pickling salt	1 cup pickling salt
alum	alum

Place cucumbers in cold water for 4-5 hours to freshen. Put a little dill into each jar. Pack with cucumbers. Add **one** hot pepper, piece horseradish and clove garlic to each jar. Sprinkle 0.5 mL (⅛ tsp.) alum over each filled jar. Combine cold water, white vinegar and pickling salt and bring to a boil. Pour brine over cucumbers. Close jars and steam in water bath canner in oven at low heat till cucumbers change colour.

Caution:

It is safer to steam cucumbers in water bath canner.

DILL PICKLES

Metric	*Standard*
Yield: Approx. 7 jars	7 qt. jars
(909 mL each)	

Ingredients:

8 L small or medium green cucumbers	8 qts. small or medium green cucumbers
7 small bunches dill	7 small bunches dill
3 L water	3 qts. water
1 L vinegar	1 qt. vinegar
250 mL pickling salt	1 cup pickling salt

Wash cucumbers well. Let stand in cold water for one hour to harden. Place a bunch of dill in bottom of each jar. Dry and pack cucumbers in sealers. Combine water, vinegar and pickling salt and bring to boil. Cool slightly and pour over cucumbers. Close and steam in canner for a few minutes, until cucumbers discolour.

DILL PICKLES

Metric	Standard
Yield: 8 jars (909 mL each)	8 qt. jars.

Ingredients:

Metric	Standard
3½-5 L small cucumbers	4-6 qts. small cucumbers
8 small pieces horseradish	8 small pieces horseradish
8 bay leaves	8 bay leaves
8 small bunches fresh dill	8 small bunches fresh dill
3 L water	3 qts. water
500-750 mL white vinegar	2-3 cups white vinegar
175 mL pickling salt	¾ cup pickling salt
175 mL sugar	¾ cup sugar
15 mL pickling spice	1 tbsp. pickling spice
5 mL celery seed or	1 tsp. celery seed or
2 mL black pepper and	½ tsp. black pepper and
2 mL celery seed	½ tsp. celery seed

Wash and dry cucumbers, pack tightly into jars. Add piece of horseradish, bayleaf, and small bunches of fresh dill to each. Combine remaining ingredients and bring to boil. Cool slightly and pour over cucumbers. Close jars and heat in steamer for about 5 minutes, or until cucumbers discolour.

COLD DILL PICKLES

Metric	Standard
Yield: 2 jars (909 mL each)	2 qt. jars

Ingredients:

Metric	Standard
50 mL pickling salt	3 tbsp. pickling salt
500 mL cold water	2 cups cold water
250 mL white vinegar	1 cup white vinegar
2 small bunches fresh dill	2 small bunches fresh dill
2 hot peppers	2 hot peppers
2 green pappers, sliced	2 green peppers, sliced
1½-2 L small cucumbers	2 qts. small cucumbers

Combine salt, cold water and white vinegar, stir until dissolved. Place bunch of dill, one hot pepper and one green pepper in each jar. Pack with small cucumbers. Pour cold brine over cucumbers. Close jars and wait a few days before serving dills.

Variation:

Dills may be steamed in canner to seal. Do not double or increase recipe, use given quantities.

CHOPPED PICKLES

Metric	Standard
Yield: 6 jars (909 mL each)	6 qt. jars

Ingredients:

1 L onions	1 qt. onions
2 L cucumbers	2 qts. cucumbers
1 medium head cauliflower	1 medium head cauliflower
3 large sweet red peppers	3 large sweet red peppers
2 large celery stalks	2 large celery stalks
6 medium sized apples	6 medium sized apples
4 L water	4 qts. water
125 mL pickling salt	½ cup pickling salt
1500 mL white vinegar	6 cups white vinegar
25 mL mustard seed	1½ tbsps. mustard seed
25 mL cloves	1½ tbsps. cloves
125 mL flour	½ cup flour
30 mL turmeric	2 tbsps. turmeric
15 mL dry mustard	1 tbsp. dry mustard
1250 mL brown sugar	5 cups brown sugar

Put onions through food chopper. Chop remaining vegetables and apples finely by hand. Combine water and pickling salt. Heat until salt is dissolved. Pour over vegetables and let stand for 8-10 hours. Drain vegetables well, discard liquid. Add vinegar to chopped vegetables, boil for ½ hour. Add mustard seed and cloves. Mix flour with a little cold water, add. Mix in remaining ingredients. Boil for 20 minutes. Pour into hot sterilized jars and close immediately to seal.

SWEET PICKLES

Metric	Standard
Yield: 6 jars (455 mL each)	6 pt. jars

Ingredients:

4 L sliced cucumbers	4 qts. sliced cucumbers
pickling salt	pickling salt
750 mL sugar	3 cups sugar
750 mL white vinegar	3 cups white vinegar
250 mL water	1 cup water
30 mL pickling spice	2 tbsps. pickling spice

Sprinkle sliced cucumbers lightly with salt. Let stand 8-10 hours. Drain and discard liquid. Combine remaining ingredients and boil for a few minutes. Strain and reheat brine. Scoop sliced, drained cucumbers into jars. Cover with boiling brine. Close jars and steam in canner for a few minutes until cucumbers turn colour.

SWEET PICKLES

Metric	Standard
Ingredients:	
4 L small to medium cucumbers	4 qts. small to medium cucumbers
2.25 L ice water	9 cups ice water
250 mL pickling salt	1 cup pickling salt
15 mL alum	1 tbsp. alum
1250 L sugar	5 cups sugar
1 L white vinegar	4 cups vinegar
500 mL water	2 cups water
30 mL pickling spice	2 tbsps. pickling spice

Wash and clean cucumbers. Make a solution of ice water, pickling salt and alum. Pour over cucumbers and let soak for 8-10 hours. Rinse and drain well and slice cucumbers into jars. Combine remaining ingredients and boil for a few minutes. Cool slightly and pour over sliced cucumbers. Close jars. Steam in canner for a few minutes or until cucumbers discolor.

PICKLES

Metric	Standard
Yield: 1 jar (909 mL)	1 qt. jar
Ingredients:	
two onion slices	two onion slices
sprig dill	sprig dill
about 750 mL cucumbers	about 1 qt. cucumbers
250 mL vinegar	1 cup vinegar
250 mL sugar	1 cup sugar
15 mL pickling salt	1 tbsp. pickling salt
1 mL celery seed	¼ tsp. celery seed
1 mL mustard seed	¼ tsp. mustard seed

Place onion slices and sprig dill in sterilized jar. Slice cucumbers thinly and pack into jar. Combine remaining ingredients and boil for three to four minutes. Pour hot syrup over thinly sliced cucumbers. Close jars and seal by steaming in hot water bath canner for about five minutes.

MUSTARD PICKLES

Metric	Standard
Yield: about 7 jars (455 mL each)	7 pt. jars

Ingredients:

18 large cucumbers	18 large cucumbers
6 L cold water	6-7 qts. cold water
750 mL pickling salt	3 cups pickling salt
5 mL turmeric	1 tsp. turmeric
5 mL dry mustard	1 tsp. dry mustard
45 mL flour	3 tbsp. flour
250 mL sugar	1 cup sugar
500 mL vinegar	2 cups white vinegar

Peel and slice cucumbers. Mix cold water and pickling salt. Pour over sliced cucumbers and let stand for 8-10 hours. Rinse two or three times with fresh water and drain well. Mix turmeric, dry mustard, flour, and sugar. Combine with vinegar in 6 L (6 qt.) preserving kettle. Heat and stir until thick. Add well drained sliced cucumbers. Heat to scalding point. Scoop into hot sterilized jars and close immediately to seal. Store in dark cool dry place.

MUSTARD PICKLES

Metric	*Standard*
Yield: About 18 jars (455 mL each)	18 pt. jars

Ingredients:

2 L small cucumbers	2 qts. small cucumbers
2 L small onions	2 qts. small onions
2 L green tomatoes (optional)	2 qts. green tomatoes (optional)
2-3 heads cauliflower	2-3 heads cauliflower
1 bunch celery	1 bunch celery
6 sweet green peppers	6 sweet green peppers
6 sweet red peppers	6 sweet red peppers
500 mL pickling salt	2 cups pickling salt
375 mL white sugar	1½ cups white sugar
375 mL brown sugar	1½ cups brown sugar
125 mL flour	½ cup flour
30 mL turmeric	2 tbsps. turmeric
375 mL dry mustard	1½ cups dry mustard
50 mL prepared mustard	¼ cup prepared mustard
3.5 L white vinegar	3½ qts. white vinegar

Cut vegetables into desired size. Mix and sprinkle pickling salt over top. Cover with cold water and let stand 8-10 hours. Drain well and rinse in cold water, drain well. Combine remaining ingredients. Bring to boiling point. Add cut, well drained vegetables. Let come to boil Scoop into hot, sterilized jars and close immediately to seal.

MUSTARD PICKLES

Metric	Standard
Yield: 3-4 jars (909 mL each)	3-4 qt. jars

Ingredients:

8 large cucumbers, sliced	8 large cucumbers, sliced
1 L onions, sliced	1 qt. onions, sliced
30 mL pickling salt	2 tbsps. pickling salt
cold water	cold water
30 mL flour	2 tbsps. flour
500 mL white vinegar	2 cups white vinegar
500 mL sugar	2 cups sugar
15 mL turmeric	1 tbsp. turmeric
15 mL dry mustard	1 tbsp. dry mustard
2 mL celery seed	½ tsp. celery seed

Sprinkle pickling salt over sliced cucumbers and onions, add cold water to cover. Let stand for 8-10 hours. Drain and rinse with fresh water once. Place in 6 L (6 qt.) pot, cover with a little water and boil for a few minutes, drain, mix flour with part of vinegar to make a smooth paste. Add remaining ingredients and mix well. Combine with drained sliced cucumbers and onions. Bring to boil. Pour into hot sterilized jars, close to seal.

Optional:

Steam in canner for about five minutes to seal.

PARTY PICKLES

Metric	Standard
Yield: 10 jars (455 mL each)	10 pt. jars

Ingredients:

6 large carrots	6 large carrots
3 red peppers	3 red peppers
3 green peppers	3 green peppers
½ head cauliflower	½ head cauliflower
cucumbers	cucumbers
250 mL salt	1 cup salt
1500 mL sugar	6 cups sugar
875 mL vinegar	3½ cups vinegar
15 mL celery seed	1 tbsp. celery seed
15 mL mustard seed	1 tbsp. mustard seed
10 mL turmeric	2 tsps. turmeric

Cut first four vegetables in desired shape and size, e.g.: sticks, coins. Measure and cut equal amount of cucumber sticks. Sprinkle cucumbers with salt. Let stand for about three hours. Drain cucumbers and combine all ingredients and steam for about 10 minutes. DO NOT OVERCOOK. Scoop into hot sterilized jars and close. No steaming needed to seal.

OVERCOOK. Scoop into hot sterilized jars and close. No steaming needed to seal.

ICICLE PICKLES

Metric	*Standard*
Yield: 9 jars (455 mL each)	9 pt. jars

Ingredients:

2 L peeled sliced cucumbers	2 qts. peeled sliced cucumbers
1.5 L sliced onions	6 cups sliced onions
1.5 L celery sticks (2 cm)	6 cups celery sticks (1 in.)
750 mL white vinegar	3 cups white vinegar
500 mL water	2 cups water
250 mL sugar	1 cup sugar
50 mL pickling salt	¼ cup pickling salt

Cover peeled sliced cucumbers with ice water. Let stand for two hours. Drain cucumbers and mix with vegetables. Pack lightly into hot sterilized jars. Bring to boil remaining ingredients. Fill jars with brine and close. Let jars stand until brine is cold before sealing in water-bath canner. (Place jars in lukewarm water in canner and heat.)

Option:

Seal some jars immediately in boiling water bath. (Approx. 5 minutes.)

BREAD AND BUTTER PICKLES

Metric	*Standard*
Yield: 4 jars (909 mL each) ı)	4 qt. jars

Ingredients:

5-6 L medium cucumbers	5-6 qts. medium cucumbers
12 onions or less	12 onions or less
1 L white vinegar	1 qt. white vinegar
750 mL sugar	3 cups sugar
125 mL pickling salt	½ cup pickling salt
10 mL mustard seed	2 tsps. mustard seed
10 mL celery seed	2 tsps. celery seed
10 mL ginger	2 tsps. ginger
5 mL turmeric	1 tsp. turmeric

Seal cucumbers in ice water for four hours. Slice (without) peeling. Slice onions and put with cucumbers into 6 L (6 qt.) preserving kettle along with remaining ingredients. Bring to boil and cook for three minutes. Pour into hot sterilized jars and close to seal. To ensure sealing place jars in canner and boil for about five minutes.

MILLION DOLLAR PICKLES

Metric	Standard
Yield: 6 jars (455 mL each)	6 pt. jars

Ingredients:

24 medium cucumbers	24 medium cucumbers
12 large onions	12 large onions
125 mL pickling salt	½ cup pickling salt
1 L white vinegar	4 cups white vinegar
1 L sugar	4 cups sugar
20 mL turmeric	4 tsps. turmeric
20 mL celery seed	4 tsps. celery seed
20 mL dry mustard	4 tsps. dry mustard
green peppers **or**	green peppers **or**
pimentos (optional)	pimentos (optional)

Slice unpeeled cucumbers and onions. Sprinkle with pickling salt. Let stand for 8-10 hours. Drain and combine with remaining ingredients. Bring to boil and cook until tender. Scoop into hot sterilized jars. Close immediately to seal.

SIX-DAY PICKLES

Metric	Standard
Yield: 5 jars (455 mL each)	5 pt. jars

Ingredients:

250 mL pickling salt	1 cup pickling salt
4 L boiling water	4 qts. boiling water
4 L small cucumbers	4 qts. small cucumbers
cold water	cold water
1 L white vinegar	1 qt. white vinegar
1 L water	1 qt. water
1500 mL sugar	6 cups sugar
15 mL pickling spice	1 tbsp. pickling spice

DAY 1:

Boil salt and water. Pour over small cucumbers and let stand overnight.

DAY 2:

Drain and rinse with cold water; discard liquid. Combine white vinegar, water, 500 mL (2 cups) sugar and pickling spice. Bring to boil and pour over small cucumbers. Let stand overnight.

DAY 3:

Drain and save brine. Add 250 mL (1 cup) sugar to brine. Boil and pour over small cucumbers. Let stand overnight.

DAY 4:

Same as Day 3.

DAY 5:
Same as Day 3.
DAY 6:
Drain and save brine. Add 250 mL (1 cup) sugar to brine; boil. Pack small cucumbers in jars. Pour brine over cucumbers and close jars. Steam in canner for about five minutes or until cucumbers turn colour.

TOMATO PICKLES

Metric	*Standard*
Yield: 13 jars (455 mL each)	13 pts.

Ingredients:

20 large ripe tomatoes	20 large ripe tomatoes
4 onions	4 onions
4 apples	4 apples
2 sweet red peppers	2 sweet red peppers
2 sweet green peppers	2 sweet green peppers
1 bunch celery	1 bunch celery
500 mL white vinegar	2 cups white vinegar
150 mL sugar	⅔ cup sugar
25 mL salt	1½ tbsps. salt
90 mL flour	6 tbsps. flour

Wash vegetables and apples. Chop vegetables, apples and onions fine. Mix with vinegar, sugar and salt. Boil 1½ hours. Mix flour with a little cold water. Add to hot mixture and bring to boil to thicken. Pour into hot sterilized jars. Close immediately to seal.

CHOW CHOW

Metric	*Standard*
Yield: 8 jars (455 mL each)	8 pt. jars

Ingredients:

4 L green tomatoes cubed	4 qts. green tomatoes cubed
1 L sliced onions	1 qt. sliced onions
75 mL salt	⅓ cup salt
750 mL white vinegar	3 cups vinegar
750 mL sugar	3 cups sugar
25 mL mixed pickling spice	1½ tbsps. mixed pickling spice

Sprinkle salt over cubed tomatoes and sliced onions. Let stand for a few hours. Drain and discard liquid. Add vinegar and sugar to vegetables. Put spices in cloth bag and add. Bring to a boil and cook for 15 minutes. Remove spice bag. Pour chow chow into hot sterilized jars; close. Seal in hot water bath for 5 minutes.

GREEN TOMATO PICKLES

Metric	Standard
Yield: 4 jars (455 mL each)	3-4 pt. jars.

Ingredients:

Metric	Standard
5 L cut green tomatoes	5 qts. cut green tomatoes
500 mL chopped celery	2 cups chopped celery
1 chopped green pepper	1 chopped green pepper
3 L cold water	3 qts. cold water
45 mL salt	3 tbsps. salt
750 mL vinegar	3 cups vinegar
500 mL brown sugar	2 cups brown sugar
5 mL cinnamon	1 tsp. cinnamon
1 mL cloves	¼ tsp. cloves
1 mL turmeric	¼ tsp. turmeric

Combine vegetables. Mix cold water and salt and pour over vegetables. Soak for a few hours. Combine remaining ingredients and bring to a boil. Drain vegetables and add to hot brine. Bring to boil and simmer for 2-3 hours. Mixture should be fairly thick. Stir frequently. Pour boiling mixture into hot sterilized jars and close immediately, to seal.

NINE-DAY CUCUMBER PICKLES

Metric	Standard
Yield: 8 jars (909 mL each)	8 qt. jars

Ingredients:

Metric	Standard
28 10 cm very thin cucumbers	28 4 in. very thin cucumbers
2 L white vinegar	2 qts. white vinegar
4 L sugar	4 qts. sugar
50 mL pickling salt	¼ cup pickling salt
15 mL whole cloves	1 tbsp. whole cloves
15 mL whole allspice	1 tbsp. whole allspice
1 stick (7 cm) cinnamon	1 stick (3 in.) cinnamon

Wash whole cucumbers and arrange in crock. Cover with fresh boiling water. Let stand for 24 hours. Drain cucumbers and repeat for three more days. On fifth day, drain cucumbers and slice very thin. Combine white vinegar, sugar, and pickling salt. Tie whole cloves, whole allspice, and stick cinnamon in spice bag. Place in vinegar mixture and bring to boil. Pour syrup over thinly sliced cucumbers. Let stand 24 hours. Drain cucumbers and reheat syrup with spice bag. Repeat for four more days. On ninth day, pack cucumbers in hot sterile jars. Cover with boiling syrup. Discard bag with spices. Close jars. Seal in canner for about five minutes at full boil (optional).

NOTE:

Cucumbers are more attractive if green colouring is added to the syrup while still boiling.

16-DAY SWEET PICKLES

Metric	*Standard*
Yield: 7 jars (909 mL each)	7 qt. jars

Ingredients:

8 L whole medium cucumbers	2 gal. whole medium cucumbers
16 L water	16 qts. water
500 mL pickling salt	2 cups pickling salt
45 mL alum	3 tbsps. alum
2750 mL sugar	11 cups sugar
1.5 L white vinegar	6 cups white vinegar
325 mL pickling spice	1⅓ cups pickling spice
15 mL celery seed	1 tbsp. celery seed
5 mL turmeric	1 tsp. turmeric

DAY 1:

Wash and put whole cucumbers in crock or canner. Boil 4 L (4 qts.) water and 500 mL (2 cups) pickling spice. Pour over cucumbers and let stand for seven days.

DAY 8:

Drain and wash cucumbers, cut in slices. Mix 4 L (4 qts.) water and 15 mL (1 tbsp.) alum. Boil and pour over cucumbers. Let stand for one day.

DAY 9:

Drain cucumbers, discarding brine. Prepare fresh brine as on previous day and pour over cucumbers.

DAY 11:

Drain cucumbers, discarding brine. Combine 1500 mL (6 cups) sugar and white vinegar. Place spices in spice bag and add to vinegar solution. Bring to boil and pour on cucumbers. Save spice bag.

DAY 12:

Drain cucumbers, save brine. Add 250 mL (1 cup) sugar and spice bag to brine. Bring to boil. Pour on cucumbers. Remove and save spice bag.

DAY 13, 14, 15:

Repeat as on Day 12.

DAY 16:

Drain cucumbers, save brine. Pack cucumbers in clean sterilized jars. Add 250 mL (1 cup) sugar, 5 mL (1 tsp.) turmeric and spice bag to brine. Bring to boil, remove spice bag. Pour hot syrup on cucumbers. Close jars. To seal, heat jars in hot water bath for a few minutes.

TOMATO RELISH

Metric	*Standard*
Yield: 2 L	2 qts.

Ingredients:

8 L ripe tomatoes	8 qts. ripe tomatoes
500 mL onions, cut fine	2 cups onions, cut fine
500 mL celery, cut fine	2 cups celery, cut fine
4 red peppers, pitted, cut fine	4 red peppers, pitted, cut fine
4 green peppers, pitted, cut fine	4 green peppers, pitted, cut fine
1 L vinegar	4 cups vinegar
1 L sugar	4 cups sugar
125 mL pickling salt	½ cup pickling salt
125 mL mustard seed	½ cup mustard seed

Peel and chop tomatoes. Drain overnight in a sack. Next morning squeeze dry and add remaining ingredients. Mix well. Pour into clean sterilized jars. Close and refrigerate. Requires no cooking.

Note:

Juice from tomatoes may be canned or used in soup.

UNCOOKED TOMATO RELISH

Metric	*Standard*
Yield: 2 L	2 qts.

Ingredients:

1.5 L red tomatoes	3 lbs. red tomatoes
3 large onions	3 large onions
500 g celery, cut fine	1 lb. celery cut fine
30 mL mustard seed	2 tbsps. mustard seed
30 mL celery seed	2 tbsps. celery seed
175 mL white cider vinegar	⅔ cup white cider vinegar
1.5 L sugar	6 cups sugar

Combine vinegar and sugar. Add spices and celery and peppers; mix well. Combine drained tomatoes and onions; add to vinegar, sugar, spices and celery. Pour into jars and close. Keeps in the refrigerator for 3-4 months. Very tasty with hamburger, hot dogs, etc.

LINDBERGH RELISH

Metric	*Standard*
Yield: 6 jars (909 mL each)	6 qt. jars

Ingredients:

Metric	Standard
2 medium heads cabbage	2 medium heads cabbage
8 medium carrots	8 medium carrots
4 red peppers	4 red peppers
12 medium onions	12 medium onions
125 mL pickling salt	½ cup pickling salt
750 mL white vinegar	3 cups white vinegar
1500 mL sugar	6 cups sugar
5 mL celery seed	1 tsp. celery seed
5 mL mustard seed	1 tsp. mustard seed
4 green peppers	4 green peppers

Grind vegetables in meat chopper or shred. Add pickling salt. Mix and let stand for two hours. Drain well and add remaining ingredients. Mix well and scoop into jars and close. Refrigerate or seal jars. Should be used within a few months.

HOT DOG RELISH

Metric	Standard
Yield: 5 jars (455 mL each)	5 pt. jars

Ingredients:

Metric	Standard
20 medium cucumbers	20 medium cucumbers
2 green peppers	2 green peppers
5 medium onions	5 medium onions
125 mL salt	½ cup salt
500 mL brown sugar	2 cups brown sugar
500 mL vinegar	2 cups vinegar
30 mL celery seed	2 tbsps. celery seed
30 mL mustard seed	2 tbsps. mustard seed
1 hot chili pepper	1 hot chili pepper
1 can (200 mL) pimento	1 can (7 oz.) pimento

Put cucumbers, peppers and onions through food chopper or blender. Sprinkle salt over vegetables and let stand 8-10 hours. Drain and discard liquid. In 2 L (2 qt.) saucepan, combine remaining ingredients, except pimento. Bring to a boil and cook for 10 minutes. Remove spices. Add strained vegetables and finely chopped pimento. Heat to boiling. Scoop into hot sterilized jars and close immediately to seal.

BEET RELISH

Metric	Standard
Yield: 3 jars (455 mL each)	3 pts.

Ingredients:

1 L diced cooked beets	4 cups diced cooked beets
2 hot red peppers chopped	2 hot red peppers chopped
75 mL chopped onion	⅓ cup chopped onion
30 mL salt	2 tsps. salt
50 mL prepared horseradish	¼ cup prepared horseradish
500 mL vinegar	2 cups vinegar
175 mL sugar	⅔ cup sugar

Combine all ingredients in 2 L (2 qt.) saucepan. Bring to boil and simmer 10 minutes stirring occasionally. Pour into clean sterilized jars and seal.

RHUBARB RELISH

Metric	Standard
Yield: 2-3 L	2-3 qt.

Ingredients:

1 L finely cut rhubarb	1 qt. finely cut rhubarb
1 L finely chopped onions	1 qt. finely chopped onion
1 L white vinegar	1 qt. white vinegar
1 L brown sugar	1 qt. brown sugar
5 mL allspice	1 tsp. allspice
5 mL salt	1 tsp. salt
5 mL cinnamon	1 tsp. cinnamon
5 mL pepper	1 tsp. pepper

Combine all ingredients. Bring to boil and cook for one hour, stirring frequently. Pour into hot sterilized jars and close to seal. Serve with hamburgers or other meat.

SANDWICH SPREAD

Metric	Standard
Yield: 6 jars (455 mL each)	6 pt. jars

Ingredients:

14 medium cucumbers	14 medium cucumbers
6 medium onions	6 medium onions
2 green peppers	2 green peppers
2 sweet red peppers	2 sweet red peppers
or pimentos	or pimentos
15 mL salt	3 tsps. salt
250-375 mL white sugar	1-1½ cups white sugar

Dressing:

Metric	Standard
125 mL butter	½ cup butter
375 mL sugar	1-1½ sugar
4 well beaten eggs	4 well beaten eggs
30 mL flour	2 tbsps. flour
5 mL celery seed (in bag)	1 tsp. celery seed (in bag)
10 mL dry mustard	2 tsps. dry mustard
250 mL heavy cream	1 cup heavy cream

Peel and slice cucumbers and onions. Remove seeds from peppers. Put vegetables through coarse food chopper. Sprinkle with salt and let stand for 8-10 hours. Drain well. Place in 1 L (1 qt.) saucepan. Barely cover with vinegar and bring to boil. Combine ingredients for dressing and mix well. Add dressing to vegetables and cook until thick, stirring frequently. Remove celery seed bag. Pour boiling mixture into hot sterilized jars, close to seal. Jars with dressing may also be heated at full boil in canner for about 5 minutes to seal.

CANNED TOMATO SOUP

Metric	*Standard*
Yield: About 9 jars (909 mL each) ·	9 qt. jars

Ingredients:

Metric	Standard
8 L ripe tomatoes	8 qt. ripe tomatoes
1 large bunch celery	1 large bunch celery
6 large onions	6 large onions
1 bunch parsley	1 bunch parsley
125 mL butter	½ cup butter
175-250 mL flour	¾-1 cup flour
125-250 mL sugar	½-1 cup sugar
50-125 mL salt	¼-½ cup salt
1 mL cayenne	¼ tsp. cayenne

Wash and cut vegetables. Boil until very soft. Press through sieve, discard solid parts. Return strained vegetables to heat. In small saucepan melt butter, add flour, sugar, salt and cayenne; stir well. When blended, slowly mix with strained vegetables. Heat to boiling point and let cook till thickened, stirring frequently. Pour into hot sterilized jars and close immediately to seal. A rich tasty soup.

Note:

Larger amounts of flour, sugar and salt yield a thicker, more spicy soup. Use amounts to suit your taste.

CHILI SAUCE

Metric	Standard
Yield: 10 jars (455 mL each)	10 pt. jars

Ingredients:

Metric	Standard
6 L ripe tomatoes	6 qts. ripe tomatoes
1 L finely chopped onions	1 qt. finely chopped onions
125 mL pickling salt	½ cup pickling salt
1.5 L chopped celery	6 cups chopped celery
2 green peppers, chopped	2 green peppers, chopped
500 mL white cider vinegar	2 cups white cider vinegar
40 mL mustard seed	2½ tbsps. mustard seed
1 mL cayenne **or** chili peppers	¼ tsp. cayenne **or** chili peppers
1250 mL sugar	5 cups sugar

Peel and cube ripe tomatoes. Place in large container, add finely chopped onions and sprinkle with pickling salt. Let stand for eight to ten hours. Drain and discard liquid. Combine vegetables, vinegar, mustard seed and cayenne in large pot. Bring to boil and cook for ten minutes. Add sugar and boil for another five minutes. Scoop into hot sterilized jars and close. An "extremely good" sauce.

TOMATO KETCHUP

Metric	Standard
Yield: 8 jars (909 mL each)	8 qt. jars

Ingredients:

Metric	Standard
12 large green apples	12 large green apples
30 large tomatoes	30 large tomatoes
1 green pepper	1 green pepper
6 medium onions	6 medium onions
250 mL white vinegar	1 cup white vinegar
1 mL cinnamon	¼ tsp. cinnamon
2 mL allspice	½ tsp. allspice
750 mL brown sugar	3 cups brown sugar
50 mL salt	¼ cup salt

Wash fruit and vegetables and remove inedible parts. Chop and soak until tender. Press through sieve. Add remaining ingredients to strained mixture. Cook mixture until thick. Pour into hot sterilized jars and close immediately to seal.

Note:

Use fresh green apples with high pectin content.

TOMATO JUICE

Metric	Standard
Yield: 3 jars (909 mL each)	3 qt. jars

Ingredients:

6 L whole tomatoes	6 qts. whole tomatoes
5 mL sugar	1 tsp. sugar
5 mL salt	1 tsp. salt

Wash tomatoes, cut into small pieces. Place in 4 L (4 qt.) pot with a small amount of water to prevent burning. Heat till juice flows freely. Put through juicer and measure juice. For each L (qt.) of juice add 5 mL (1 tsp.) each sugar and salt. Return to heat and boil for five minutes. Pour at once into hot sterilized jars and close. Steam in canner for five minutes (optional).

Note:

For less acidic thicker juice, allow juice to settle overnight before pouring into jars. Strain off clear acidic liquid from surface. Return remaining juice to heat and process as above.

FROZEN TOMATO JUICE

Metric	Standard
Yield: 2 L	2 qt.

Ingredients:

4 L ripe tomatoes	4 qts. ripe tomatoes
250 mL water	1 cup water
10 mL salt	2 tsps. salt
20 mL sugar	4 tsps. sugar

Wash and cut ripe tomatoes into large chunks. Add water, and bring to boil. Cook over low heat stirring frequently. When tomatoes are soft, remove from heat. Strain through sieve or fruit press. Add salt and sugar and stir well. Pour juice into jars or plastic containers allowing space to expand in container. Cool and freeze. Allow plenty of time to thaw juice before serving.

RHUBARB KETCHUP

Metric	*Standard*
Yield: approx. 1 L	1 qt.

Ingredients:

1 L stewed rhubarb	1 qt. stewed rhubarb
1 L chopped onion	1 qt. chopped onion
1 L white vinegar	1 qt. white vinegar
750 mL brown sugar	3 cups brown sugar
15 mL salt	1 tbsp. salt
25-50 mL mixed spices **or** pickling spices	1½-3 tbsps. mixed spices **or** pickling spices

Combine all ingredients. Bring to boil and simmer for 1½ hours; stirring frequently. Strain and pour into hot sterilized jars. Close to seal. Serve with meat or sausage.

RHUBARB JUICE

Metric	*Standard*
Yield: 5 L	5 qts.

Ingredients:

5 L cubed rhubarb	5 qts. cubed rhubarb
2.5 L water	10 cups water
unsweetened pineapple juice	unsweetened pineapple juice
sugar	sugar

Combine rhubarb and water in 10 L (10 qt.) kettle. Cook till tender. Strain and sieve two or three times beginning with large and ending with small sieve. Measure strained juice. To each L (qt.) of juice add 125 mL (½ cup) each unsweetened pineapple juice and sugar. Boil for five minutes. Pour into hot sterilized jars and close immediately to seal. To serve, chill juice; add fruit such as frozen strawberries or fresh orange slices. Add chilled ginger ale if desired. A lovely tart punch.

RHUBARB SAUCE

Metric	*Standard*
Yield: 600 mL	2 cups
Serves: 4	

Ingredients:

1 L cubed rhubarb	1 qt. cubed rhubarb
50 mL water	¼ cup water

grated ring of 1 lemon **or** orange	grated ring of 1 lemon **or** orange
125 mL sugar	½ cup sugar

Place cubed rhubarb in 2 L (2 qt.) saucepan. Add water and grated lemon rind. Bring to boil and cook until tender. Stir frequently. Remove from heat. Add sugar and stir until dissolved. Cool and serve as dessert with whipped cream. Makes a nice tart topping for cakes or ice cream.

CRABAPPLE PRESERVE

Metric	*Standard*
Yield: 6 jars (909 mL each)	9 qt. jars

Ingredients:

3 L crabapples	3-3½ qts. crabapples
3 L water	12 cups water
1500 mL sugar	6 cups sugar

Wash crabapples and place with stems into clean jars. Combine water and sugar; bring to boil, stirring until sugar is dissolved. Pour syrup over crabapples. Close jars and steam in canner for 10-15 minutes or until apples being to crack. Cool and store in cool, dark, dry place.

QUICK PICKLED CRABAPPLES

Metric	*Standard*
Yield: 2 jars (909 mL each)	2 qt. jars

Ingredients:

500 mL white vinegar	2 cups white vinegar
1250 mL brown sugar **or**	5 cups brown sugar **or**
½ brown and	½ brown and
½ white sugar	½ white sugar
5-15 mL whole cloves	1-3 tsps. whole cloves
5-15 mL whole allspice	1-3 tsps. whole allspice
1-2 sticks cinnamon	1-2 sticks whole cinnamon
2 L crabapples	2 qts. crabapples

Combine white vinegar and sugar in pot. Add spices or tie into cheese cloth and add. (For less spicy pickles use smaller amount.) Bring to boil. Add crabapples and simmer for a few minutes until tender or beginning to crack. Spoon crabapples and syrup into hot sterilized jars. Close to seal — no steaming needed.

PICKLED CRABAPPLES

Metric	Standard
Yield: 4-5 jars (909 mL each)	4-5 qt. jars

Ingredients:

Metric	Standard
1250 mL sugar	5 cups white sugar
750 mL white vinegar	3 cups white vinegar
375 mL water	1½ cups water
1 mL pickling salt	¼ tsp. pickling salt
3 sticks cinnamon	3 sticks cinnamon
10 mL whole allspice	2 tsps. whole allspice
5 mL whole cloves	1 tsp. whole cloves
2 pieces ginger root	2 pieces ginger root
4 L crabapples	4 qts. crabapples

Combine first four ingredients in pot. Tie spices into cheese cloth and add to liquid. Bring liquid and spices to boil. Lower heat and simmer for 15 minutes. Let cool. Add some crabapples carefully to cooled syrup; just enough to cover surface of syrup. Bring slowly to boil and simmer until fruit is barely tender or begins to crack. Turn frequently. When all fruit is done, cool syrup and return apples. Let stand for 8-10 hours. Remove apples and pack cold into sterilized jars. Bring syrup to boil and pour over fruit. Close jars and steam in canner briefly to seal jars. Do not overcook. A tedious method but a very tasty pickle.

FRUIT PRESERVE

Metric	Standard
Yield: 3 jars (909 mL each)	3 qt. jars

Ingredients:

Metric	Standard
500 mL sugar	2 cups sugar
1-1.5 L water	4-6 cups water
1 kg fruit	2 lbs. fruit

Combine sugar, and water, boil until sugar dissolves. (Use proportions of sugar to water depending on natural sweetness of fruit or personal taste.) Prepare fruit; wash; pit and peel if using large peaches or pears. Add fruit to syrup and bring to a boil. Scoop fruit and juice into hot sterilized jars. Cover fruit well with juice. Close immediately to seal or close and steam in canner for about five minutes to ensure sealing. Avoid long steaming to prevent fruit from over-cooking.

NOTE:

Pears if peeled should be placed in mild salt water for a few minutes before cooking to prevent browning.

SAUERKRAUT

Metric	*Standard*
Yield: 1 L	1 qt.

Ingredients:

2 L shredded cabbage	2 qts. shredded cabbage
10-15 mL salt	2-3 tbsps. salt

Place some shredded cabbage in large crock or similar container. Sprinkle with a little salt. Knead or pound till cabbage is limp. Add a little more cabbage, salt and pound. Repeat till all cabbage is used. Continue pounding till moisture covers cabbage. Place clean cloth over cabbage. Place heavy object on cloth to keep cabbage under moisture. Allow to ferment in cool place for two weeks to one month, depending on quantity of sauerkraut in pot. Check occasionally to remove excess foam. Moisture level will suddenly drop when sauerkraut is done. Put into containers and freeze to preserve.

NOTE:

Above recipe may be multiplied to make large quantity of sauerkraut.

PICKLED HERRINGS

Metric	*Standard*
Yield: 1 L	1 qt.
Serves: 6-8	

Ingredients:

2 herrings	2 herrings
125 mL vinegar	½ cup vinegar
240 mL water	1 cup water
2 bay leafs	2 bay leafs
5 mL pickling salt	1 tsp. pickling salt
1 small onion	1 small onion
30 mL sugar	2 tbsps. sugar
15 mL oil	1 tbsp. oil
Sliced onions as desired	

Clean herrings and chop off heads and tails. Soak in cold water changing water 3-4 times for several hours or overnight. Combine ingredients for brine and bring to a boil. Cool. Drain herrings and cover with sliced onions. Cover with cold brine. Store in closed container in refrigerator. Ready for eating in 48 hours.

CANNED BEANS

Metric	Standard
jars (455 mL each)	pt. jars

Ingredients:

yellow **or** green beans	yellow **or** green beans
2 mL salt	½ tsp. salt
5 mL vinegar	1 tsp. vinegar
cold water	cold water

Wash and cut beans, amount desired. Put into clean sterilized jars. Add salt and vinegar to each jar (amount given above). Fill nearly full with cold water. Close and steam in canner for one hour.

NOTE: The pressure cooker is a safe means to can beans. Check canning booklet for directions.

CANNED CHICKEN

Metric	Standard
jars (909 mL each)	1 qt. jars

Ingredients:

fresh chicken	fresh chicken
cold water	cold water
5 mL salt	1 tsp. salt

Wash and cut chicken in desirable pieces. Place in clean sterilized jars. Fill with cold water; add salt. Close and process in canner for three hours. May be served cold or reheated.

NOTE: Processing chicken in pressure cooker is a safer preserving method. Check booklet accompanying pressure cooker.

CANNED FISH

Metric	Standard
jars (909 mL each)	1 qt. jars

Ingredients:

salmon, suckers	salmon, suckers
15 mL white vinegar	1 tbsp. white vinegar
15 mL safflo oil **or** butter	1 tbsp. safflo oil **or** butter
10 mL salt	2 tsps. salt

Clean and cut fish in small pieces. Put in sterilized jars. To each add given amounts of white vinegar, safflo oil and salt. Close lids. Process in canner for seven hours.

NOTE: Processing fish in pressure cooker is a safer preserving method. Follow instructions as given in booklet accompanying pressure cooker.

MAIN DISHES

STUFFED PEPPERS

Metric	Standard
2 L casserole dish	2 qt. casserole dish
180°C	350°F
45 min.	
Serves: 4	

Ingredients:

Metric	Standard
50 mL uncooked rice	¼ cup uncooked rice
125 mL water	½ cup water
50 mL chopped onion	3 tbsps. chopped onion
15 mL butter **or** margarine	1 tbsp. butter **or** margarine
4 green peppers	4 green peppers
500 g hamburger	1 lb. hamburger
2 eggs	2 eggs
salt to taste	salt to taste
750 mL tomato juice	3 cups tomato juice

Cook rice in water till almost done. Rinse and drain. Brown onion in butter. Cut peppers lengthwise in half and remove seeds. Combine rice, onion, hamburger, eggs and salt. Stuff pepper halves. Place in greased casserole and cover with tomato juice. Bake and serve hot.

FALSE CABBAGE ROLLS

Metric	Standard
3 L cooking pot	3 qt. cooking pot
30-40 min.	
Serves: 4-6	

Ingredients:

Metric	Standard
500 g ground beef	1 lb. ground beef
1 medium onion, sliced	1 medium onion, sliced
1 medium cabbage, sliced	1 medium cabbage, sliced
2 cans (284 mL each) tomato soup	2 cans (10 oz. each) tomato soup
75 mL sour cream	⅓ cup sour cream
salt and pepper to taste	salt and pepper to taste

Brown ground beef and sliced onion in cooking pot, stirring frequently. Add sliced cabbage, tomato soup and spices. Cover and simmer till cabbage is tender. Stir occasionally. Add sour cream and serve over rice, mashed potatoes or noodles.

HAM ROLL-UPS

Metric	Standard
200°C	400°F
15 min.	
Serves: 3-4	

Ingredients:

250 mL minute rice	1 cup minute rice
250 mL consomme	1 cup consomme
30 mL butter	2 tbsps. butter
50 mL minced green pepper	¼ cup minced green pepper
50 mL minced onion	¼ cup minced onion
6 sliced cooked ham	6 slices cooked ham
30 mL prepared mustard	2 tbsps. prepared mustard
season to taste	season to taste

Cook minute rice in consomme and drain. Melt butter in skillet and saute minced green pepper and onion. Mix with drained, cooked rice. Spread slices of cooked ham with prepared mustard. Place rice/vegetable mixture on ham slices. Roll up and place in shallow baking dish with open side down. Bake and serve with tossed salad.

SAUERKRAUT UND SCHWEINERIPPCHEN
(Sauerkraut and Spareribs)

Metric	Standard
4 L casserole dish	4 qt. casserole dish
160°C — 30 min.	325°F
180°C — 1 to 1½ hours	350°F
Serves: 6	

Ingredients:

1 kg spareribs	2 lbs. spareribs
6 large potatoes	6 large potatoes
1 can (398) mL sauerkraut	1 can (14 oz.) sauerkraut
500 g smoked sausage	1 lb. smoked sausage
500 mL hot water	2 cups hot water

Place spareribs on cookie sheet. Bake for 30 minutes to brown. Drain fat. Peel and slice potatoes. Cover sauerkraut with water and drain. Lightly grease casserole and dish and place in layers: sliced potatoes, sauerkraut, spareribs and sliced sausage. Repeat layers ending with a mixture of sauerkraut and potato slices to keep meat moist. Pour hot water over and cover tightly. Bake till tender. If casserole seems too dry, add additional hot water.

EGGS ON TOAST WITH CHEESE SAUCE

Metric	*Standard*
Serves: 6	

Ingredients:

6 eggs	6 eggs
6 slices toast bread	6 slices toast bread
30 mL butter	2 tbsps. butter
30 mL flour	2 tbsps. flour
250 mL hot milk	1 cup hot milk
2 mL salt	½ tsp. salt
125 mL grated cheese	½ cup grated cheese

Hard cook 6 eggs, peel and chop. Toast bread and cover with chopped eggs. In 1 L (1 qt.) saucepan melt butter. Add flour and stir until frothy. Add hot milk and stir constantly until mixture boils and thickens. Add salt and grated cheese. Stir and pour over eggs and toast. Sprinkle with fresh chopped parsley or pimento. Makes a delicious lunch dish.

MEAT STEW CASSEROLE DISH

Metric	*Standard*
3 L casserole dish	3 qt. casserole dish
180°C	350°F
30-45 min.	
Serves: 4	

Ingredients:

500 g stewing beef **or** leftover meat, cubed	1 lb. stewing beef **or** leftover meat, cubed
25-50 mL fat	2-3 tbsps. fat
150 mL hot water	⅔ cup hot water
250 mL diced carrots	1 cup diced carrots
250 mL diced potatoes	1 cup diced potatoes
500 mL canned tomatoes with juice	2 cups canned tomatoes with juice
30 mL flour	2 tbsps. flour
1 bay leaf	1 bay leaf
1 onion, chopped	1 onion, chopped
salt and pepper to taste	salt and pepper to taste

Brown meat in fat. Add hot water and transfer mixture into casserole. Cover and bake for 1 hour. (Omit if leftover meat is used.) Add vegetables and spices. Bake until vegetables are tender. Mix flour with a little cold water to make a thin paste. Add flour mixture during the last few minutes of baking time to thicken casserole. Casserole is delicious with dumplings.

Variation: Dish may also be prepared on top of stove.

SHEPHERDS PIE

Metric	*Standard*
1.5 L casserole dish	1½ casserole dish
180°C	350°F
35-40 min.	
Serves: 4-6	

Ingredients:

500 mL chopped roast **or** ground beef	2 cups chopped roast **or** ground beef
30 mL chopped onion	2 tbsps. chopped onion
250 mL gravy	1 cup gravy
salt and pepper to taste	salt and pepper to taste
500 mL mashed potatoes	2 cups mashed potatoes
1 egg, beaten	1 egg, beaten

Combine meat, onion, gravy and seasonings. Place in buttered casserole and cover with mashed potatoes. Brush with beaten egg. Bake until potatoes are slightly browned.

ROMAN HOLIDAY DISH

Metric	*Standard*
3 L baking dish	3 qt. baking dish
180°C	350°F
40 min.	
Serves: 4-6	

Ingredients:

50 mL Crisco	¼ cup Crisco
125 mL chopped onion	½ cup chopped onion
1 L cooked spaghetti	4 cups cooked spaghetti
500 g hamburger	1 lb. hamburger
5 mL salt	1 tsp. salt
1 mL pepper	¼ tsp. pepper
375 mL tomatoes (canned)	1½ cups tomatoes (canned)
175 mL grated cheese	¾ cup grated cheese

Saute onion in melted Crisco. Add meat and seasonings; cook 5 minutes. Place a layer of spaghetti in baking dish; add meat, another layer of spaghetti, repeating until all ingredients are used. Pour in tomatoes, sprinkle with grated cheese. Bake covered 30 minutes, uncover and bake another 10 minutes to brown cheese. A nice quick supper dish.

HUNGARIAN GOULASH

Metric   *Standard*

30 min.
Serves: 4

Ingredients:

250 mL macaroni	1 cup macaroni
500 g cubed steak **or** stewing beef	2 lbs. cubed steak **or** stewing beef
2 medium onions, sliced	2 medium onions, sliced
30 mL oil	2 tbsps. oil
1 can (540 mL) tomatoes	1 can (19 oz.) tomatoes
salt and pepper to taste	salt and pepper to taste
dash of Worcestershire sauce	dash of Worcestershire sauce
50 mL ketchup (optional)	¼ cup ketchup (optional)

Cook and drain macaroni. In large skillet, brown cubed steak and sliced onions in oil. Add remaining ingredients and simmer till onions are tender. Very tasty served with tea biscuits.

Note:

If stewing beef is used, brown, add a little hot water and simmer till tender before adding remaining ingredients.

NOODLE DISH

Metric   *Standard*

3 L casserole dish   3 qt. casserole dish
180°C   350°F
30-45 min.
Serves: 8-9

Ingredients:

500 g hamburger	½ lb. hamburger
125 mL chopped onion	½ cup chopped onion
50 mL chopped green pepper	¼ cup chopped green pepper
1 can (284 mL) cream of chicken soup	1 can (10 oz.) cream of chicken soup
1 can (284 mL) cream of mushroom soup	1 can (10 oz.) cream of mushroom soup
50 mL milk	¼ cup milk

Cook 1.25 L fine noodles according to package direction. While noodles cook, brown hamburger in skillet and add remaining ingredients to make sauce. Place noodles in casserole. Pour sauce over noodles. Cover and bake, adding more liquid if mixture seems dry.

CHILI CON CARNE

Metric	Standard
2 L skillet or heavy saucepan	2 qt. skillet or heavy saucepan

Serves: 4

Ingredients:

500 g ground beef	1 lb. ground beef
1 medium onion, chopped	1 medium onion, chopped
250 mL chopped celery	1 cup chopped celery
1 can (284 mL) cream of tomato soup	1 can (10 oz.) cream of tomato soup
2 cans (398 mL each) red kidney beans	2 cans (15 oz. each) red kidney beans
150 mL water	⅔ cup water
5 mL salt	1 tsp. salt
7 mL chili powder	1½ tsps. chili powder

Brown beef, onion and celery in heavy skillet. Add remaining ingredients. Simmer, stirring occasionally for 30 minutes. Serve.

CHICKEN ALMOND SUPREME

Metric	Standard

Serves: 6-8

Ingredients:

60 mL butter	4 tbsps. butter
125 mL sliced mushrooms	½ cup sliced mushrooms
250 mL thinly sliced onions	1 cup thinly sliced onions
1 green pepper sliced	1 green pepper sliced
250 mL chicken broth	1 cup chicken broth
500 mL sliced celery	2 cups sliced celery
750 mL cooked sliced chicken	3 cups cooked sliced chicken
125 mL water chestnuts	½ cup water chestnuts
250 mL bean sprouts	1 cup bean sprouts
15 mL cornstarch	1 tbsp. cornstarch
125 mL blanched almonds	½ cup blanched almonds
25 mL butter	1½ tbsps. butter
Chow Mein Noodles **or** steamed Rice	Chow Mein Noodles **or** steamed Rice
Soya sauce	Soya sauce

Melt 50 mL (3 tbsps.) butter in large skillet. Cook sliced mushrooms, onions and green pepper in butter till limp. Add chicken broth and celery. Cook till celery is barely tender. Add chicken. Drain water chestnuts and bean sprouts, and heat thoroughly. Combine cornstarch with a little cold water. Blend with liquid in skillet. Bring just to boil. Brown almonds in remaining butter. Serve chicken vegetable sauce over oven warmed chow mein noodles or steamed rice with soya sauce. Garnish with browned almonds. Add seasonings of your choice.

SPANISH STYLE NOODLES

Metric	Standard

Serves: 4

Ingredients:

Metric	Standard
½ pkg (170 g) fine noodles	½ pkg fine noodles
15 mL butter	1 tbsp. butter
1 can (398 mL) canned tomatoes	1 can (14 oz.) canned tomatoes
125 g diced bacon	¼ lb. diced bacon
125 mL onion, chopped fine	½ cup onion, chopped fine
salt and pepper to taste	salt and pepper to taste

Cook noodles according to package directions and top with butter. Boil tomatoes until fairly thick. While tomatoes boil, fry bacon and onions until bacon begins to brown. Add tomatoes and boil 5 minutes longer. Pour over buttered noodles and mix well. Season and let simmer a few minutes. Serve.

CURRIED RICE

Metric	Standard
1.5 L casserole dish	1½ qt. casserole dish
190°C	375°F
60 mins.	

Ingredients:

Metric	Standard
1 diced onion	1 diced onion
1 diced green pepper	1 diced green pepper
50 mL butter	¼ cup butter
250 mL uncooked rice	1 cup uncooked rice
1 can (540 mL) tomatoes	1 can (19 oz.) tomatoes
750 mL water	3 cups water
7-10 mL curry powder	1½-2 tsps. curry powder

Saute diced onion and green pepper in butter. Mix with remaining ingredients and put in well greased casserole dish. Bake till done, and serve hot. Season to taste.

SPANISH RICE

Metric	Standard
Serves: 3-4	

Ingredients:

Metric	Standard
4 slices side bacon	4 slices side bacon
250 mL chopped onion	1 cup chopped onion
50 mL minced green pepper	¼ cup minced green pepper
2 cans (284 mL ea.) cream of tomato soup **or**	2 cans (14 oz. ea.) cream of tomato soup **or**
1 can (540 mL) tomatoes	1 can (19 oz.) tomatoes
1 bay leaf	1 bay leaf
2-4 whole cloves	2-4 whole cloves
125 mL water	½ cup water
125 mL uncooked rice	½ cup uncooked rice

Cook bacon until crisp in large skillet. Remove and break into bits. Add chopped onion and minced pepper to bacon drippings; cook until soft. Return bacon bits to skillet, add remaining ingredients; cover, and simmer for 30 minutes, stirring occasionally. Remove bay leaf and whole cloves. Serve hot.

POTATOES AND ONIONS IN CREAM

Metric	Standard
3 L casserole dish	3 qt. casserole dish
180°C	350°F
60-75 mins.	
Serves: 4-6	

Ingredients:

Metric	Standard
5 medium potatoes	5 medium potatoes
8 small onions	8 small onions
30 mL butter	2 tbsps. butter
15 mL flour	1 tbsp. flour
50 mL heavy cream	¼ cup heavy cream
175 mL water	¾ cup water
7 mL salt	1½ tsps. salt
pepper and paprika	pepper and paprika

Grease casserole. Peel and quarter potatoes. Place in greased casserole along with small onions. Melt butter in small saucepan. Stir in flour. Combine heavy cream and water and add. Cook until mixture thickens, stirring frequently. Add salt and pepper to taste. Pour over potatoes and onions. Bake until tender. Sprinkle with paprika and serve.

SCALLOPED POTATOES

Metric	Standard
2.5 L casserole dish	2½ qt. casserole dish
180°C	350°F
1-1¼ hrs.	
Serves: 8	

Ingredients:

1.5 L thinly sliced raw potatoes	6 cups thinly sliced raw potatoes
1 small onion, finely chopped	1 small onion, finely chopped
7 mL salt	1½ tsps. salt
1 mL pepper	⅛ tsp. pepper
60 mL flour	4 tbsps. flour
30 mL butter	2 tbsps. butter
600 mL hot milk	2½ cups hot milk

Place a layer of thinly sliced raw potatoes in buttered casserole. Add some finely minced onion, salt, pepper, flour and dot with butter. Repeat layers until ingredients are used. Pour hot milk over dish and bake till top is golden brown and potatoes are done.

HAMBURGER POTATO PIE

Metric	Standard
2.5 L casserole dish	2½ qt. casserole dish
180°C	350°F
20-30 mins.	
Serves: 6	

Ingredients:

1 medium onion	1 medium onion
30 mL fat	2 tbsps. fat
500 g ground beef	1 lb. ground beef
2 mL salt	½ tsp. salt
1 mL pepper	¼ tsp. pepper
250 mL cooked peas	1 cup cooked peas
250 mL canned tomatoes	1 cup canned tomatoes
125 mL ketchup	½ cup ketchup
750 mL hot mashed potatoes	3 cups mashed potatoes
1 beaten egg	1 beaten egg

Chop onion and fry in hot fat until golden. Add ground beef and seasonings; cook until meat is browned. Add cooked peas, canned tomatoes and ketchup. Mix well and pour into casserole. Combine seasoned mashed potatoes and beaten egg. Spread over meat mixture. Bake until mashed potatoes are thoroughly heated and golden in color.

SUPPER DISH
(with leftover meat)

Metric	Standard
2 L casserole	2 qt. casserole
180°C	350°F
20-30 mins.	
Serves: 4	

Ingredients:

Metric	Standard
500 g leftover meat (beef, pork, chicken)	2 lbs. leftover meat (beef, pork, chicken)
250 mL brown gravy	1 cup brown gravy
50 mL chopped onion	¼ cup chopped onion
5 mL salt	1 tsp. salt
1 mL pepper	¼ tsp. pepper
150 mL canned tomatoes	⅔ cup canned tomatoes
15 mL butter	1 tbsp. butter
3 slices dry bread	3 slices dry bread

Grease casserole. Cut meat fine. Simmer meat, gravy, chopped onion, salt and pepper in 2 L (2 qt.) saucepan about 15 mins. Add canned tomatoes and bring to a boil. Transfer into greased casserole. Butter bread, and cut into 2 cm (1 in.) cubes. Place with buttered side up on top of meat mixture. Bake. Serve over buttered noodles.

BAKED BEANS

Metric	Standard
2 L casserole	2 qt. casserole
150°C	300°F
1-1½ hours	
Serves: 4	

Ingredients:

Metric	Standard
375 mL dry white beans	1½ cups white beans
50 mL chopped onion	¼ cup chopped onion
500 g smoked sausage or other cured meat sliced	1 lb. smoked sausage or other cured meat sliced
75 mL brown sugar	⅓ cup brown sugar
30 mL molasses	2 tbsps. molasses
5 mL dry mustard	1 tsp. dry mustard
5 mL salt	1 tsp salt
50 mL ketchup	¼ cup ketchup
250-375 mL tomato juice	1-1½ cups tomato juice

Cover beans with water and cook until beans break. Drain and place in casserole. Add copped onion and sliced smoked sausage.

Mix remaining ingredients using sufficient tomato juice to cover beans. Cover and bake until ingredients are well done. Add hot water if necessary to prevent drying.

MACARONI AND CHEESE BAKE

Metric	*Standard*
3 L shallow casserole dish	3 qt. shallow casserole dish
160°C	325°F
50 mins.	
Serves: 4	

Ingredients:

375 mL scalded milk	1½ cups scalded milk
250 mL soft bread cubes	1 cup soft bread cubes
15 mL minced onion	1 tbsp. minced onion
50 mL melted butter **or** margarine	¼ cup melted butter **or** margarine
250 mL macaroni	1 cup macaroni
375 mL grated cheese	1½ cups grated cheese
2 mL salt	½ tsp. salt
1 mL pepper	⅛ tsp. pepper
3 eggs, slightly beaten	3 eggs, slightly, beaten

Grease shallow casserole dish. Pour scalded milk over soft bread cubes in large bowl. Add minced onion and melted butter; stir in. Boil macaroni in salted water. Add grated cheese to bread cube mixture. (A sharp smooth-melting kind of cheese is suggested). Add salt and pepper; mix lightly. Add slightly beaten eggs, and cooked, drained macaroni. Mix lightly and pour into greased casserole dish. Bake and serve. A quick, economical lunch dish or pot luck casserole.

GREEN BEAN DISH

| *Metric* | *Standard* |
| Serves: 6 | |

Ingredients:

50 mL minced onions	¼ cup minced onions
25 mL margarine	1½ tbsps. margarine
1 can (284 mL) cream of mushroom **or** cream of celery soup	1 can (10 oz.) cream of mushroom **or** cream of celery soup
125 mL milk	½ cup milk
2 hard cooked eggs, sliced	2 hard cooked eggs, sliced
25 mL chopped pimento	1½ tbsps. chopped pimento
1 can (220 g) drained salmon **or** tuna	1 can (7¾ oz.) drained salmon **or** tuna
750 mL cut green beans	3 cups cut green beans

Combine minced onions and margarine in 2 L (2 qt.) saucepan. Cook till soft, but not brown. Blend in soup, milk, eggs, pimento and fish. Heat, stirring frequently. Cook green beans till tender; drain. Arrange hot, drained beans on platter. Pour sauce over beans and serve. Do not stir.

CHEESE SOUFFLE

Metric	*Standard*
1 L casserole dish	1 qt. casserole dish
160°C	325°F
30-45 mins.	
Serves: 3-4	

Ingredients:

30 mL butter	2 tbsps. butter
125 mL milk	½ cup milk
3 eggs, separated	3 eggs, separated
2 mL salt	½ tsp. salt
30 mL flour	2 tbsps. flour
250 mL grated cheese	1 cup grated cheese
dash of cayenne	dash of cayenne

Grease casserole dish. Melt butter in saucepan. Stir in flour. Remove from heat and stir in milk (works best if milk is at room temperature). Return to heat, add salt and bring to boil to thicken. Boil 1 minute. Add grated cheese; cool until melted. As white sauce cools, beat egg whites to stiff peaks. Beat egg yolks separately. When sauce is cooled, add egg yolks, then fold in beaten egg whites. Pour into casserole and bake. Souffle should be puffed and slightly browned when done.

MEATS

BAKED HAM SLICE

Metric	Standard
1-2 L baking dish	1-2 qt. baking dish
150°C	300°F
1 hr.	
Serves: 4	

Ingredients:

1 slice ham 3 cm thick	1 slice ham 1¼ in. thick
30 mL prepared mustard	2 tbsps. prepared mustard
30 mL brown sugar	2 tbsps. brown sugar
a few whole cloves	a few whole cloves
15 mL flour	1 tbsp. flour
250 mL hot water	1 cup hot water
50 mL raisins	¼ cup raisins

Spread ham slice with prepared mustard. Sprinkle with brown sugar and whole cloves. Bake.

Sauce:

Scrape topping from ham. Remove ham from pan. Add flour, stirring continuously. Add hot water gradually. Add raisins and simmer till thick. Pour over ham and serve.

SIMPLE SWEET AND SOUR SPARERIBS

Metric	Standard
160°C	325°F
60 mins.	
Serves: 4	

Ingredients:

1 kg spareribs	2 lbs. spareribs
250 mL sugar	1 cup sugar
250 mL ketchup	1 cup ketchup
200-250 mL vinegar	¾-1 cup vinegar
5 mL dry mustard	1 tsp. dry mustard

Cut spareribs in 5 cm (2 in.) pieces. Brown ribs in roaster at 200°C (400°F) or in frying pan. Turn ribs occasionally until evenly browned. In 1 L (1 qt.) saucepan, mix and bring to boil remaining ingredients. Pour over spareribs in roaster. Cover and bake until tender. Serve with hot fluffy rice.

SWEET AND SOUR SPARERIBS

Metric	Standard
220°C	425°F

1 hr.
Serves: 4

Ingredients:

1 kg spareribs	2 lbs. spareribs
1 mL pepper	¼ tsp. pepper
5 mL salt	1 tsp. salt
30 mL brown sugar	2 tbsps. brown sugar
30 mL cornstarch	2 tbsps. cornstarch
50 mL white vinegar	¼ cup white vinegar
50 mL cold water	¼ cup cold water
250 mL pineapple juice	1 cup pineapple juice
15 mL soya sauce	1 tbsp. soya sauce

Cut spareribs in 5 cm (2 in.) pieces. Place in 2 L (2 qt.) pan, sprinkle with pepper and part of salt. Bake until ribs are crisp, brown and tender, turning once or twice. Meanwhile, mix brown sugar, cornstarch and remaining salt in large skillet. Stir in remaining ingredients; cook on low heat. Stir vigorously until juice becomes transparemt. Drain spareribs of fat and place in large, deep serving platter. Pour sauce over ribs and serve with fluffy rice.

HAWAIIAN PORK CHOPS

Metric	Standard

Serves: 4-6

Ingredients:

6 pork chops	6 pork chops
15 mL flour	1 tbsp. flour
5 mL salt	1 tsp. salt
dash of pepper	dash of pepper
30 mL oil	2 tbsps. oil
30 mL white vinegar	2 tbsps. white vinegar
125 mL pineapple juice	½ cup pineapple juice
50 mL ketchup	¼ cup ketchup
1 small onion	1 small onion
1 medium green pepper	1 medium pepper
5 pineapple slices	5 pineapple slices

Trim excess fat from pork chops. Combine flour, salt and pepper. Dredge pork chops in flour mixture. Brown in oil in large skillet. Combine vinegar, pineapple, juice, ketchup; quarter small onion. Cut green pepper in 2 cm (½ in.) squares. Add onion, green pepper and pineapple slices cut in wedges to vinegar mixture. Pour over pork chops. Cover and simmer for 45 minutes or until meat is tender. A little hot water may be added if more sauce is needed. Serve with fluffy rice.

DILL PORK CHOPS

Metric	Standard
45 mins.	
Serves: 4	

Ingredients:

Metric	Standard
4 loin pork chops	4 loin pork chops salt
salt and pepper to taste	and pepper to taste
75 mL flour	⅓ cup flour
15 mL salad oil	1 tbsp. salad oil
10 mL Worchestershire	2 tsps. Worchestershire
sauce	sauce
2 small onions,	2 small onions,
chopped fine	chopped fine
125 mL hot water	½ cup hot water
50 mL finely chopped dill	3 tbsps. finely chopped
pickles	dill pickles

Season pork chops with salt and pepper. Roll in flour. Brown well on both sides in salad oil in skillet. Add Worchestershire sauce, chopped onion and hot water. Cover and simmer for 20 minutes. Turn pork chops and simmer for another 25 minutes or until chops are tender. Drain off excess fat. Place some finely chopped dill pickle on each chop and serve. Remaining sauce may be used as gravy.

ROAST TURKEY
(Uncovered Method)

Metric	Standard
160°C	325°F
3½-4 hours	

Ingredients:

Metric	Standard
6 kg turkey	12-13 lb. turkey

Place turkey, breast side up, on rack in shallow roasting pan. Brush with melted butter. Roast uncovered. Season halfway through the baking period. Baste every 30 minutes. If desired, drumsticks, tail and wings may be covered with foil for latter part of cooking time to prevent excessive browning and drying.

ROAST TURKEY
(Covered Roaster Method)

Metric	Standard
160°C	325°F
7 hrs.	7 hrs.
Serves: 10-15	

Ingredients:

Metric	Standard
6.5 kg turkey	14 lb. turkey
125 mL melted butter	½ cup melted butter
salt and pepper to taste	salt and pepper to taste
250 g side bacon, sliced	½ lb. side bacon, sliced

Place turkey breast side up on rack in deep roaster. Brush with melted butter, sprinkle with salt and pepper. Place bacon strips over turkey to prevent white meat from drying out. Cover and roast. If desired, remove cover for last ½ hour of roasting, to brown and crisp the surface. For turkeys of various sizes, follow cooking chart in any reliable cookbook.

BREAD STUFFING

Metric	Standard
Yield: 2 L, enough dressing for a 7 kg turkey	2 qts., enough dressing for a 15 lb. turkey

Ingredients:

Metric	Standard
250 mL butter **or** margarine	1 cup butter **or** margarine
175 mL finely minced onion	¾ cup finely minced onion
2.5 L day old bread cubes	3 qts. day old bread cubes
125 mL chopped celery, stalks and leaves	½ cup chopped celery, stalks and leaves
10 mL salt	2 tsps. salt
5 mL pepper	1 tsp. pepper
5-15 mL crumbed herbs i.e. sage, thyme, poultry seasoning	1-3 tsps. crumbed herbs i.e. sage, thyme, poultry seasoning

Melt butter in large skillet. Add and cook minced onion until yellow. Stir in some bread cubes. Continue cooking for a brief time, stirring to prevent excessive browning. Turn into large bowl and mix with remaining ingredients. Cool and place stuffing in bird.

Variation: For dry stuffing, add none or very little moisture; for moist stuffing, mix in lightly with fork just enough hot water to moisten cubes.

Stuffing Tips: A 700 g (24 oz.) loaf makes 2.5 L (2 qts.) loosely packed cubes. Place 200 mL (5 cups) of dressing, or somewhat less, for 1 kg (2 lbs.) of bird.

BREAD DRESSING FOR TURKEY

Metric	Standard
Yield: 1 L	1 qt.
Serves: 4-6	

Ingredients:

1 L bread crumbs	1 qt. bread crumbs
5 mL salt	1 tsp. salt
30 mL chopped parsley	2 tbsps. chopped parsley
1 small onion	1 small onion
finely chopped	finely chopped
7 mL poultry seasoning	1½ tsps. poultry seasoning
1 mL pepper	¼ tsp. pepper
50 mL melted butter	¼ cup melted butter

Mix bread crumbs and seasonings. Add to melted butter and stir with fork. Cool and stuff into turkey. Dressing is enough for a 2 kg (5 lb.) bird. Recipe may be easily doubled or tripled for a larger turkey.

TURKEY OR CHICKEN CURRY

Metric	Standard
1-2 L saucepan	1-2 qt. saucepan
Serves: 6	

Ingredients:

250 mL mushrooms	1 cup mushrooms
75 mL minced onion	⅓ cup minced onion
750 mL cooked turkey, cubed	3 cups cooked turkey, cubed
75 mL oil	⅓ cup oil
2 mL salt	½ tsp. salt
50 mL flour	3 tbsps. flour
7 mL curry powder	1½ tsps. curry powder
500 mL turkey stock	2 cups turkey stock
5 mL milk **or** cream	1 tsp. milk **or** cream

Sauté first three ingredients in oil. Remove from heat, add salt, flour and curry powder. Add liquids and stir thoroughly. Cook till thickened (about 15 minutes) to blend flavors. Serve over hot rice.

CHICKEN WITH TOMATOES

Metric	Standard
4 L casserole dish	4 qt. casserole dish
160°-170°C	325°F
30-45 min.	
Serves: 6	

Ingredients:

Metric	Standard
1½-2 kg chicken	3-3½ lbs. chicken
75 mL flour	⅓ cup flour
15 mL salt	1 tbsp. salt
1 mL pepper	¼ tsp. pepper
10 mL paprika	2 tsps. paprika
50 mL margarine	¼ cup margarine
1 medium onion, chopped	1 medium onion, chopped
1 clove garlic, crushed	1 clove garlic, crushed
50 mL slivered almonds (optional)	¼ cup slivered almonds (optional)
50 mL flour	¼ cup flour
1 can (398 mL) tomatoes	1 can (14 oz.) tomatoes
15 mL tomato paste	1 tbsp. tomato paste
250 mL chicken stock or consomme	1 cup chicken stock or consomme
175 mL sweet cream	¾ cup sweet cream
75 mL grated cheddar cheese	⅓ cup grated cheddar cheese

Quarter chicken. Coat with mixture of flour, salt, pepper and paprika. Brown in large skillet with margarine. Place browned chicken in casserole. Over low heat, cook chopped onion, crushed garlic and slivered almonds in large skillet with margarine remaining from browned chicken. Use additional margarine if necessary. Stir and cook until onions are limp and almonds are beige. Stir in 50 mL (¼ cup) flour till smooth. Add canned tomatoes, tomato paste and chicken stock. Cook until mixture bubbles, stirring constantly. Remove from heat and stir in cream, small amounts at a time to prevent curdling. Pour sauce over chicken. Bake 30-40 minutes, or until chicken is tender when tested with fork. Just before serving, sprinkle top with grated cheddar cheese and broil untll cheese melts.

CHICKEN CURRY

Metric	Standard
2.5 L casserole dish	2.5 qt. casserole dish
150°C	300°F
15 min.	
Serves: 4-6	

Ingredients:

Metric	Standard
50 mL minced onions	¼ cup minced onions
50 mL fat	¼ cup fat
1 can (284 mL) mushrooms	1 can (10 oz.) mushrooms
750 mL cooked chicken, cubed	3 cups cooked chicken, cubed
2 mL salt	½ tsp. salt
50 mL flour	¼ cup flour
5-7 mL curry powder	1-1½ tsps. curry powder
500 mL chicken stock	2 cups chicken stock

Using a large skillet, sauté minced onions in fat until tender. Drain and add mushrooms and cooked chicken. Heat through. Add salt, flour, curry powder and stir thoroughly. Add chicken stock and cook until thickened. Transfer into lightly greased casserole dish and cook for at least 15 minutes to blend flavours. Serve over hot, fluffy rice.

SWISS STEAK

Metric	Standard
4 L casserole dish	4 qt. casserole dish
180°C	350°F
2 hours.	
Serves: 4	

Ingredients:

Metric	Standard
1 kg round steak	2 lbs. round steak
75 mL flour	⅓ cup flour
5 mL salt	1 tsp. salt
1 mL pepper	¼ tsp. pepper
30 mL fat	2 tbsps. fat
1 onion, sliced	1 onion, sliced
500 mL boiling water	2 cups boiling water

Wipe meat clean. Mix flour, salt and pepper. Sprinkle meat with flour mixture. Pound flour into meat. Heat frying pan till quite hot; add fat. Brown meat on both sides. Add sliced onion and boiling water. Place in casserole dish. Cover tightly and cook for two hours or until tender. Vegetables may be placed over meat for last hour.

Variation:

Substitute half of boiling water with 1 can (284 mL) (10 oz.) tomatoes or mushroom soup.

BEEF STROGANOFF

Metric	*Standard*
Serves: 4	

Ingredients:

500 g round steak	1 lb. round steak
30 mL flour	2 tbsps. flour
10 mL salt	2 tsps. salt
30 mL shortening *or* oil	2 tbsps. shortening *or* oil
50 mL chopped onion	¼ cup chopped onion
250 mL thinly sliced mushrooms	1 cup thinly sliced mushrooms
30 mL tomato paste	2 tbsps. tomato paste
250 mL water	1 cup water
50 mL flour	3 tbsps. flour
50 mL water	¼ cup water
75 mL sour cream	⅓ cup sour cream

Dredge meat in 30 mL (2 tbsps.) flour and salt. Melt or heat shortening in large skillet and brown meat quickly. Add chopped onion, sliced mushrooms, tomato paste and 250 mL (1 cup) water. Simmer for 1 hour. Mix remaining ingredients and add to meat mixture. Bring to boil and serve over hot noodles. A delicious dish.

PENNSYLVANIA DUTCH DINNER

Metric	*Standard*
60 mins.	
Serves: 4-6	

Ingredients:

500 g ground beef	1 lb. ground beef
125 mL fine bread crumbs	½ cup fine bread crumbs
1 egg	1 egg
2 mL salt	½ tsp. salt
1 mL pepper	¼ tsp. pepper
30 mL oil	2 tbsps. oil
2 medium onions	2 medium onions
500 mL sauerkraut, drained	2 cups sauerkraut, drained
500 mL canned tomatoes with juice	2 cups canned tomatoes with juice

Combine ground beef, fine bread crumbs, egg, salt and pepper; shape into small meatballs. Heat oil in heavy skillet and brown meatballs, turning occasionally. Cut onions in wedges and add with drained sauerkraut and canned tomatoes to meatballs. Simmer in covered skillet for about 1 hour. Serve with dumplings or buttered noodles.

MEAT PORCUPINES

Metric	Standard
3 L saucepan	3 qt. saucepan

Serves: 4-6

Ingredients:

200-300 g hamburger meat	½ lb. hamburger meat
125 mL uncooked rice	½ cup uncooked rice
1 small onion, finely chopped	1 small onion, finely chopped
salt and pepper to taste	salt and pepper to taste
1 can (284 mL) tomato soup	1 can (10 oz.) tomato soup
425 mL water	1½ cups water

Combine hamburger meat, uncooked rice, finely chopped onion, salt and pepper; form into small balls. Combine tomato soup and water in saucepan. Bring to boil. Drop meatballs into hot liquid. Simmer one hour; serve.

MEAT LOAF

Metric	Standard
1.5 L loaf pan (20 x 10 x 7 cm)	8 x 4 x 3 in. loaf pan
190°C-30 mins.	375°F
150°C-30 mins.	300°F

Serves: 6-8

Ingredients:

1 kg ground beef	2 lbs. ground beef
2 eggs	2 eggs
175 mL quick cooking oats	¾ cup quick cooking oats
250 mL ketchup	1 cup ketchup
5 mL dry mustard	1 tsp. dry mustard
15 mL Worchestershire Sauce	1 tbsp. Worchestershire Sauce
salt and pepper to taste	salt and pepper to taste
1 pkg (42 g) Lipton Onion Soup Mix	1 pkg Lipton Onion Soup Mix
250 mL diced celery	1 cup diced celery
125 mL diced green pepper	½ cup diced green pepper

Grease loaf pan. Mix all ingredients well. Turn mixture into loaf pan and bake, reducing heat as suggested to prevent excessive browning during second half of cooking time. Turn onto platter, slice and serve.

MEAT LOAF

Metric	Standard
2 L loaf pan (23 x 13 x 7 cm)	9 x 5 x 3 in. loaf pan
180°C	350°F
45 mins.	
Serves: 6-8	

Ingredients:

Metric	Standard
1 egg	1 egg
125 mL milk **or** canned tomatoes	½ cup milk **or** canned tomatoes
700 g ground beef	1½ lbs. ground beef
250 mL bread crumbs	1 cup bread crumbs
10 mL salt	2 tsp. salt
1 mL pepper	¼ tsp. pepper
5 mL chopped onion	1 tsp. chopped onion
5 strips side bacon, fried and chopped	5 strips side bacon, fried and chopped

Grease loaf pan. Beat egg, add milk and remaining ingredients. Mix well. Pat into greased loaf pan. Sprinkle with a few bread crumbs. Bake and serve with gravy or tomato sauce. May also be served cold.

MEAT LOAF

Metric	Standard
2 L loaf pan (23 x 13 x 7 cm)	9 x 5 x 3 in. loaf pan
190°C	375°F
1 hour	

Ingredients:

Metric	Standard
1 kg ground beef	2 lbs. ground beef
2 eggs	2 eggs
175-250 mL quick cooking oats	¾-1 cup quick cooking oats
250 mL ketchup	1 cup ketchup
5 mL dry mustard	1 tsp. dry mustard
15 mL Worchestershire Sauce	1 tbsp. Worchestershire Sauce
250 mL diced celery	1 cup diced celery
1 pkg. (1½ oz.) Lipton Onion Soup Mix	1 pkg. (42.5 g) Lipton Onion Soup Mix
125 mL diced green pepper	½ cup diced green pepper
salt and pepper to taste	salt and pepper to taste

Mix all ingredients together. Place in loaf pan and bake. Reduce heat to 150°C (300°F) if edges of loaf get too brown before center is done. A delicious meat loaf!

SALMON LOAF

Metric	Standard
2 L loaf pan (23 x 13 x 7 cm)	9 x 5 x 3 in. loaf pan
180°C	350°F
45 min.	
Serves: 4	

Ingredients:

1 can (440 g) salmon	1 can (15½ oz.) salmon
75 mL milk	⅓ cup milk
125 mL buttered bread crumbs	½ cup buttered bread crumbs
15 mL finely chopped onion	1 tbsp. finely chopped onion
2 eggs	2 eggs
2 mL salt	½ tsp. salt

Grease loaf pan lightly. Drain and clean salmon. Combine all ingredients, mix well and pack into prepared loaf pan. Bake and serve.

SALMON LOAF

Metric	Standard
1.5 L loaf pan (20 x 10 x 7 cm)	8 x 4 x 3 in. loaf pan
160°C	325°F
1 hr.	
Serves: 6	

Ingredients:

2 cans (220 g each) salmon	2 cans (7¾ oz. each) salmon
2 eggs	2 eggs
2 mL pepper	½ tsp. pepper
3 mL salt	¾ tsp. salt
125 mL milk	½ cup milk
6 soda biscuits	6 soda biscuits
sage (optional)	sage (optional

Grease loaf pan. Drain and clean salmon. Mix with eggs, pepper, salt and milk. Crush soda biscuits until fine and add to salmon mixture. Turn into greased loaf pan and bake. Makes a lovely hot or cold meat dish.

SALMON FRITTERS

Metric	*Standard*
Serves: 6-8	

Ingredients:

Metric	Standard
1 can (220 g) salmon	1 can (7¾ oz.) salmon
250 mL flour	1 cup flour
5 mL baking powder	1 tsp. baking powder
2 mL salt	½ tsp. salt
2 eggs, separated	2 eggs, separated
150 mL milk	⅔ cup milk
15 mL lemon juice	1 tbsp. lemon juice

Drain and flake salmon. Sift flour. Add baking powder and salt and sift again. Beat egg yolks, combine with milk and lemon juice. Pour into flour mixture and stir till smooth. Add flaked salmon. Beat egg whites to stiff peaks and fold in. Drop batter by spoonfuls into deep fat 180°-190°C (365°-375°F) and fry until well browned, about three to five minutes. May also be sautéd in shallow frying pan, and browned on both sides. Drain on absorbent paper and serve hot.

SALMON FRITTERS

Metric	*Standard*
Yield: 20 fritters	

Ingredients:

Metric	Standard
2 cans (220 g each) salmon	2 cans (7¾ oz. each) salmon
250 mL flour	1 cup flour
5 mL baking powder	1 tsp. baking powder
2 mL salt	½ tsp. salt
2 eggs, separated	2 eggs, separated
150 mL milk	⅔ cup milk
15 mL lemon juice	1 tbsp. lemon juice

Sift flour, add baking powder and salt, sift again. Combine beaten egg yolks, milk and lemon juice. Pour into flour mixture and stir until smooth. Add flaked salmon. Beat egg whites to stiff peaks; fold into egg salmon mixture. Drop by spoonfuls into deep fat 180°-190°C (350°-375°F) and fry until well browned (3-5 min.) or sauté in fat in shallow pan, browning on both sides. Drain on absorbent paper. Serve.

JELLIED VEAL

Metric	Standard
Yield: about 700 mL	2½ cups

Ingredients:

2 kg veal with shank	4-5 lbs. veal with shank
1 large onion	1 large onion
cold water	cold water
2 celery stalks	2 celery stalks
salt and pepper to taste	salt and pepper to taste

Place veal shank and onion in 4 L (4 qt.) pot; cover with cold water. Add sliced celery and bring to a boil. Cook for about two hours or until only ⅓ of liquid remains. Drain meat, saving stock. Refrigerate for 8-10 hours. Remove fat from stock. Note the firmness of cooled stock. If stock is not firmly set, add 5 mL (1 tsp.) unflavoured gelatin to 500 mL (2 cups) liquid; heat to dissolve gelatin, but DO NOT BOIL. Add to meat stock. Reheat meat stock. While stock heats, remove meat from bones and chop fine. Return to stock; season to taste. Pour into large or individual molds. Chill to set. Serve on lettuce leaf garnished with hard cooked eggs, radishes, olives, parsley or your favorite garnishes. A lovely summer salad.

VEAL BIRDS

Metric	Standard
Serves: 6-8	

Ingredients:

1 kg veal steak	2 lbs. veal steak
500 mL soft bread crumbs	2 cups soft bread crumbs
1 medium onion, chopped fine	1 medium onion, chopped fine
2 mL sage **or** chopped parsley	½ tsp. sage **or** chopped parsley
salt and pepper to taste	salt and pepper to taste
30 mL ketchup	2 tbsps. ketchup
flour	flour
shortening	shortening

Cut steak into pieces of equal size about 8 cm by 10 cm (3 in. by 4 in.). Combine soft bread crumbs, finely chopped onion, sage, salt and pepper to form dressing. Combine 50 mL (3 tbsps.) warm water and ketchup. Moisten dressing with ketchup mixture, spread evenly over veal squares. Roll up individually and fasten with toothpicks or string; sprinkle with salt and pepper. Roll lightly with flour. Brown quickly in hot melted shortening, in heavy pan. Add 125 mL (½ cup) hot water, cover tightly and simmer until meat is tender.

HAM ROLLS WITH CHEESE SAUCE

Metric	Standard
3 L baking dish (30 x 20 x 5 cm)	12 x 8 x 2 in. baking dish
220°C	425°F
20 min.	
Serves: 4-6	

Ingredients:

Ham Rolls:

500 mL ground ham	2 cups ground ham
50 mL soft butter	3 tbsps. soft butter
15 mL prepared mustard	1 tbsp. prepared mustard
750 mL flour	3 cups flour
20 mL baking powder	4 tsps. baking powder
2 mL salt	½ tsp. salt
60 mL shortening	4 tbsps. shortening
175 mL milk	¾ cup milk

Combine ground ham, soft butter and prepared mustard; mix well. Sift together flour, baking powder and salt. Add shortening, mix well. Add milk to make soft dough. Toss dough lightly on floured surface till smooth. Roll out to 1 cm (½ in.) thickness. Spread with ham mixture. Roll up and cut in 4 cm (1½ in.) slices. Flatten each slice to 2 cm (1 in.) thickness. Bake on greased pan, and serve with following:

Cheese Sauce:

Metric	Standard
30 mL butter	2 tbsps. butter
30 mL flour	2 tbsps. flour
5 mL salt	1 tsp. salt
500 mL milk	2 cups milk
125 mL grated cheese	½ cup grated cheese

In a 1 L (1 qt.) saucepan, melt butter; add flour and salt, stirring well to blend. Slowly add milk, stirring until thick and smooth. Bring to boil and cook two minutes. Add grated cheese. Stir until cheese has melted. Pour over ham rolls and serve.

CURRY AND RICE

Metric	Standard
1-2 L skillet or saucepan	1-2 qt. skillet or saucepan
Serves: 4-6	

Ingredients:

Curry:

125 mL chopped onion	½ cup chopped onion
15 mL butter	1 tbsp. butter
200-300 g chopped meat (chicken, beefsteak, veal)	¾ lbs. chopped meat (chicken, beefsteak, veal)
125 mL water	½ cup water
flour	flour
15 mL curry powder	1 tbsp. curry powder
15 mL vinegar	1 tbsp. vinegar
pinch of salt	pinch of salt
1 can (540 mL) tomatoes	1 can (19 oz.) tomatoes

Sauce:

canned tomatoes	canned tomatoes
50 mL chopped onion	¼ cup chopped onion
10 mL vinegar	2 tsps. vinegar
salt and pepper to taste	salt and pepper to taste
250 mL uncooked rice	1 cup uncooked rice

For Curry:

Sauté chopped onion in butter just till limp. Dredge chopped meat in a little flour, add to onion and brown. Add water, curry powder, vinegar (if meat is tough), salt and 250 mL (1 cup) of canned tomatoes (keep remainder for sauce).

For Sauce:

Combine all ingredients. Cook rice and serve with curry and sauce.

BROWN GRAVY

Metric	Standard
Yield: About 500 mL	2 cups

Ingredients:

50 mL drippings	¼ cup drippings
50 mL flour	¼ cup flour
500 mL liquid	2 cups liquid
(water, meat or vegetable stock)	(water, meat or vegetable stock)
salt and pepper to taste	salt and pepper to taste

Always make gravy in the pan in which meat was cooked. When meat is done, remove from pan to a hot platter. Keep warm in oven with heat off or on low. Pour off excess fat, leaving drippings in pan. Add flour and cook, stirring constantly until flour becomes brown but not burned. Remove pan from direct heat and add cool liquid. Return to low heat and cook, stirring constantly until gravy boils and thickens. Season to taste. Serve.

Note:

To prevent gravy from becoming lumpy, put cold water in a small container with a lid. Add necessary flour and shake well. Pour into gravy drippings and add remaining liquid. Return to heat and complete as above.

Variations:

Milk Gravy:

Use milk as all or part of the liquid. Serve with roast, poultry, veal, pork chops or cutlets.

Giblet Gravy:

Add finely chopped, cooked, steamed or baked giblets to brown or milk gravy. Serve with roast poultry.

Onion Gravy:

Add 125 mL (½ cup) raw sliced onions to drippings. Cook until clear and golden brown, stirring occasionally to prevent burning. Add flour and proceed as for brown gravy. Serve with roast beef, baked heart, baked or fried liver or meat loaf.

Tomato Gravy:

Use sieved canned tomatoes or tomato juice as all or part of the liquid. Serve with roast beef, veal, lamb, pork, baked or fried liver, baked heart, chops, cutlets, meat or liver loaf.

PIES

PIE PASTRY

Metric	Standard
Yield: pastry for 3 double **or** 6 single crust pies	

Ingredients:

Metric	Standard
1500 mL flour	6 cups flour
5 mL baking powder	1 tsp. baking powder
15 mL salt	1 tbsp. salt
500 mL Crisco shortening	2 cups Crisco shortening
1 egg	1 egg
15 mL white vinegar	1 tbsp. white vinegar
150-175 mL milk	½-¾ cup milk

Sift dry ingredients. Add Crisco and mix in well. Break egg into measuring cup. Stir just to break up. Add vinegar and milk to make 225 mL (⅞ cup). Mix and add to flour mixture, stirring just to moisten. Place on well floured surface. Flour hands well and work dough into a ball. Divide into six sections and roll out for crusts.

Note:

Pastry sections may be wrapped individually in saran wrap and foil and frozen. Take out to thaw six hours before using. An excellent pastry.

FRUIT PIE FILLING

Metric	Standard
3 jars (455 mL each)	3 pt. jars
Yield: 1.5 L	6 cups

Ingredients:

Metric	Standard
2 L raw fruit	2 qts. raw fruit
1250 mL sugar	5 cups sugar
75 mL water	⅓ cup water
45 mL tapioca	3 tbsps. tapioca

Sterilize jars and keep hot. Peel and slice fruit, removing pits or seeds. Pour 500 mL (2 cups) sugar over fruit. Let stand till sugar is dissolved. Add water and boil in 3 L (3 qts.) sauce pan for one minute. Add remaining sugar and tapioca. Boil for another minute. Pour into hot sterilized jars and close immediately with hot lids to seal. One jar should be enough for a 750 mL (8 in.) pie.

Note:

Suggested fruit: peaches, apricots, cherries, strawberries.

PASTRY MIX

Metric	Standard
Yield: pastry for 2 double crust pies and one pie shell	

Ingredients:

Metric	Standard
2500 mL sifted pastry flour	10 cups sifted pastry flour
5 mL salt	1 tsp. salt
500 mL shortening	2 cups shortening

With a pastry blender or 2 knives, cut in 250 mL shortening until the texture resembles cornmeal (assures tenderness). Then cut in remaining shortening to the size of peas (for flakiness). DO NOT OVERMIX. Store in container with tight fitting lid in a cool place (need not be in refrigerator).

Two Crust Pie:

Metric	Standard
675 mL pastry mix	2⅔ cups pastry mix
60 mL cold water	¼ cup cold water
3 mL vinegar	¾ tsp. vinegar

Mix to form soft dough (as with any pastry). Roll out on floured board. Bake as required for filling.

One Crust Pie Shell:

Metric	Standard
375 mL pastry mix	1½ cups pastry mix
30 mL cold water	2 tbsps. cold water
1 mL vinegar	¼ tsp. vinegar

Combine as above. Bake at 240°C (475°F) 8-10 minutes or as directed for filling used.

PINEAPPLE PIE

Metric	Standard
1 L pie (23 x 3 cm)	9 in. pie

Ingredients:

Metric	Standard
250 mL crushed pineapple	1 cup crushed pineapple
125 mL water	½ cup water
30 mL flour	2 tbsps. flour
50 mL sugar	¼ cup sugar
pinch of salt	pinch of salt
2 eggs, beaten	2 eggs, beaten
baked pie shell	baked pie shell

Bring crushed pineapple (undrained) and water to a boil. Mix dry ingredients, add beaten eggs. Add to pineapple mixture. Boil until thick. Pour into baked pie shell; chill. Top with whipped cream and serve.

APPLE PIE

Metric	Standard
1 L pie pan (23 x 4 cm)	9 in. pie pan
190-200°C	375-400°F
30-45 min.	

Ingredients:

425 mL peeled, sliced apples	1¾ cups peeled, sliced apples
125 mL sugar	½ cup sugar
15 mL flour	1 tbsp. flour
1 mL cinnamon	¼ tsp. cinnamon
7 mL butter	1½ tsps. butter
pastry for double-crust pie	pastry for double-crust pie

Combine first four ingredients. Prepare pie shell. Fill with apple mixture. Dot with butter. Cover with top crust. Slit with scissors to allow steam to escape. Bake till filling bubbles and crust is golden.

DUTCH APPLE PIE

Metric	Standard
1 L pie pan	9 in. pie pan
220°C — 10 min.	425°F
160°C — 45 min.	325°F

Ingredients:

pastry for one pie shell	pastry for one pie shell
6 or 8 apples	6 or 8 apples
200 mL brown sugar	⅞ cup brown sugar
75 mL white sugar	⅓ cup white sugar
2 mL cinnamon	½ tsp. cinnamon
75 mL flour	⅓ cup flour
200 mL light **or** sour cream	⅞ cup light **or** sour cream

Line pie pan with pastry. Pare, core and quarter or slice apples. Mix sugars, cinnamon and flour. Place half of mixture in bottom of pie shell. Over this arrange quartered apples in rows. Mix light cream with remainder of sugar mixture. Pour over apples. Bake at higher temperature for 10 minutes. Reduce heat and bake for about 45 minutes until apples are translucent and tender. Serve hot. A delicious pie.

RHUBARB PIE

Metric	Standard
1 L pie pan (2343 mm)	9 in. pie pan
220°C — 10 min.	425°F — 10 min.
160°C — 30 min.	325°F — 30 min.

Ingredients:

Metric	Standard
	Pastry for double crust pie
Pastry for double crust pie	
625 mL diced rhubarb	1½-3 cups diced rhubarb
250 mL sugar	1 cup sugar
50 mL flour	3 tbsps. flour
2 egg yolks	2 egg yolks
15 mL lemon juice	1 tbsp. lemon juice
15 mL melted butter or margarine	1 tbsp. melted butter or margarine

Line pie pan with pastry. Arrange rhubarb in pie pan. Combine sugar and flour, add egg yolks, lemon juice and melted butter. Stir to a smooth paste. Pour over rhubarb. Cover with top crust, slit to allow for steam escape. Bake at higher temperature for 10 minutes. Reduce temperature and bake for 30 minutes.

Variation:

Omit top crust. Top pie with meringue and bake for an additional 10 minutes at 220°C (425°F).

RHUBARB CUSTARD PIE

Metric	Standard
1 L pie pan (23 x 3 cm)	9 in. pie pan
220°C — 20 min.	425°F
200°C — 20 min.	400°F
160°C — 15-20 min.	325°F

Ingredients:

Metric	Standard
Pastry for one pie shell	Pastry for one pie shell
750 mL diced rhubarb	3 cups diced rhubarb
125 mL sugar	½ cup sugar
50 mL flour	3 tbsps. flour
2 egg yolks	2 egg yolks
5 mL lemon extract (optional)	1 tsp. lemon extract (optional)
pinch of nutmeg	pinch of nutmeg
250 mL milk	1 cup milk

Line pie pan with pastry. Fill shell with diced rhubarb. Mix remaining ingredients in order given. Pour over rhubarb. Bake at high temperature for 20 minutes. Reduce heat and continue baking for 20 minutes. Prepare meringue from 2 egg whites. Remove pie from oven and top with meringue. Return to oven, reduce heat to 160°C (325°F). Bake until meringue is firm and golden brown.

RAISIN CREAM PIE

Metric	Standard
1 L pie pan (23 x 3 cm)	9 in. pie pan
160°C	325°F
40-45 min.	

Ingredients:

250 mL raisins	1 cup raisins
hot water	hot water
250 mL cream **or** whole milk	1 cup cream **or** whole milk
250 mL sugar	1 cup sugar
30 mL flour	2 tbsps. flour
1 mL cinnamon	¼ tsp. cinnamon
grated rind of one lemon **or**	grated rind of one lemon **or**
1 mL lemon extract	¼ tsp. lemon extract
2 eggs, separated	2 eggs, separated
30 mL icing sugar	2 tbsps. icing sugar
baked pie shell	baked pie shell

Cover raisins with hot water, stew till tender and thick. Drain, add cream to raisins. Mix sugar, flour, cinnamon, grated lemon rind and add to raisins. Cook slowly for five minutes. Stir in beaten egg yolks and cook a few minutes longer, till mixture is well thickened. Pour into baked pie shell. Bake for about 30 minutes. Beat egg whites, adding icing sugar gradually. Remove pie from oven, top with meringue. Return to oven and bake for another 12 minutes or until meringue is golden and done.

CHOCOLATE CREAM PIE

Metric	Standard
2 L double boiler	2 qt. double boiler
Yield: pudding for 1 22.5 cm pie crust	pudding for 1 9" pie crust

Ingredients:

2 sqs. chocolate **or** 50 mL cocoa	2 sqs. chocolate **or** 3 tbsps. cocoa
500 mL milk	2 cups milk
250 mL sugar	1 cup sugar
15 mL butter	1 tbsp. butter
2 mL salt	½ tsp. salt
50 mL cornstarch **or** 60 mL flour	3 tbsps. cornstarch **or** 4 tbsps. flour
2 eggs, separated	2 eggs, separated
5 mL vanilla	1 tsp. vanilla
pastry for 1 22.5 cm crust	pastry for 1 9" crust

Melt chocolate in top of double boiler. Add 375 mL (1½ cups) milk and bring to boiling point. Combine sugar, salt and cornstarch. Add remaining milk to make a smooth paste. Add paste to chocolate mixture; cook until thickened. Stir egg yolks with a fork. Pour a small amount of hot mixture over egg yolks, mix and **then** add to remaining hot mixture. Cook 2 minutes. Remove from heat, add butter and vanilla. Cool and pour into baked pie shell. Cover with whipped cream or meringue.

RAISIN PIE

Metric	Standard
1 L pie pan (23 x 3 cm)	9 in. pie pan
200°C	400°F
25-30 min.	

Ingredients:

250 mL chopped raisins	1 cup chopped raisins
250 mL hot water	1 cup hot water
2 mL butter	½ tsp. butter
½ lemon rind, grated	½ lemon rind, grated
250 mL brown sugar	1 cup brown sugar
10 mL cornstarch	2 tsps. cornstarch
1 mL salt	¼ tsp. salt
1 egg, beaten	1 egg, beaten
15 mL lemon juice	1 tbsp. lemon juice
pastry for double-crust pie	pastry for double-crust pie

Combine raisins, water, butter and lemon rind. Bring to boil and cook for five minutes. Cool and mix in beaten egg; blend well. Pour into unbaked pie shell. Cover with top pastry and bake.

LEMON PIE

Metric	Standard
1 L pie pan (23 x 3 cm)	9 in. pie pan

Ingredients:

Metric	Standard
1 small lemon, juice and rind	1 small lemon, juice and rind
500 mL water	2 cups water
250 mL sugar	1 cup sugar
50 mL cornstarch	¼ cup cornstarch
1 mL salt	¼ tsp. salt
3 eggs, separated	3 eggs, separated
15 mL butter	1 tbsp. butter
baked 1 L pie shell	baked 9 in. pie shell

Combine lemon juice and rind with 375 mL (1½ cups) of water. Place in double boiler and bring to boil. Meanwhile mix sugar, cornstarch, salt and remaining water. Add to hot mixture and cool for 15 minutes. Beat egg yolks slightly and add to hot mixture. Cook for 1 minute. Add butter and stir in. Remove from heat and cool. Pour into baked pie shell. For meringue, use remaining egg whites. Follow "MILE HIGH MERINGUE" recipe to complete pie.

MILE HIGH MERINGUE

Metric	Standard
160°C	325°F
12 min.	
Yield: Sufficient for one pie or 12 tarts	

Ingredients:

Metric	Standard
3 egg whites	3 egg whites
30 mL cold water	2 tbsps. cold water
pinch of salt	pinch of salt
1 mL cream of tartar	¼ tsp. cream of tartar
1 mL flavouring	¼ tsp. flavouring
50 mL granulated sugar **or** icing sugar	3 tbsps. granulated sugar **or** icing sugar

Combine egg whites and cold water in large bowl. Beat until frothy. Add salt, cream of tartar, and flavouring. Beat until stiff. Add sugar and beat to stiff peaks. Pile on to hot pie, tarts or cake and bake for time suggested or until golden.

BAKED LEMON PIE

Metric	Standard
1 L pie pan (23 x 3 cm)	9 in. pie pan an
220°C — 5 min.	425°F
160°C — 30 min.	325°F

Ingredients:

30 mL butter	2 tbsps. butter
125 mL sugar	½ cup sugar
2 eggs, separated	2 eggs, separated
30 mL flour	2 tbsps. flour
juice and rind of 1 lemon	juice and rind of 1 lemon
2 mL salt	½ tsp. salt
250 mL milk	1 cup milk
unbaked pie shell	unbaked pie shell

Cream butter and sugar together. Add egg yolks, flour, juice and rind of lemon, and salt. Mix well. Add milk and mix well. Beat egg whites to stiff peaks and fold in. Line DEEP, DARK pie pan with pastry. Pour in filling and bake for five minutes at high temperature. Lower heat and continue baking until knife comes out lean when placed in center.

Note: Filling usually separates in layers, but make the pie none the less tasty.

PUMPKIN PIE

Metric	Standard
1 L pie pan (23 x 3 cm)	9 in. pie pan
180°C	350°F
35 min.	

Ingredients:

375 mL pumpkin	1½ cups pumpkin
30 mL flour	2 tbsps. flour
250 mL sugar	1 cup sugar
5 mL ginger	1 tsp. ginger
5 mL cinnamon	1 tsp. cinnamon
dash of nutmeg	dash of nutmeg
2 mL mace	½ tsp. mace
1 mL salt	¼ tsp. salt
3 eggs	3 eggs
125 mL milk	½ cup milk
pastry for 1 23 cm. pie	pastry for 1 9 in. pie

Combine pumpkin, flour, sugar, spices and salt. Beat eggs, add milk. Combine egg mixture with pumpkin; mix well. Pour into pastry lined pie plate. Bake until firm.

CHIFFON PUMPKIN PIE

Metric	Standard
Yield: 1 L pie (23 x 3 cm)	9 in. pie

Ingredients:

Metric	Standard
1 pkg. (7 g) unflavoured gelatin	1 pkg. unflavoured gelatin
125 mL cold water	½ cup cold water
300 mL cooked pumpkin	1¼ cups cooked pumpkin
125 mL milk	½ cup milk
250 mL sugar	1 cup sugar
3 eggs, beaten separately	3 eggs, beaten separately
2 mL ginger	½ tsp. ginger
2 mL nutmeg	½ tsp. nutmeg
2 mL cinnamon	½ tsp. cinnamon
2 mL salt	½ tsp. salt
1 baked pie shell	1 baked pie shell

Soak unflavoured gelatin in cold water and allow to stand for a few mintues. Mix cooked pumpkin, milk, sugar, egg yolks and spices. Cook in double boiler until thick, add gelatin and stir till dissolved. When filling begins to set, fold in stiffly beaten egg whites. Pour into baked pie shell. Chill and serve with whipped cream. A delicious refreshing pie.

MINCEMEAT PIE

Metric	Standard
Two 1 L pie pans (23 c 3 cm)	Two 9 in. pie pans
220°C — 190°C	425°F — 375°F
45 min.	

Ingredients:

Metric	Standard
500 mL chopped apples	2 cups chopped apples
375 mL raisins	1½ cups raisins
125 mL currants	½ cup currants
50 mL citron peel	¼ cup citron peel
50 mL chopped nuts	¼ cup chopped nuts
125 mL chopped suet	½ cup chopped suet
250 mL brown sugar	1 cup brown sugar
25 mL mixed juice	2 tbsps. mixed juice
75 mL rich fruit juice	⅓ cup rich fruit juice
pastry for two double-crust pies	pastry for two double-crust pies

Combine ingredients in order given. Line pie pans with pastry. Distribute filling evenly in pans. Top with remaining pastry, slitting steam holes in top. Bake for 15 minutes at higher temperature. Reduce heat and bake for another 30 minutes or until pastry is golden brown and filling bubbles. Serve hot.

FLAPPERS PIE

Metric	Standard
1 L pie pan (23 x 3 cm)	9 in. pie pan
160°F	325°F
20 min.	

Ingredients:
Crust:

14 Graham wafers (rolled fine)	14 Graham wafers (rolled fine)
50 mL melted butter	¼ cup melted butter
50 mL sugar	¼ cup sugar
5 mL cinnamon	1 tsp. cinnamon

Combine and reserve 125 mL (½ cup) for top of pie. Use balance to line pie pan.

Filling:

500 mL milk	2 cups milk
2 egg yolks	2 egg yolks
50 mL cornstarch	¼ cup cornstarch
5 mL vanilla extract **or** fruit if desired	1 tsp. vanilla extract **or** fruit if desired
50 mL sugar	¼ cup sugar

Combine ingredients in 1 L (1 qt.) saucepan. Bring to a boil and cook until thick. While hot, spread over pie crust.

Topping:

2 egg whites	2 egg whites
45 mL icing sugar	3 tbsps. icing sugar

Beat egg whites to stiff peaks. Add sugar gradually, beating as you add. Spread over filling and sprinkle crumbs over top. Bake.

APPLE DUMPLINGS

Metric	Standard
3.5 L baking dish (33 x 21 x 5 cm)	13 x 9 x 2 in. baking dish
190°-200°C	375°-400°F
20 min.	
Yield: 15-18	

Ingredients:

750 mL flour	3 cups flour
5 mL salt	1 tsp. salt
30 mL butter	2 tbsps. butter
1 egg	1 egg
175 mL (approx.) heavy sweet cream	¾ cup (approx.) heavy sweet cream
7-9 baking apples	7-9 baking apples

Mix flour and salt. Cut in butter to make crumbs. Beat **egg** and add cream to make 250 mL (1 cup). Combine flour and **egg** mixtures. Mix well to make a uniform dough. Roll out on floured surface to 0.5 (¼ in.) thickness. Cut in 7 cm (3 in.) squares. Peel, halve and core apples. On each piece of dough, place an apple half. Fold over corners and press together. Place in slightly greased pan. Bake. Brush each with milk and sprinkle with brown sugar; return to oven and bake until slightly brown and apples are done when tested with a fork.

Optional:
Apple halves may be cut in slices instead of leaving whole. Apple pie filling may be substituted for fresh apples.

BUTTER TARTS

Metric	*Standard*
200°C, 180°C	400°F, 350°F
15-20 min.	
Yield: 12 medium tarts	

Ingredients:

250 mL brown sugar	1 cup brown sugar
50 mL butter	¼ cup butter
2 eggs	2 eggs
pinch of salt	pinch of salt
2 mL vanilla	½ tsp. vanilla
75 mL corn syrup **or**	⅓ cup corn syrup **or**
maple syrup	maple syrup
(optinal)	(optional)
250-375 mL raisins **or**	1-1½ cups raisins **or**
currants	currants
pastry for 12	pastry for 12
medium tarts	medium tarts

Prepare pastry dough. Wash and dry raisins. Cream brown sugar and butter. Add eggs, salt, vanilla and corn syrup; mix well. Fold in raisins. Place pastry (or cookie dough may be used) into muffin or tart tins. Place filling by spoonfuls into tart shells. Bake at higher temperature for 8 minutes. Reduce heat and bake for an additional 5-10 minutes, or until pastry is delicately browned.

FILLING FOR BUTTER TARTS

Metric	Standard
2 L saucepan	2 qt. saucepan

Yield: filling for 12 tarts

Ingredients:

500 mL brown sugar	2 cups brown sugar
30 mL flour	2 tbsps. flour
dash of salt	⅛ tsp. salt
500 mL raisins	2 cups raisins
500 mL boiling water	2 cups boiling water
45 mL lemon juice	3 tbsps. lemon juice
30 mL lemon rind	2 tbsps. lemon rind
125 mL nuts (optional)	½ cup nuts (optional)

Combine sugar, flour, salt and raisins in saucepan. Pour in boiling water. Bring mixture to a boil; simmer until raisins are plump and the mixture thickens. Remove from heat and stir in remaining ingredients. This filling may be used in baked or unbaked tart shells. For unbaked shells, bake at 160°C (325°F) for about 20-25 minutes. Top with whipped cream if desired.

SALADS

PINEAPPLE SALAD

Metric | Standard

Serves: 6

Ingredients:

1 pkg. (85 g) lemon jello powder
450 mL boiling water
250 mL crushed pineapple, drained
125 mL whipping cream **or** 1 pkg. (42.5 g) Dream Whip **plus** 100 mL milk

1 pkg. (3 oz.) lemon jello powder
2 cups boiling water
1 cup crushed pineapple, drained
½ cup whipping cream **or** 1 pkg. Dream Whip **plus** ½ cup milk

Dissolve jello in boiling water and let thicken. Add drained pineapple and let set. Whip cream and spread over surface of set jello. Serve on lettuce leaf with grated cheese or nuts on top.

Variation:

This could also be a dessert by folding whipped cream into jello before it sets.

ORANGE CARROT SALAD

Metric | Standard

1 L jelly mold
Serves: 4-6

1 qt. jelly mold

Ingredients:

1 pkg. (85 g) lemon jello powder
250 mL boiling water
200 mL cold water
1 mL salt
30 mL vinegar
4-6 medium carrots
125 mL finely cut celery (optional)
1 mL finely grated orange peel

1 pkg. (3 oz.) lemon jello powder
1 cup boiling water
1 cup cold water
¼ tsp. salt
2 tbsps. vinegar
4-6 medium carrots
½ cup finely cut celery (optional)
¼ tsp. finely grated orange peel

Dissolve lemon jello powder in boiling water, stir. Add cold water, salt and vinegar. Grate carrots, finely and add with remaining ingredients. Rinse jelly mold with water and add jello mixture. Chill till firm. Unmold on crisp lettuce. Serve with mayonnaise.

GINGERALE FRUIT SALAD

Metric	Standard
1 1.5 L mold **or**	1 1½ qt. mold **or**
10 125 mL molds	10 ½ cup molds
Serves: 8-10	

Ingredients:

Metric	Standard
20 mL unflavoured gelatin	4 tsps. unflavoured gelatin
75 mL cold juice	⅓ cup cold juice
125 mL boiling orange juice	½ cup boiling orange juice
50 mL lemon juice	¼ cup lemon juice
50 mL sugar	¼ cup sugar
250 mL gingerale	1 cup gingerale
250 mL grapes	1 cup grapes
2 oranges	2 oranges
1 apple	1 apple
1 banana	1 banana
50 mL chopped nuts (optional)	¼ cup chopped nuts

Soak gelatin in cold juice for five minutes. Then dissolve in boiling juice. Add lemon juice, sugar and gingerale; chill. Cut grapes in half and remove seeds. Peel and section oranges, removing membranes. Peel and chop apple. Peel and slice bananas. Mix fruit to prevent apple and banana from turning brown. When gelatine begins to thicken, add fruit and nuts. Pour into one large or several individual molds to set. Serve on crisp lettuce leaves with fruit and dressing.

Note:

Add a few drops of food colouring to gelatine mixture while still warm and mix well.

PINEAPPLE SALAD

Metric	Standard
1.5 L dish	1½ qt. dish
Serves: 10-12	

Ingredients:

Metric	Standard
2 pkg. (85 g ea.) lime Jello powder	2 pkg. (3 oz. ea.) lime Jello powder
150 mL drained pineapple juice and water	⅔ cup drained pineapple juice and water
125 mL crushed pineapple, drained	½ cup crushed pineapple, drained
125 mL Philadelphia cream cheese	½ cup Philadelphia cream cheese
250 mL chopped celery	1 cup chopped celery

250 mL whipped cream	1 cup whipped cream
125 mL chopped nuts	½ cup chopped nuts
Lettuce	Lettuce

Drain pineapple, measure juice and add water to measure 175 mL (⅔ cup). Bring liquid to a boil, pour over Jello powder and stir to dissolve. Cool until partly set. Add remaining ingredients. Allow to set firmly. Cut and serve on a lettuce leaf.

FRUIT SALAD WITH A COOKED DRESSING

Metric   *Standard*

Serves: 8-10

Ingredients:

Metric	Standard
1 can (540 mL) tidbit **or** crushed pineapple	1 can (19 oz.) tidbit **or** crushed pineapple
1 can (284 mL) fruit cocktail	1 can (10 oz.) fruit cocktail
2 cans (284 mL ea.) mandarin oranges **or** meat of 1 fresh orange	2 cans (10 oz. ea.) mandarin oranges **or** meat of 1 fresh orange
2 eggs beaten	2 eggs beaten
50 mL sugar	¼ cup sugar
30 mL vinegar	2 tbsps. vinegar
30 mL butter	2 tbsps. butter
150 mL drained fruit juice	⅔ cup drained fruit juice
250 mL whipping cream **or** 1 pkg. (42.5 g) Dream Whip **plus** 100 mL milk	1 cup whipping cream **or** 1 pkg. Dream Whip **plus** ½ cup milk
500 mL miniature marshmallows	2 cups miniature marshmallows

Drain fruit well and save juice. Combine beaten eggs, sugar, vinegar, butter and drained fruit juice. Boil in double boiler till thick; chill. Whip cream and add to chilled dressing. Combine fruit, marshmallows and dressing; chill. Garnish with maraschino cherries, coconut or nuts.

Note:

Salad is even more delicious if refrigerated for a day before serving.

JELLIED VEGETABLE SALAD

Metric	Standard
Serves: 6	

Ingredients:

Metric	Standard
1 pkg. (85 g) lemon Jello powder	1 pkg. (3 oz.) lemon Jello powder
225 mL boiling water	1 cup boiling water
125 mL cold water	½ cup cold water
15 mL onion, minced	1 tbsp. minced onion
2 mL salt	½ tsp. salt
15 mL vinegar	1 tbsp. vinegar
125 mL finely shredded cabbage	½ cup finely shredded cabbage
125 mL finely shredded carrots	½ cup finely shredded carrots
125 mL chopped celery	½ cup chopped celery
15 mL chopped pimento (optional)	1 tbsp. chopped pimento (optional)

Place Jello powder in a 1 L (1 qt.) bowl. Add boiling water and stir until completely dissolved. Pour in cold water; stir well. Add onion, salt, and vinegar; stir until blended. Chill in refrigerator until mixture is thick and syrupy (approx. 1 hr.) Shred cabbage and carrots. Chop celery and pimento. Fold vegetables into thickened gelatine (distribute evenly). Pour into 750 mL (3 cups) loaf pan. Chill until firm (3 hours or longer). Unmold on platter and trim with crisp lettuce or other greens. Cut and serve.

Optional:

Use individual 125 mL (½ cup) salad molds. Serve on individual salad plates.

CHRISTMAS SALAD

Metric	Standard
Yield: 1 L	1 qt.
Serves: 6-8	

Ingredients:

Metric	Standard
15 mL gelatine	1 tbsp. gelatine
125 mL cold water	½ cup cold water
200 mL hot water	¾ cup hot water
75 mL sugar	⅓ cup sugar
2 mL salt	½ tsp. salt
60 mL lemon juice **or** weak vinegar	4 tbsps. lemon juice **or** weak vinegar
250 mL cooked beets (chopped fine)	1 cup cooked beets (chopped fine)

125 mL chopped nuts	½ cup chopped nuts
15 mL horseradish	1 tbsp. horseradish
salad dressing	salad dressing

Soak gelatine in cold water for 2 minutes, then add hot water and stir until gelatine dissolves. Add sugar and salt, stirring until they dissolve. Add lemon juice. Put aside until mixture begins to set. Then add remaining ingredients, turn mixture into a mold. Allow to set firmly. Unmold and serve with salad dressing.

BEET SALAD

Metric	*Standard*
1 L pot	1 qt. pot
Serves: 6-8	

Ingredients:

1 can (540 mL) diced beets	1 can (19 oz.) diced beets
or freshly cooked beets	**or** freshly cooked beets
15 mL flour	1 tbsp. flour
15 mL vinegar	1 tbsp. vinegar
15 mL water	1 tbsp. water
175 mL sugar	¾ cup sugar
5 mL salt	1 tsp. salt

Drain beets, measuring liquid. Replace liquid with equal amount of water. Heat to boiling. Mix remaining ingredients and add to beets. Bring to boil, stirring occasionally. Serve hot or cold.

Variation:

Add freshly sliced onion rings or diced celery to beet salad.

SAUERKRAUT SALAD

Metric	*Standard*
Yield: 1.25 L	5 cups

Ingredients:

1 can (398 mL) sauerkraut, drained	1 can (14 oz.) sauerkraut, drained
250 mL chopped green peppers	1 cup chopped green peppers
250 mL chopped onion	1 cup chopped onion
250 mL chopped celery	1 cup chopped celery
50 mL grated carrots	¼ cup grated carrots
375 mL sugar	1½ cup sugar
175 mL vinegar	⅔ cup vinegar

Drain sauerkraut, prepare vegetables. Measure sugar and vinegar into 1 L (1 qt.) saucepan; bring to a boil. Cool. Pour cooled vinegar mixture over vegetable mixture. Toss to mix. Refrigerate 24 hours to blend. Store in refrigerator. Stays fresh indefinitely.

FRUIT SALAD DELIGHT

Metric	Standard
Serves: 8-10	

Ingredients:

Metric	Standard
1 pkg. (113 g) instant vanilla pudding **plus** 450 mL cold milk	1 pkg. (4 oz.) instant vanilla pudding **plus** 2 cups cold milk
1 grapefruit	1 grapefruit
2 oranges	2 oranges
2 bananas	2 bananas
1 can (540 mL) fruit cocktail	1 can (19 oz.) fruit cocktail
1 can (540 mL) pineapple chunks	1 can (19 oz.) pineapple chunks
500 mL miniature marshmallows	2 cups miniature marshmallows
125 mL whipping cream	½ cup whipping cream

Prepare pudding following package directions. Peel, section and skin fresh fruit. Drain well. Drain canned fruit. Add fruit and miniature marshmallows to chilled pudding. Beat whipping cream and fold in. Place in fridge to chill and serve.

Variation:

Instant pudding may be replaced by cooked pudding. Any kind of fruit may be used but should be well drained. Fruit should be coated generously with pudding.

MYSTERY SALAD

Metric	Standard
Yield: 1 L	1 qt.

Ingredients:

Metric	Standard
1 can (796 mL) drained sauerkraut	1 can (28 oz.) drained sauerkraut
250 mL chopped celery	1 cup chopped celery
125 mL chopped onion	½ cup chopped onion
125 mL chopped green peppers	½ cup chopped green peppers
pimento strips (optional)	pimento strips (optional)
250 mL sugar	1 cup sugar
125 mL vinegar	½ cup vinegar

Combine vegetables. Bring sugar and vinegar to a boil, stirring until sugar dissolves. Cool slightly and pour over vegetables. Let stand overnight to marinate. Serve cold and store remainder in refrigerator.

FOAMY SALAD

Metric	*Standard*
Serves: about 10	

Ingredients:

250 mL sweet cherries	1 cup sweet cherries
250 mL canned orange **or** mandarin slices	1 cup canned orange **or** mandarin slices
250 mL crushed pineapple	1 cup crushed pineapple
500 mL shredded cabbage	2 cups shredded cabbage
250 mL chopped nuts	1 cup chopped nuts
250 mL chopped marshmallows	1 cup chopped marshmallows
1 pkg. (42.5 g) Dream Whip **plus** 125 mL milk **or** 250 mL whipping cream	1 pkg. Dream Whip **plus** ½ cup milk **or** 1 cup whipping cream
250 mL mayonnaise	1 cup mayonnaise

Drain fruit well and measure. Combine fruit, cabbage, nuts and marshmallows. Prepare Dream Whip and add to mayonnaise. Pour this dressing over salad mixture and fold in. Chill in refrigerator for 1 hour before serving.

STUFFED TOMATOES

Metric	*Standard*
Serves: 4	

Ingredients:

4 medium tomatoes	4 medium tomatoes
salt and pepper	salt and pepper
2 hard cooked eggs	2 hard cooked eggs
125 mL chopped celery	½ cup chopped celery
5 mL chopped onion	1 tsp. chopped onion
15 mL chopped nuts	1 tbsp. chopped nuts
15 mL chopped green pepper	1 tbsp. chopped green pepper
75 mL mayonnaise	⅓ cup mayonnaise
15 mL chopped dill pickles	1 tbsp. chopped dill pickles
paprika	paprika

Cut round capsule from stem end of tomatoes. Scoop out flesh, drain, chop and save. Sprinkle tomatoes with salt and pepper on the inside. Chop hard cooked eggs and mix with remaining ingredients including tomato flesh. Stuff well drained tomatoes and sprinkle with paprika. Chill and serve as side salad on lettuce cup.

COLE SLAW

Metric	Standard
Serves: about 6	

Ingredients:

Metric	Standard
1 L shredded cabbage	4 cups shredded cabbage
3 medium carrots, grated	3 medium carrots, grated
chopped green onion	chopped green onion
to taste	to taste
45 mL lemon juice	3 tbsps. lemon juice
45 mL sugar	3 tbsps. sugar
2 mL salt	½ tsp. salt

Combine vegetables and mix lightly. Combine remaining ingredients in tightly closing container. Shake well and pour over vegetables. Toss lightly and serve this delicious salad.

QUICK COLE SLAW

Metric	Standard
Serves: 6-8	

Ingredients:

Metric	Standard
1 L finely shredded cabbage	1 qt. finely shredded cabbage
¼ green pepper	¼ green pepper
¼ sweet pepper	¼ sweet pepper
a few drops onion juice	a few drops onion juice
5 mL salt	1 tsp. salt
5 mL sugar	1 tsp. sugar
dash pepper	dash pepper
75 mL mayonnaise	⅓ cup mayonnaise
30 mL vinegar	2 tbsps. vinegar

To finely shredded cabbage add red and green peppers cut in thin strips. Add onion juice, salt, sugar and pepper; mix. Combine mayonnaise and vinegar. Pour over cabbage and mix well.

HEAT WAVE FRUIT PLATE

Serves: 1 or many, depending on amount of ingredients.

Ingredients:

Lettuce
Pineapple **or** cantaloupe slice
Scoop of lime sherbet
Grated chocolate **or** cream cheese and chopped nuts
Fresh red berries (strawberries, raspberries, etc.)

Banana
Quartered **or** miniature marshmallows
Apricot halves
Blueberries **or** saskatoons
Nut bread
Jellied fruit mold
Arrange as follows:

Make bed of lettuce on plate. On lettuce, place pineapple slice. Top with scoop of lime sherbet. Sprinkle with grated chocolate. Fill lettuce cup with fresh red berries. Dice banana and place beside lettuce cup, along with marshmallows. Fill apricot halves with blueberries to overflowing and arrange on plate. Add sliced, lightly buttered nut bread and ready to serve jellied fruit mold. Serve on a hot summer day with lemonade and additional nut bread.

SALAD PLATE IDEAS FOR A HOT SUMMER DAY
Yield: one or more servings, depending on ingredients used.
Ingredients:
Crisp lettuce leaves
Cold sliced meat **or** cheese
Fruit **or** vegetable jello mold
Green onion
Rice salad **or** bun
Pickles
Cucumber slices **or** sticks
Celery stick stuffed with cream **or** processed cheese
Stuffed tomato **or** tomato wedges
Scoop of macaroni **or** potato salad
Radish rose **or** parsley sprig to garnish
Dab of salad dressing

Place crisp lettuce leaf as base on dinner plate. Arrange combinations of above ingredients to your liking. Serve as individual salad plate or arrange ingredients on a large platter from which each person may choose.
Variation:
Meat or cheese may be replaced by a scoop of creamed cottage cheese, canned tuna or salmon moistened with mayonnaise.

PEARS WITH CRISPED CREAM SALAD

Metric	Standard
Serves: 6	

Ingredients:

Metric	Standard
1 pkg. (113 g) Philadelphia cream cheese	1 pkg. (4 oz.) Philadelphia cream cheese
30 mL mayonnaise	2 tbsps. mayonnaise
50 mL minced green peppers	¼ cup minced green peppers
50 mL minced celery	¼ cup minced celery
30 mL minced onions	2 tbsps. minced onions
2 mL salt	½ tsp. salt
6-8 canned pear halves	6-8 canned pear halves
6 lettuce cups	6 lettuce cups

Cream cheese and mayonnaise together. Drain minced vegetables well. Add minced vegetables and salt to creamed mixture. Fill cavities of pears with cheese mixture. Serve on crisp lettuce cup as side salad.

HAM AND POTATO SALAD

Metric	Standard
Serves: 4-6	

Ingredients:

Metric	Standard
250 mL diced cooked ham	1 cup diced cooked ham
500 mL diced cooked potatoes	2 cups diced cooked potatoes
3 hard cooked eggs, chopped	3 hard cooked eggs chopped
125 mL diced celery	½ cup diced celery
125 mL mayonnaise	½ cup mayonnaise
25 mL prepared mustard	1½ tbsps. prepared mustard
salt and pepper to taste	salt and pepper to taste
crisp lettuce	crisp lettuce

Combine ham, potatoes, eggs and celery. Mix mayonnaise and prepared mustard together and combine with other ingredients. Add salt and pepper to taste. Serve on a bed of crisp lettuce.

HOT POTATO SALAD

Metric	Standard
Serves: 4-6	

Ingredients:

Metric	Standard
6 medium potatoes	6 medium potatoes
3 eggs, hard cooked	3 eggs, hard cooked

3 strips side bacon	3 strips side bacon
15 mL chopped onion	1 tbsp. chopped onion
25 mL chopped celery	1½ tbsps. chopped celery
125 mL mayonnaise	½ cup mayonnaise
salt and pepper to taste	salt and pepper to taste
sprig of parsley	sprig of parsley

Cook potatoes, peel and cube. (Do not overcook.) Dice two of the hard cooked eggs. Chop side bacon and fry. Add chopped onion and celery; cook till limp. Combine potatoes, eggs, mayonnaise, salt and pepper with onion and celery. Heat through, stirring constantly. Remove from heat. Decorate wlth remaining egg and sprig of parsley. Serve hot.

TOMATO ASPIC

Metric	Standard

Serves: 4-6

Ingredients:

1 envelope (7g) unflavoured) gelatin powder	1 envelope unflavoured gelatin powder
500 mL tomato juice	2 cups tomato juice
30 mL sugar	2 tbsps. sugar
30 mL vinegar	2 tbsps. vinegar
pinch of salt	pinch of salt
2 onion slices	2 onion slices
1 small bay leaf	1 small bay leaf
4 whole cloves	4 whole cloves
small piece chili pepper	small piece chlli pepper
stalk of celery, cut (optional)	stalk of celery, cut (optional)

Dissolve unflavoured gelatin powder in 100 mL (⅓ cup) of tomato juice to soften. Combine and simmer remaining ingredients about 10 minutes. Strain, add softened remaining gelatin to liquid; mix. Pour into 1 large or several smaller jello molds. Let set and serve.

Variation:

Add shrimp or peas before gelatin sets.

MACARONI SALAD

Metric	*Standard*
Serves: 4	

Ingredients:

500 mL cooked macaroni	2 cups cooked macaroni
4 hard cooked eggs, chopped chopped	4 hard cooked eggs, chopped
4 medium sized tomatoes, chopped	4 medium sized tomatoes, chopped
1 can (184 g) salmon **or** tuna fish	1 can (7-8 oz.) salmon **or** tuna fish
125 mL salad dressing	½ cup salad dressing
salt and pepper to taste	salt and pepper to taste

Combine all ingredients. Chill and serve on lettuce leaf with crisp crackers or toast. A tasty main dish salad.

BEAN SALAD

Metric	*Standard*
Serves: 6-8	

Ingredients:

2 cans (398 mL each) green beans	2 cans (14 oz. each) green beans
1 can (398 mL) yellow wax beans	1 can (14 oz.) yellow wax beans
1 can (398 mL) kidney beans	1 can (14 oz.) kidney beans
1 can (398 mL) lima beans (optional)	1 can (14 oz.) lima beans (optional)
1 medium onion	1 medium onion
1 green pepper	1 green pepper
150 mL white vinegar	⅔ cup white vinegar
75 mL salad oil	⅓ cup salad oil
125-150 mL sugar	½-⅔ cup sugar
salt and pepper to taste	salt and pepper to taste

Drain beans well. Slice onion and green pepper in rings; add to beans. Combine remaining ingredients; mix well and pour over vegetables. Marinate 24 hours before serving.

DEEP SEA SALAD

Metric	*Standard*
Serves: 4	

Metric	Standard
250 mL (1 can, 220 g) salmon	1 cup (1 can, 7¾ oz.) salmon
125 mL cooked peas	½ cup cooked peas
125 mL diced celery	½ cup diced celery
5 mL minced onion	1 tsp. minced onion
75 mL salad dressing	⅓ cup salad dressing
salt and pepper to taste	salt and pepper to taste
tomatoes and cucumber	tomatoes and cucumber
to garnish	to garnish

Flake salmon and mix lightly with peas, celery, and onion. Moisten with salad dressing and season to taste. Pile on crisp lettuce leaf in salad bowl and garnish with sections of tomato and sliced cucumber.

FRENCH DRESSING

Metric	*Standard*
Yield: 700 mL	approx. 3 cups

Ingredients:

250 mL salad oil	1 cup salad oil
1 can (284 mL) tomato soup	1 can (10 oz.) tomato soup
150 mL vinegar	⅔ cup vinegar
3 mL salt	¾ tsp. salt
5 mL paprika	1 tsp. paprika
chopped onion **or**	chopped onion **or**
garlic (optional)	garlic (optional)

Combine all ingredients; mix or shake well. Store in refrigerator. Shake well before using.

FRENCH DRESSING

Metric	*Standard*
Yield: 750 mL	3 cups

Ingredients:

250 mL salad oil	1 cup salad oil
150 mL vinegar	⅔ cup vinegar
125 mL sugar	½ cup sugar
5 mL dry mustard	1 tsp. dry mustard
dash of paprika	dash of paprika
5 mL grated onion **or**	1 tsp. grated onion **or**
onion salt	onion salt
5 mL salt	1 tsp. salt
15 mL Worcestershire sauce	1 tbsp. Worcestershire sauce
1 can (284 mL) tomato soup	1 can (10 oz.) tomato soup

Mix ingredients well in blender. A tasty dressing, ready to serve.

SHRIMP SALAD

Metric	Standard
Serves: 4-6	

Ingredients:

Metric	Standard
3 hard cooked eggs (sliced)	3 hard cooked eggs (sliced)
250 mL chopped celery **and/or** peas	1 cup chopped celery **and/or** peas
50 mL chopped green pepper	¼ cup chopped green pepper
50 mL chopped pickle	¼ cup chopped pickle
125 mL mayonnaise	½ cup mayonnaise
1 can (113 g) shrimp	1 can (4 oz.) shrimp
salt and pepper to taste	salt and pepper to taste
lettuce	lettuce
cucumber	cucumber

With two forks, toss all ingredients together lightly **except** lettuce and cucumber. Place salad in lettuce cups and garnish with cucumber slices.

Variation:

Shrimp may be substituted with salmon.

HERBED CROUTONS

Metric	Standard
110°C	225°F
1 hour	
Yield: 1.25-1.5 L	5-6 cups

Ingredients:

Metric	Standard
50 mL grated parmesan cheese	¼ cup grated parmesan cheese
15 mL oregano	1 tbsp. oregano
15 mL garlic powder	1 tbsp. garlic powder
15 mL basil (optional)	1 tbsp. basil (optional)
2 mL salt	½ tsp. salt
2 mL pepper	½ tsp. pepper
1.25-1.5 L dry bread cubes	5-6 cups dry bread cubes
45 mL oil	3 tbsps. oil.

In small bowl mix cheese and herbs. In large bowl toss bread cubes with oil, mix well. Toss bread cubes with cheese and herb mixture, until well blended. Spread on ungreased cookie sheet. Bake till crisp and light golden. Stir occasionally to toast sides. Cool and store in closed plastic bag. Serve as a garnish on soups or fresh green salads.

SALAD DRESSING

Metric	*Standard*
1 L saucepan	1 qt. saucepan
Yield: 400-500 mL	1½-2 cups

Ingredients:

125 mL vinegar	½ cup vinegar
125 mL water	½ cup water
15 mL flour	1 tbsp. flour
5 mL mustard	1 tsp. mustard
5 mL salt	1 tsp. salt
125 mL sugar	½ cup sugar
2 eggs, beaten	2 eggs, beaten

Heat vinegar and water. Mix dry ingredients and add beaten eggs. Add hot liquid and stir vigorously. Return to stove and cook until thick, stirring. Chill and serve.

Variation:

Add a little paprika to give colour to dressing. Dry or fresh chopped parsley may also be added before serving. Store in refrigerator.

SALAD DRESSING

Metric	*Standard*
1 L double boiler	1 qt. double boiler
Yield: approx. 500 mL	approx. 2 cups

Ingredients:

2 eggs	2 eggs
60 mL sugar	4 tbsps. sugar
5 mL salt	1 tsp. salt
60 mL vinegar	4 tbsps. vinegar
45 mL flour	3 tbsps. flour
2 mL dry mustard	½ tsp. dry mustard
375 mL sour cream	1½ cups sour cream
15 mL butter	1 tbsp. butter

Beat eggs well. Add sugar, salt, mustard and flour; beat until thoroughly blended. Bring vinegar to a boil. Pour over egg mixture; continue beating as you pour. Stir in sour cream and butter. Place mixture in double boiler and cook until thick and smooth. Cool and serve. Refrigerate.

SALAD DRESSING

Metric	*Standard*
Yield: 400-500 mL	1½-2 cups

Ingredients:

75-90 mL sugar	5-6 tbsps. sugar
15 mL dry mustard	1 tbsp. dry mustard
15 mL flour	1 tbsp. flour
75 mL vinegar	⅓ cup vinegar
2 eggs	2 eggs
250 mL milk **or** water	1 cup milk **or** water
15 mL butter	1 tbsp. butter

Mix dry ingredients. Add vinegar. Beat in eggs. Add milk and butter; mix well. Cook in 1 L (1 qt.) double boiler until creamy. Beat occasionally with egg beater for smooth consistency. Pour into jar, close and refrigerate to store.

SOUPS

RICE AND TOMATO SOUP

Metric	Standard
3 L saucepan	3 qt. saucepan
Serves: 3-4	

Ingredients:

1 L beef stock	1 qt. beef stock
30 mL uncooked rice	2 tbsps. uncooked rice
250 mL canned tomatoes	1 can canned tomatoes
1 small piece ginger root	1 small piece ginger root
2-3 whole pepper kernels	2-3 whole pepper kernels
1 bay leaf	1 bay leaf
1 small onion chopped	1 small onion chopped
2 stalks celery chopped	2 stalks celery chopped
fresh parsley chopped	fresh parsley chopped
salt to taste	salt to taste
30 mL light cream	2 tbsps. light cream
15 mL butter	1 tbsp. butter

In saucepan combine all ingredients except cream and butter. Cook until rice and vegetables are tender. Remove from heat. Add cream and butter and serve.

CREAM OF TOMATO SOUP

Metric	Standard
2 L saucepan	2 qt. saucepan
Yield: 1 L	1 qt.
Serves: 2-4	

Ingredients:

1 small onion chopped	1 small onion chopped
15 mL butter	1 tbsp. butter
45 mL flour	3 tbsp. flour
1 can (540 mL) tomatoes	1 can (19 oz.) tomatoes
500 mL cold milk	2 cups cold milk
salt and pepper to taste	salt and pepper to taste
fresh chopped parsley	fresh chopped parsley

Saute chopped onion in butter. Add flour and stir. Add canned tomatoes and bring to boil; stirring. Add tomato mixture to cold milk. Season with salt and pepper. Bring near boiling point. Sprinkle fresh parsley over soup and serve.

CONSOMME

Metric	*Standard*
5 L saucepan	5 qt. saucepan
Yield: about 2 L stock	2 qt. stock

Ingredients:

Metric	Standard
30 mL fat	2 tbsps. fat
1 medium onion chopped	1 medium onion chopped
2 large **or** 4 medium soup bones (beef, veal)	2 large **or** 4 medium soup bones (beef, veal)
3 L cold water	3 qts. cold water
1 bay leaf	1 bay leaf
2 large stalks celery chopped	2 large stalks celery chopped
1 small carrot	1 small carrot
small bunch parsley	small bunch parsley
15 mL salt	1 tbsp. salt

Melt fat and saute chopped onion. Add soup bones and cold water. Bring to boil and let simmer for four hours. Skim off foam occasionally. Add remaining ingredients. (additional vegetables if desired) Bring to boil and simmer for one hour. Strain through a sieve and cool broth. Remove fat and use as soup base.

VEGETABLE SOUP

Metric	*Standard*
Yield: 5 L	5 qt.
Serves: 10 or more	

Ingredients:

Metric	Standard
1-1½ kg soup bone	2-3 lbs. soup bone
3 L cold water	3 qts. cold water
15-25 mL salt	1-2 tbsps. salt
1 medium onion	1 medium onion
1 medium head cabbage	1 medium head cabbage
4 medium carrots	4 medium carrots
3 medium parsnips	3 medium parsnips
2 medium potatoes	2 medium potatoes
125 mL pot barley	½ cup pot barley
2 bay leaves	2 bay leaves
4 small chili peppers	4 small chili peppers
large bunch dill	large bunch dill
large bunch parsley	large bunch parsley
1 can (284 mL) peas	1 can (10 oz.) peas
1 L cut tomatoes	1 qt. cut tomatoes
1 container (284 mL) heavy cream	1 container (10 oz.) heavy cream

Place soup bone and water in 6 L (6 qt.) pot. Bring to boil and simmer two hours. Add salt. Slice onion and cabbage. Grate carrots and parsnips. Peel and cube potatoes. Add fresh vegetables, pot barley and herbs. Let simmer for one hour. Add peas, tomatoes and heavy cream. Bring to boil and serve.

MINESTRONE (SOUP)

Metric	Standard
Yield: 4½-5 L	4-6 qts.
Serves: 8-10	

Ingredients:

Metric	Standard
175 mL chopped celery	¾ cup chopped celery
175 mL finely chopped onion	¾ cup finely chopped onion
2 cloves garlic chopped fine	2 cloves garlic chopped fine
30 mL oil	2 tbsps. oil
2.5-3 L boiling water	2½-3 qts. boiling water
125 mL cubed carrots	½ cup cubed carrots
375 mL quartered and sliced zucchini	1½ cups quartered and sliced zucchini
250 mL diced potatoes	1 cup diced potatoes
250 mL coarsely chopped cabbage	1 cup coarsely chopped cabbage
150 mL tomato paste	⅔ cup tomato paste
15 mL salt (or more to taste)	1 tbsp. salt (or more to taste)
1 mL pepper	¼ tsp. pepper
15 mL sweet basil	1 tbsp. sweet basil
5 mL chopped parsley	1 tsp. chopped parsley
125 mL wagon wheel macaroni	½ cup wagon wheel macaroni
1 can (398 mL) chickpeas	1 can (14 oz.) chickpeas

Saute celery, onion and garlic in oil for 5-10 minutes. Put in 6 L (6 qt.) soup pot and add boiling water. Add remaining ingredients **except** macaroni and chickpeas. Bring to boil and simmer 1½ hours. For last ten minutes add macaroni and chickpeas. Serve — a delicious soup.

CREAM OF CELERY SOUP

Metric	Standard
2.5 L saucepan	2½ qt. saucepan
Yield: 2 L	2 qt.
Serves: 4	

Ingredients:

1 medium bunch celery	1 medium bunch celery
250 mL water	1 cup water
15 mL butter	1 tbsp. butter
30-45 mL flour	2-3 tbsps. flour
750 mL milk	3 cups milk
10 mL salt	2 tsps. salt
pepper to taste	pepper to taste

Chop stalks and leaves of celery bunch. Add water and boil for about 15 minutes or until tender. Melt butter in saucepan, add flour stirring well. Gradually add milk and spices. Bring to boil stirring continuously. Add sauce to celery. Serve with croutons.

VEGETABLES

BREADED PARSNIPS

Metric	*Standard*
Serves: 4	

Ingredients:

4 medium parsnips	4 medium parsnips
2 mL salt	½ tsp. salt
1 egg	1 egg
125 mL fine bread crumbs	½ cup fine bread crumbs
15-30 mL butter **or** shortening	1-2 tbsps. butter **or** shortening

Peel and slice parsnips lengthwise in four or more pieces. Place in 1.52 (1½ qt.) saucepan. Sprinkle with salt and add cold water to barely cover parsnips. Cook until nearly tender, about 10 minutes. Drain. Slightly beat egg and roll parsnips in egg and then in fine bread crumbs. Fry in butter until brown on both sides. Serve as vegetable.

ASPARAGUS AU GRATIN

Metric	*Standard*
1 L casserole	1 qt. casserole
180°C	350°F
30 min.	
Serves:4	

Ingredients:

300 g asparagus	½-¾ lb. asparagus
2 mL salt	½ tsp. salt
250 mL water	1 cup water
30 mL butter	2 tbsps. butter
30 mL flour	2 tbsps. flour
250 mL milk	1 cup milk
2 hard cooked eggs, sliced	2 hard cooked eggs, sliced
125 mL grated cheese	½ cup grated cheese
salt and pepper	salt and pepper
45 mL crumbs	3 tbsps. crumbs

Cut asparagus in 3 cm (1 in.) pieces and cook in salted water for about 10 minutes. Drain well. Melt butter, blend in flour. Add milk slowly and cook till thick and smooth, stirring constantly. In greased baking dish arrange in layers asparagus, sliced eggs, grated cheese, salt and pepper and sauce. Brown crumbs in a little butter and sprinkle over top. Bake and serve.

EGGPLANT

Metric	Standard
2 L casserole	2 qt. casserole
180°C	350°F
15 min.	
Serves: 4-6	

Ingredients:

1 medium eggplant	1 medium eggplant
1 egg	1 egg
2 mL salt	½ tsp. salt
1 mL pepper	¼ tsp. pepper
250 mL bread crumbs	1 cup bread crumbs
15 mL butter	1 tbsp. butter
30 mL oil	2 tbsps. oil
1 medium onion sliced	1 medium onion sliced
2 large ripe tomatoes sliced	2 large ripe tomatoes sliced

Peel eggplant and cut in 2 cm (¾ in.) slices. Add salt and pepper to egg; and beat. Dip eggplant in egg mixture then bread crumbs. Heat butter and oil in frying pan. Quickly brown both sides of eggplant slices. and remove from pan. Cook sliced onion in remaining fat until clear and soft but not brown. Place alternate layers of eggplant and onion into casserole. Top with tomato slices. Cover and bake just to heat through. Serve as hot vegetable.

CAULIFLOWER

Metric	Standard
Serves: 4-6	

Ingredients:

1 medium head cauliflower	1 medium head cauliflower
5 mL salt	1 tsp. salt
50 mL butter	¼ cup butter
125 mL bread crumbs	½ cup bread crumbs

Split cauliflower into small florets. Place in 1 L(1 qt.) pot and cover with cold water. Add salt and boil briefly until tender. Drain. In saucepan melt butter, add bread crumbs just to brown. Pour over hot cauliflower and serve.

Variations:

Broccoli may be prepared in same manner. A white sauce sprinkled with grated parmesan cheese also makes a good topping.

GLAZED CARROTS

Metric	Standard
2 L saucepan	2 qt. saucepan
Serves: 4-6	

Ingredients:

700 g carrots	1½ lbs. carrots
175 mL water	¾ cup water
4 mL salt	¾ tsp. salt
30 mL butter	2 tbsps. butter
30 mL white **or** brown sugar	2 tbsps. white **or** brown sugar
5 mL grated orange **or** lemon rind	1 tsp. grated orange **or** lemon rind
50 mL orange juice	¼ cup orange juice
5 mL fresh chopped parsley **or** mint	1 tsp. fresh chopped parsley **or** mint

Peel carrots and cut lengthwise in quarters. Place into saucepan, add water and salt. Boil for about 10 minutes, till crisp-tender stage. Drain. Combine butter, sugar, orange rind and juice. Add to carrots. Stir and cook till carrots are glazed. Sprinkle with fresh chopped parsley and serve.

VEGETABLE MEDLEY

Metric	Standard
2 L saucepan	2 qt. saucepan
Serves: 4-6	

Ingredients:

500 mL canned whole kernel corn	2 cups canned whole kernel corn
500 mL cooked fresh frozen peas	2 cups cooked fresh frozen peas
5 mL salt	1 tsp. salt
5 mL sugar	1 tsp. sugar
15-25 mL flour	1-1½ tbsps. flour
125 mL light cream	½ cup light cream
50 mL finely chopped pimento	¼ cup finely chopped pimento

Drain vegetables. Combine vegetables, salt, sugar, flour and light cream in saucepan. Heat thoroughly, stirring occasionally. Add finely chopped pimento and serve.

FRIED CABBAGE

Metric	Standard
Serves: 4	

Ingredients:

Metric	Standard
125 mL chopped onion	½ cup chopped onion
125 mL chopped green pepper	½ cup chopped green pepper
30 mL butter **or** margarine	2 tbsps. butter **or** margarine
1 L chopped cabbage	1 qt. chopped cabbage
50 mL water	¼ cup water
salt and pepper to taste	salt and pepper to taste

Saute chopped onion and green pepper in butter, for 10 minutes. Add chopped cabbage and water. Simmer for 10 minutes. Season and serve.

YELLOW WAX BEANS AND CARROTS

Metric	Standard
Serves: 6	

Ingredients:

Metric	Standard
375 mL carrot coins	1½ cups carrot coins
500 mL cut wax beans	2 cups cut wax beans
1 small fresh onion	1 small fresh onion
small bunch parsley	small bunch parsley
2 mL sugar	½ tsp. sugar
salt to taste	salt to taste
15 mL butter	1 tbsp. butter
small bunch summer savory	small bunch summer savory

Combine all ingredients except butter in 1 L (1 qt.) saucepan. Add a little water, cover and cook for about 15 minutes or until tender. Drain, remove parsley, summer savory and onion. Add butter, shake and serve.

SPRING VEGETABLE DISH

Metric	Standard
Serves: 4-6	

Ingredients:

Metric	Standard
500 mL young tender peas in pods	2 cups young tender peas in pods
125 mL water	½ cup water
small bunch summer savory	small bunch summer savory

4 medium fresh potatoes	4 medium fresh potatoes
3 small fresh carrots	3 small fresh carrots
salt to taste	salt to taste
30 mL margarine	2 tbsps. margarine
2 hard cooked eggs	2 hard cooked eggs
75 mL sour cream	⅓ cup sour cream

Combine peas, water and summer savory in 2 L (2 qt.) sauce pot. Cook for five minutes. Add peeled sliced fresh potatoes and whole small fresh carrots. Cover and cook for 15 minutes or until vegetables are tender. Drain and remove summer savory. Add salt to taste, margarine and finely chopped hard cooked eggs. Bring just to boil, stirring carefully. Remove from heat. Just before serving add sour cream and stir in. Makes a lovely hot vegetable.

BAKED CARROTS AND POTATOES

Metric	*Standard*
2 L casserole	2 qt. casserole
150°C	300°F
1½-2 hours	
Serves: 4-6	

Ingredients:

4 medium potatoes	4 medium potatoes
4 medium carrots	4 medium carrots
1 large onion	1 large onion
5 mL salt	1 tsp. salt
30 mL butter	2 tbsps. butter
500 mL milk	2 cups milk
1 mL paprika	¼ tsp. paprika

Peel and slice vegetables. Grease casserole and place sliced vegetables in alternate layers in dish. Season and dot with butter between layers. Pour milk over vegetables and bake until tender. Sprinkle with paprika and serve.

Notes

MENNONITE RECIPES

BEVERAGES

QUICK BREADS

263

SALADS

SOUPS

VEGETABLES

Additional Favourite Recipes

Additional Favourite Recipes

Additional Favourite Recipes

Additional Favourite Recipes

Additional Favourite Recipes

Additional Favourite Recipes

Additional Favourite Recipes

Additional Favourite Recipes

Additional Favourite Recipes